A Traveller's Guide to Cape Breton

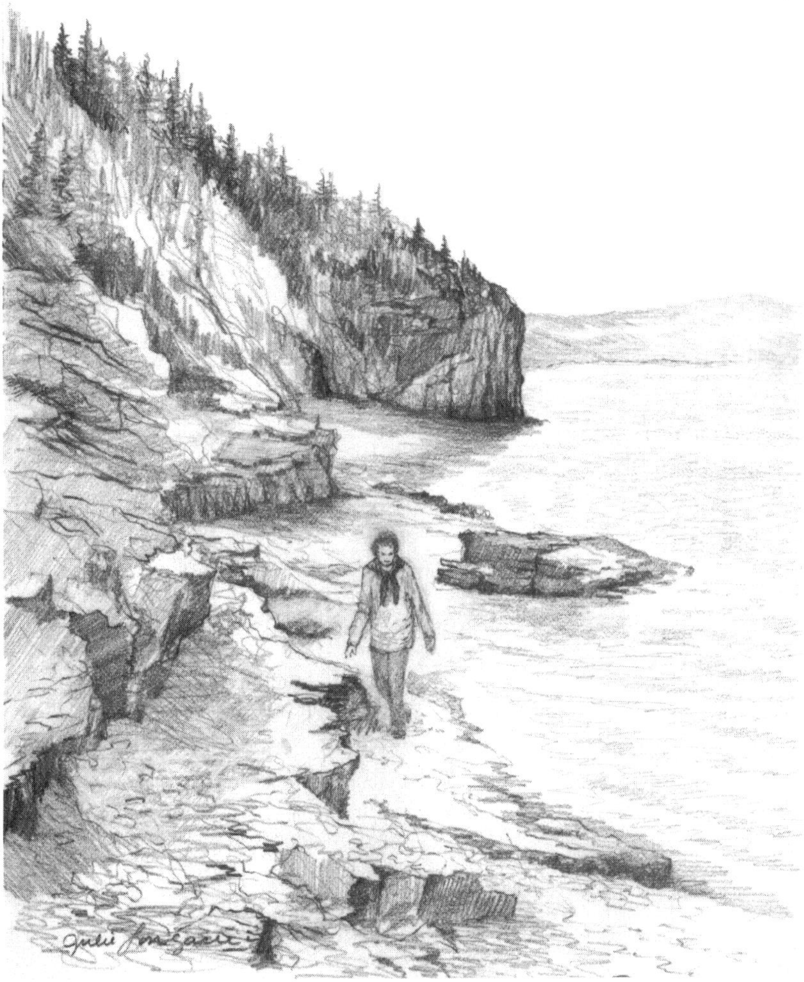

A Traveller's Guide to Cape Breton

Pat O'Neil

Solus Publishing
Sydney, Cape Breton

Cover Painting by Julia Longacre
Printed by City Printers, Sydney N.S.

Solus Publishing
14 Beacon St
Sydney, Nova Scotia B1P 4S9
902-562-8195

Printed and bound in Cape Breton.

Canadian Cataloguing in Publication Data

O'Neil, Pat, 1946-

A Traveller's Guide to Cape Breton

Includes index.
ISBN 1-896792-00-6

1. Cape Breton Island (N.S.) — Guidebooks. I. Title.

FC2343.2.053 1996 917.16'9044 C96-950095-5
F1039.C2053 1996

To Sarah and Eva

About Cover Artist, JULIA LONGACRE

When asked about her work as an artist, 'Julie' replies simply, "I love to paint."

Well known for her drawings, paintings and book illustrations, her style and sensitivity to subject matter has earned her the respect of private and corporate collectors alike.

An artist of the people, as she is frequently called, Julie concentrates on rural landscape, responding to the demand for historic detail on a rapidly changing horizon.

Whether she is painting in her studio in Barto, Pennsylvania, or in her Lighthouse Cottage in Port Hood, she captures the mood and detail of her surroundings. The work she has contributed to *A Traveller's Guide to Cape Breton* is just a sampling of paintings and drawings she has done over the years, reflecting her fondness for the beauty of the island and the warm and friendly people she has met here.

"Each time I return to Cape Breton I discover something new. From the scenic village harbours to the breathtaking highlands, the drama of the seasons unfold each year and I am happy to be part of it.

Julie graduated with her Bachelor of Fine Arts Degree from Bethany College in Lindsborg, Kansas.

In addition to the cover image, Julie contributed the drawings on the following pages, most of which were generously produced especially for this book.

Julia's illustrations can be found on pages:

Title page, this page (below), 1, 19, 26, 37, 50, 57, 62, 69, 79, 84, 90, 98, 109, 124, 131, 137, 143, 146, 168, 183, 190, 210, 217, 223, 242, 248, 252, 265, 269, 271, 283, 287.

ACKNOWLEDGEMENTS

I would like to thank my husband Ken and my children Daniel and Kate; Fran Baldner; Beatrice MacNeil; Vange Deschepper; Mark Flannery; Martin MacLellan of ECBC; Sylvia Ho of ArtPlus Advertising, Harve Grant of City Printers and the many people who volunteered information and time to help get this book into print.

I would also like to thank these Cape Breton artists who have generously allowed me to use their artwork in the book. Their artwork can be found on the pages indicated.

Vernon Amos, page 152
Christopher Gorey, page 155
Beryl Davis, 260
Ollie MacKinnon, pages 226, 239
Kenny Boone, page 212
Thorn Morrow, pages 175, 231
Adrian Syms, page 24
Michael Armentrout, pages 97, 105
Teena Marie Saunders, pages 201, 291
William Rogers, page 45

And I would especially like to thank Julie Longacre, regular summer visitor and true Cape Bretoner in spirit, who has been overwhelmingly generous in her encouragement, advice and interest in this project, and who has contributed the greater part of the artwork in the book, including the cover painting. Many thanks, Julie!

Some Emergency Numbers

Ambulance

C.B. Regional Ambluance Service 902-842-0000
Baddeck Ambulance Service 902-295-2360
Clarke's Ambulance, Sydney Mines 902-736-3400
T. W. Curry Ambulance Service, Sydney 902-564-8196
Rescue 1 EMS Ambulance Service 902-562-2230
long distance 1-800-333-3911
Unity Ambulance, Glace Bay 902-849-2222
New Waterford Ambulance Service 902-862-2266
Cheticamp Ambulance Services 902-224-2316
Judique Ambulance Service 902-787-2299
Inverness Ambulance 902-258-2879
T. W. Curry, Eskasoni 902-379-2597
Sydney Ambulance Service 902-564-8196
Boudreau Ambulance, Arichat, 902-226-3300
Margaree Valley Ambulance 902-248-2486.

Royal Canadian Mounted Police

Emergency number accessible from the whole Island **564-1323.**

Table of Contents

Cape Breton Island

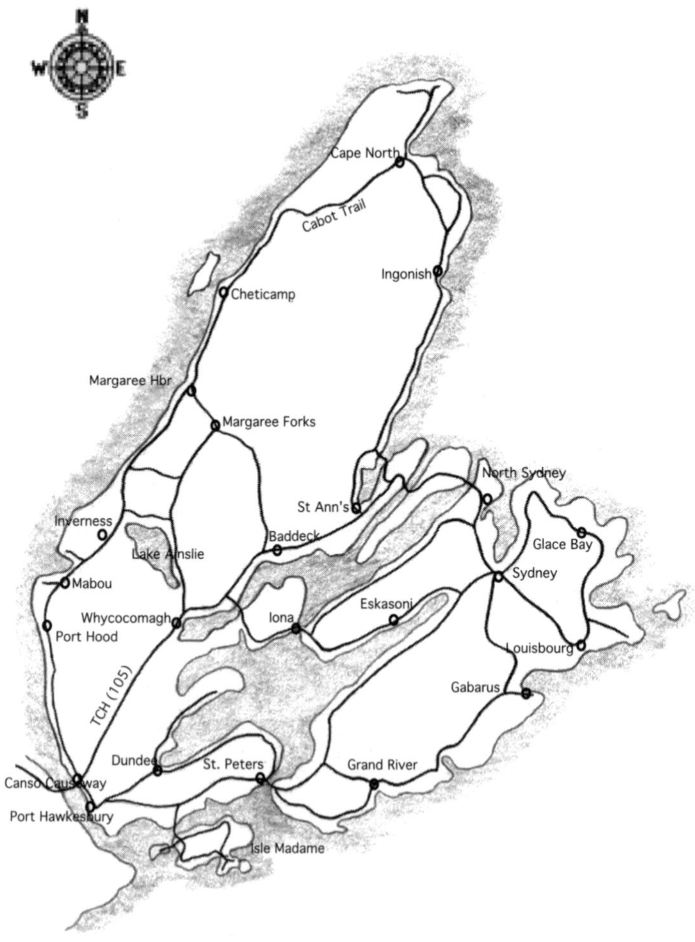

INTRODUCTION

As I see it, there are three kinds of travellers: the '***planners***' who work out every detail of their holidays long before most of us have even decided where to go; the '***vagabonds***' to whom 'plan' is a four-letter word and for whom "Let's find out when we get there!" is a code of behaviour; and the '***middle-of-the-roaders***', who plan a little, guess a little, and usually discover a little.

A *Traveller's Guide to Cape Breton* is designed with all three species in mind.

It's a valuable resource for the 'planners'..no need to guess where to find the nearest beach, restaurant or gas station.

It's a useful reference for the 'vagabonds'...leaving lots of room for freedom and discovery.

And for the 'middle-of-roaders' (which probably includes the majority of us), it's a handy mixture of planning and discovery, information and ideas.

Cape Breton - with its scenic trails and back roads, country inns and woodland retreats, glorious beaches and awsome hiking trails, Acadian villages, Mi'kmaq legends and Celtic roots, fiddlers, festivals, ceilidhs and concerts - is a perfect place for a holiday.

If this is your first visit, it is my wish that this book will guide you through one of the most memorable holidays away from home ever.

If you are a returning visitor, I hope this book will entice you to venture a little farther off the beaten path to discover some of Cape Breton's hidden treasures.

And if, like me, you are lucky enough to call Cape Breton home, I hope this book will inspire you to rediscover your island now and for many holidays to come.

The Lure of Cape Breton

✠ Geography

Cape Breton Island lies off the north east coast of Nova Scotia, separated from the mainland by the Strait of Canso. The Canso Causeway, completed on December 10, 1954, is the one and only 'road to the Isle'. There's a story about an elderly Cape Breton woman who was praying with her family on the night the Causeway was finished. When she had finished her regular prayers, she added, "...and thank God for at last making Canada part of Cape Breton." (That about sums up how Cape Bretoners feel about their Island!)

Cape Breton's origins began 1200 to 600 million years ago as an island off Africa. Great ferns grew in the swamps that covered most of the land and dragonflies, the size of gulls, thrived. Eventually our island made a slow journey northward and all that shifting and colliding caused the Highlands and canyons to form.

The Island itself is 6,352 sq km (3,970 sq mi) of rocky shores, rolling farmland, barren headlands, mountains, forests and plateaus. It is 175 km (110 mi) long and 140 km (87 mi) wide and, to our great delight, has over 1,000 km (650 mi) of Atlantic coastline. In the middle of it all is the Bras d'Or Lakes, a salt-water lake system 80 km (50 mi) long and 32 km (20 mi) wide, stretching across the Island from East Bay to West Bay.

✠ History

The history books tell us that John Cabot 'discovered' Cape Breton in 1497. He apparently landed at Aspy Bay in Northern Cape Breton and erected a cross there claming the land for the King of England.

But long before that, Norsemen are believed to have stopped off here on their many voyages of discovery across the ocean. There is evidence, too, that Cape Breton was inhabited by Indians as far back as 6000 BC and that the Mi'kmaqs have been here for a thousand years.

In the early 1500's European fishermen began to fish in our waters and occasionally visit our shores. By the early 1600's, English, French, Portuguese and Spanish fishermen were using Cape Breton as a place to dry their fish and trade furs with the natives.

The first permanent settlement, though, wasn't established until 1629. A Scotsman by the name of Sir James Stewart, Lord Ochiltree, settled with sixty others at Baleine Cove, near Louisbourg.

The 1713 Treaty of Utrecht, officially gave Cape Breton to France. To protect 'Isle Royale, as it was then called, France set about building its great fortress at Louisbourg. For a short time Louisbourg was one of the busiest ports in North America and a vital commercial centre of New France. But the struggle for supremacy in the 'New World' was never far away, and in 1745 the British attacked and captured the town. It was returned to the French only to be captured a second time in 1758. Two years later the British destroyed the Fortress.

The history of Cape Breton is a fascinating subject and far too extensive to relate here in any great detail. I have, however, tried to provide snippits here and there to whet the appetite just enough, I hope, to entice the traveller into the many community museums and historical sites found all over the Island.

What's *A Traveller's Guide to Cape Breton* All About?

In a word, *A Traveller's Guide to Cape Breton* is about **information**. Information that will help make your Island travels a worry-free and memorable experience. Information that will take the guess work out of finding a place to eat or sleep, what to do on a hot summer afternoon or how to find your way to the Cabot Trail. And information that will help you discover not just the incredible physical beauty of our island, but the soul and spirit of its people as well, for these two features of our Island are, I believe, inextricably linked.

A Traveller's Guide to Cape Breton will take you around Cape Breton town by town, village by village, small community by small community. It will tell you where to find gas stations, banks, beaches, hospitals, museums, pharmacies, churches, restaurants, accommodations and more. It will tell you stories, introduce you to special people and take you back to our intriguing past. It will show you Alternate Routes, take you on Side Trips, enlighten you with maps and lure you with pictures.

And most of all, it will let you sit back, relax and enjoy our Island as it deserves to be enjoyed.

GETTING FAMILIAR

Travel Options at a Glance

To help you plan your trip, and to make your travels as hassle-free as possible, I divided the Island into six Travel Options. Some of them follow the official tourist trails, like the Ceilidh Trail and the Cabot Trail, and others have been created just for this book. You won't find these Travel Option designations anywhere else.

The purpose of the Travel Options is to give you, the traveller, a choice as to how you would like to travel the Island. Each Travel Option shows you a different part Cape Breton. You can follow Travel Option 1, for instance, to go from the Canso Causeway to Sydney by way of Baddeck, and you can follow Travel Option 3 to go back by way of the Cabot Trail. The choices are yours.

Information Galore

Each Travel Option has its own special place in the book and in each Travel Option section you'll find the following information:

- general overview of the Travel Option
- communities you'll travel through on the Travel Option
- map showing the Travel Option
- Side Trips and Alternate Routes
- outline of the special features of the Travel Option
- pictures, historical notes, stories and legends
- a community-by-community listing of hotels/motels, campgrounds, cabins and inns, restaurants, museums and historical sites, beaches, hiking trails, gas stations, craft and gift shops, outdoor adventures, etc.

To further help you find what you're looking for, a Table of Contents and Index are included.

How to Use *A Traveller's Guide to Cape Breton*

Because the book is set up as a series of Travel Options, the simplest way to make use of the book is to decide where you want to go then find the Travel Options that will take you there.

If, on the other hand, you have no idea where you want to

go and are just in the planning stages of your trip, read through all the Travel Options to find out what there is to see on the Island, then choose the Travel Options that appeal to you.

The Travel Options are written in a west to east direction. When you are travelling in the opposite direction, from east to west, follow the Travel Options in reverse. Special instructions are given when necessary.

Which Way is North?

When you're using the book - looking up directions, following travel routes - it's important first to become familiar with how the Island is situated. Take a look at the map opposite page 1 and familiarize yourself with North, South, East and West. Very often in the book I say things like "...2 km (1.2 mi) north of Ingonish, or 40 km (24 mi) west of Sydney." The more familiar you are with the Island's compass points, the easier it will be for you to get around. Here are a few reference points:

- √ Canso Causeway/Port Hastings are **WEST**
- √ Sydney/Glace Bay are **EAST**
- √ Louisbourg is **SOUTH-EAST**
- √ Ingonish/Cape North are **NORTH**
- √ Isle Madame/Gabarus are **SOUTH**

A Word About Listings

Throughout each Travel Option you will find entries for the facilities you will come upon along that route.

In large villages and towns where there are many facilities, not every facility is listed; for example, convenience stores, fast food outlets, or gas stations may be left out. However, in areas where facilities are scarce, I have tried to include everything.

Because of the nature of the tourism industry - new businesses start up frequently, others close down - you may notice on your travels some discrepancies in the list of facilities. To minimize this, *A Traveller's Guide to Cape Breton* will be reprinted each year with any changes that occur. To provide further current information you will find an insert in the book listing the current year's major festivals, concerts and events.

And one more note on this: the listings for each facility

contain information regarding season and times of operation. It's possible that some businesses will make last minute changes that will contradict what is written in the book. Here's an example: you're travelling from point A to point B and you're getting low on gas. You don't worry because the book says there's a gas station 50 km down the road that's open until 11 pm. If you keep going you'll make it just before closing time. You get there at 10:45 and the gas station is closed - owners decided to close early this week. There are no more gas stations for another 30 km and you don't have enough gas to get there. That darn book! My advice - if you're cutting it that close, you should probably call ahead.

Prices and Ratings

✠ Prices

You will notice that in the book "price ranges" are used instead of specific prices for facilities like accommodations, meals, activities, etc. The reason for that, of course, is that prices change constantly making it very difficult to keep the information current.

"Price ranges" are intended only as a guideline to give you a general idea of what you might expect to pay. The following is a list of the "Price ranges" used throughout the book:

Accommodations

Price ranges are for high season, double occupancy. Expect to pay between $5 and $15 for each additional person; in some cases children under a certain age are free.

Low	0 - $40
Med-low	$41 - $55
Mid-range	$56 - $80
Med-high	$81 - $95
Upper end	$96 and over

Campgrounds

Avg	under $15
Avg plus	$15 and over

Restaurants

Price Ranges are for an average full dinner, per person.

Low	0 - $8
Mid-range	$9 - $15
Med-high	$16 - $20
Upper end	$21 and over

Activities (including museums, historical sites, amusements, etc.)

For many activities family and group rates are available. Often, too, there are children's and seniors' rates.

Low	0 - $5
Med	$6 - $15
Upper range	over $15

Boat Tours

All boat tours on the island seem to be within the $20 to $25 range for adults, $10 to $15 for children 6 to 12, and small children under 5 or 6 are usually free; some offer a discount for seniors.

✠ Ratings

You will not find "quality ratings" in *A Traveller's Guide to Cape Breton*. The rating of accommodation, restaurants, craft shops and other facilities is beyond the scope of this book.

I do, however, occasionally comment on a particular restaurant, lodging or shop that has caught my attention. These comments reflect my own personal tastes and experience, and shouldn't be taken as my endorsement of one facility over another.

In my opinion the overall quality of the majority of the facilities on the Island is very good. In a lot of cases it is excellent. And in some cases it is supurb.

If you feel you didn't get your money's worth for a service or product, you should make your feelings known to the provider of that service or product.

✠ Use of Abbreviations

I tried to keep my use of abbreviations to a bare minimum as I find them annoying! Some that have sneaked in are as follows:

TCH	- Trans Canada Highway
o/s	- off season
VS	- Visa
MC	- Master Card
AE	- American Express
DC	- Diner's Club
Disc	- Discover Card

✠ **Responsibility & Liability**

Owners of the facilities listed in the book are under no obligation to comply with the information given in the book and the author and/or publisher do not guarantee that the information is and will always remain accurate. The author and/or publisher are not responsible for price or time changes with regard to the facilities listed. The author and/or publisher are not responsible for any injuries or fatalities that may occur while a traveller is using this book. Please be sure to heed 'cautions' where noted.

TRAVELLING IN CAPE BRETON - GENERAL INFORMATION

Getting Here

There are several ways you can come to Cape Breton. The most frequently used one is by car. If you are travelling by car, there are two entry points to the Island - the Canso Causeway at Port Hastings and the car ferries from Newfoundland. The car ferries to and from Port-aux-Basques and Argentia, Newfoundland, run from the Marine Atlantic terminal in North Sydney. (For more information see page 56.)

You can also take a bus - either a tour bus or a regularly scheduled bus like the Acadian Lines buses which run back and forth from Halifax every day.

If air travel is your choice, Sydney Airport will no doubt be able to accommodate you. There are several flights a day into and out of Sydney and connections for other Canadian cities as well as international destinations are good. (See page 281 for more information about Sydney Airport.)

Every year a number of visitors come to Cape Breton in private vessels. If you're lucky enough to be among them, you'll find full-service marinas throughout the Island.

Distances

Here is a list of some distances between Cape Breton and other parts of eastern North America:

Boston	1352 km	840 mi
Buffalo	2070 km	1286 mi
Chicago	2910 km	1808 mi
Detroit	2482 km	1542 mi
Fredericton	698 km	434 mi

Halifax	423 km	263 mi
Montreal	1568 km	974 mi
New York	1683 km	1046 mi
Ottawa	1772 km	1101 mi
Philadelphia	1844 km	1146 mi
Pittsburg	2277 km	1415 mi
Portland, Me	1181 km	734 mi
Quebec City	1308 km	813 mi
St.John, N.B.	660 km	410 mi
St.John's Nfld	909 km	565 mi
Sudbury	2269 km	1410 mi
Thunder Bay	3174 km	1972 mi
Toronto	2108 km	1310 mi
Washtn, DC	2058 km	1279 mi

Advance Reservations

Nova Scotia has a free reservation and information service from anywhere in North America. It's called "Check In-Nova Scotia". Many of the accommodations in Cape Breton are members of Check In -Nova Scotia, which means by calling the toll-free number below, you can make a reservation free of charge for those facilities. The best way to find out if a certain accommodation is a member of Check In-Nova Scotia is to call the toll-free number and ask. Many accommodations on the Island have their own toll-free numbers, which you will find with the listings for those facilities.

Check In-Nova Scotia Toll-Free Number:
1-800-565-0000 (North America)
1-902-425-5781 (from outside North America)
Note: this is not toll-free
425-5781 (in greater Halifax)

Health Services Tax

A Health Services Tax (also called Sales Tax) of 11% is charged on many goods and services in Nova Scotia. Purchases of clothing and footwear under $100 are exempt as are most grocery items. Non-residents of Nova Scotia are entitled to a rebate of this tax on goods removed from the Province. You have 90 days after leaving the Province to apply. Receipts or photocopies are required. Forms are available from the Visitor Information Centres.

Information

There are several official Visitor Information Centres around the Island at Port Hastings, just over the Canso Causeway, Baddeck, Louisbourg, Sydney River, Port Hood, St. Peters, Little Narrows, Margaree Forks and North Sydney. The Travel Option listings will give you more information about each of these centres.

In addition, you can call Check In-Nova Scotia toll free 1-800-565-0000 (North America) or call Tourism Cape Breton toll-free 1-800-565-9464.

Other Cape Breton Travel & Guide Books

Explore Cape Breton - by Pat O'Neil. Nimbus Publishing, 1994, reprinted 1995.

A take-along guide to hiking trails and outdoor adventures in some of Cape Breton's most delightful and out-of-the-way spots, as well as notes on looking up your Cape Breton roots.

A Nature and Hiking Guide to Cape Breton's Cabot Trail, by David Lawley. Nimbus Publishing, 1994.

A fascinating guide to the natural history of Cape Breton's Cabot Trail written by an interpretive naturalist who works in the Cape Breton Highlands National Park.

Birding Cape Breton's Historic East, by Cathy Murrant.

A comprehensive guide to all the birds you will find, or that have ever been sighted, in the eastern part of Cape Breton.

Rules of the Road

✠ **Speed Limits**

Speed limits in Nova Scotia are as follows, except where otherwise posted:

- 100 km per hr (62 mi per hr) on Trans Canada Highway;
- 80 km per hr (50 mi per hr) on secondary highways;
- 50 km per hr (30 mi per hr) in cities, towns and school zones.

There is a minimum fine of $77.50 for violations of the speed limit.

✠ **Seat Belts**
All dirvers and passengers are required to wear seat belts in Nova Scotia.

✠ **Drinking and Driving**
There are stiff penalities (including loss of license) in Nova Scotia for anyone caught driving with a blood-alcohol level over .08%.

Climate

Cape Breton is an Island of many faces...ocean, lakes, highlands, valleys, plateaus, rolling farmland and wilderness forests. Is it any wonder we have trouble predicting the weather?

The fact is that you can be sweltering on a July day in a certain part of the Island, but a few miles away, if the ocean breezes are just so, you might need a sweater.

Generally our summer months are wonderful...warm, often hot, days; almost always cooler, refreshing nights. In the fall, probably our most predictable and overall pleasant time of year, the skies are almost always clear, sunshine is abundant and the scenery is...well, indescribable.

For up-to-date weather information, you can call Environment Canada at 902-564-7788 or 7299; or you can tune in to CBC radio, Information Morning, each weekday morning from 6 am to 9 am - you'll hear the weather at twenty minutes to each hour.

Liquor Regulations

The following are a few tidbits of information regarding Nova Scotia liquor laws and practices:

√ You must be 19 years old or over to buy any type of alcoholic beverage; a proof of age ID is often asked for.

√ Liquor, wine or beer can only be bought in Nova Scotia Liquor Commission outlets. Normal hours are from 10 am to 6 pm Mon to Thurs; 10 am to 10 pm Fri; and 10 am to 5 pm Sat; however, some stores have extended hours during the summer months. All Nova Scotia Liquor Commissions are closed on Sundays and holidays.

√ An under-aged person may eat in a beverage room or tavern until 8:30 pm only if accompanied by a parent, legal guardian or spouse.

√ Nova Scotia imposes heafty penalties on anyone caught driving a vehicle under the influence of alcohol. The legal acceptable blood-alcohol level if .08%.

Warnings and Good Advice

√ When you're driving, be aware that deer and moose frequently roam or cross highways, especially in the highlands and on the lesser-travelled roads. Early morning and dusk seem to be their favourite times for road travel; don't under-estimate the size and weight of these animals, moose especially. Deer will generally run away as soon as they spot danger, moose often stand on the side (or in the middle) of the road and watch. Just drive around them slowly and don't get out of the car for a closer look.

√ I mention this quite frequently throughout the book, but I will say it again...when swimming in the ocean, be aware that high waves create undertows that can be dangerous for children and those who are not strong swimmers; some beaches on the Island are supervised, but many are not.

√ When walking on cliffs, be careful not to walk too close to the edge. Many cliffs have very unstable overhangs that will not support any weight; what looks like an innocent patch of grass could be a very dangerous overhang.

√ Cape Breton, and all of Nova Scotia, are in the Atlantic Time Zone, which is one hour ahead of the Eastern Time Zone. Daylight Saving time is in effect from the first Sunday in April to the last Sunday in October.

√ You cannot pass a school bus from either direction when it has a red light flashing; when its amber light is flashing, you can pass with caution.

√ Blackflies and mosquitoes can be quite pesky, especially inland and near fresh water. Be sure to bring along good insect repellent and if you're walking in the woods, a long-sleeved sweater and long pants wouldn't be a bad idea.

√ The minimum fine for littering in Nova Scotia is in the vicinity of $350.00.

AMERICAN AND OTHER OUT-OF-COUNTRY VISITORS

Getting Here

There are three ways you can get from the United States to Nova Scotia - by land, by air and by sea.

Land Travel

Since Cape Breton is an island and is connected to mainland Nova Scotia solely by the Canso Causeway, the only road leading onto the Island is the Trans Canada Highway.

Regardless of the point at which you choose to enter Canada from the U.S. - whether it's from Maine to New Brunswick, from Vermont to Quebec, or even from way out west - the Trans Canada Highway and its connector highways will eventually lead you to Cape Breton.

There is a daily bus service from Halifax, Nova Scotia, to Sydney, Cape Breton (Acadian Lines, 902-454-9321/8279) which makes connections with American bus lines.

Alas, there are no more passenger trains to Cape Breton!

Ocean Travel

There are two car ferries from the United States to Nova Scotia. One is from Bar Harbour, Maine to Yarmouth, Nova Scotia, and the other is from Portland, Maine to Yarmouth, Nova Scotia.

For more information about the ferry service, check out these addresses and telephone numbers:

For **Bar Harbour to Yarmouth ferry**:
Marine Atlantic
Bar Harbour, Maine 04690
1-800-341-7981 (from U.S. only)

For **Portland to Yarmouth ferry**:
Prince of Fundy Cruises Ltd.
Box 4216, Station "A"
Portland, Maine, 04101
1-800-341-7540 (U.S. & Can)
1-800-482-0955 (Maine only)

You may also want to consider driving to St. John, New Brunswick and taking a ferry across the Bay of Fundy to Digby, Nova Scotia.

For **St. John, N.B. to Digby, N.S. ferry**:
1-800-341-7981 (from U.S. only)

How We Do Things

✠ That Darned Metric!

Don't feel bad, most of us aren't used to it yet either!

Here are some equivalents you might find useful. Keep in mind that gasoline comes in litres, not gallons; mileage is in kilometres, not miles; and we buy steak by kilograms, not pounds.

1 kilometre (km) = .6 mile (mi)
1 litre (l) = 0.26 gallons U.S. (gal)
1 kilogram (kg) = 2.2 pounds (lb)
1 centimetre (cm) = .39 inches (in)
1 mile (mi) = 1.6 km (kilometres)
1 U.S. gallon (gal) = 3.8 litres
1 pound (lb) = .45 kg (kilograms)
1 inch (in) = 2.5 centimetres (cm)

Celsius and Fahrenheit

To convert Fahrenheit to Celsius, subtract 30 and divide by 2

To convert Celsius to Fahrenheit, multiply by 2 and add 30.

For instance: 21° celsius = 21 x 2 = 42 + 30 = 72° Fahrenheit

✠ That Double-Darned GST (Goods and Service Tax) and other Pesky Taxes.

Canadians have to pay 7% GST on almost all goods and services we purchase. Although out-of-country visitors do have to pay the GST as well, you can get a rebate on certain purchases. Exceptions include such things as gas, cigarettes and alcohol and items that tend to increase in value like paintings and jewellery.

Short-term accommodations (less than 30 days) are eligible for rebate, but not meals or camping and trailer park fees.

The minimum amount eligible for rebate is $100 worth of goods and/or services. Rebate forms are available from Visitor Information Centres and: Revenue Canada, Customs & Excise, Visitors' Rebate Program, Summerside Tax Centre, Summerside, P.E.I., C1N 6A2; toll-free 1-800-668-4748 in Canada; outside Canada not toll-free (613) 991-3346.

Save your receipts!

Currency Exchange and Banking

As you are no doubt aware, U.S. dollars are worth more than Canadian dollars. Banks on the Island will cash Travellers' Cheques and exchange currency at the going rate. There are banking machines in larger centres and Interac is available in some grocery stores and shops. Most shops and businesses will accept American dollars at the going exchange rate as well.

Customs Information

U.S. citizens require only a proof of citizenship or permanent resident status (birth certificate or Alien Registration Card) to enter Canada.

Residents from other countries require valid passports.

Currently you are permitted to take back into the U.S. $400 U.S. worth of tax-exempt goods after 48 hours. For more information, contact Customs Border Services, Box 3080 South, Halifax, N.S. B3J 3G6; 902-426-2911; toll-free in Canada 1-800-461-9999; Fax 902-426-2652.

Insurance and Licenses

Drivers in Canada are required by law to carry liability insurance on their vehicles. U.S. residents can obtain from their insurance companies what is knows as a 'Non-Resident Inter-Province Motor Vehicle Liability Insurance Card'. This card will be accepted by Canadian police as evidence of financial responsibility.

A valid U.S. driver's license is valid in Nova Scotia. Driver must have proof of car registration.

Note: For further general information on travelling in Cape Breton, see page 8.

Cape Breton Island

Travel Options

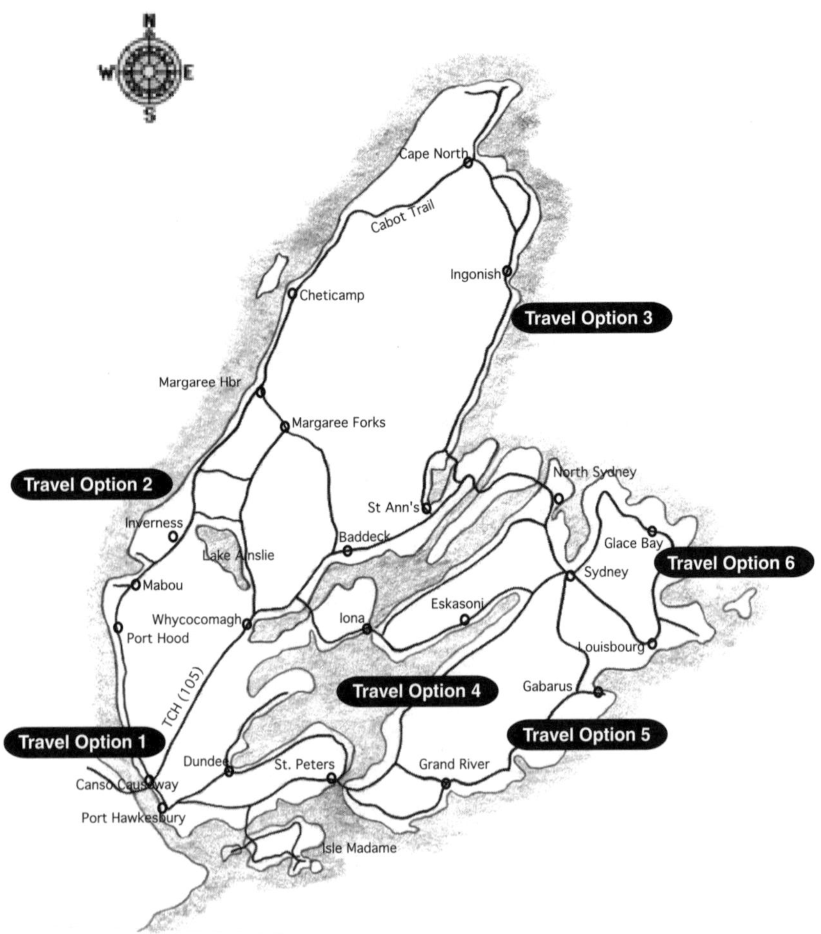

Travel Options at a Glance

TRAVEL OPTION 1 - Trans Canada Highway
- Canso Causeway to Sydney
- Sydney to Canso Causeway (reverse)
VIA Baddeck, with Alternate Route to Iona

TRAVEL OPTION 2 - Ceilidh Trail
-Canso Causeway to Margaree Harbour
-Margaree Harbour to Canso Causeway (reverse)
VIA Port Hood, Mabou, Inverness, with Side Trip to Lake Ainslie

---

TRAVEL OPTION 3 - Cabot Trail
- Nyanza to St Ann's/South Haven
-St Ann's/South Haven to Nyanza (reverse)
VIA the Margarees, Cheticamp, Ingonish with Side Trips to Bay St Lawrence, Smelt Brook & Englishtown

---

TRAVEL OPTION 4
- Canso Causeway to Sydney
-Sydney to Canso Causeway (reverse)
VIA St Peters, Big Pond, with Alternate Routes via Dundee or Isle Madame

---

TRAVEL OPTION 5 - Fleur-de-lis Trail
- Canso Causeway to Louisbourg
- Louisbourg to Canso Causeway (reverse)
VIA L'Ardoise, Grand River, Gabarus

TRAVEL OPTION 6
- Sydney to Louisbourg
- Louisbourg to Sydney
VIA Hwy 22, Colliery Route or Marconi Trail

Travel Option 1

Trans Canada Highway

Canso Causeway to Sydney
Sydney to Canso Causeway
VIA Baddeck, with Alternate Route to Iona

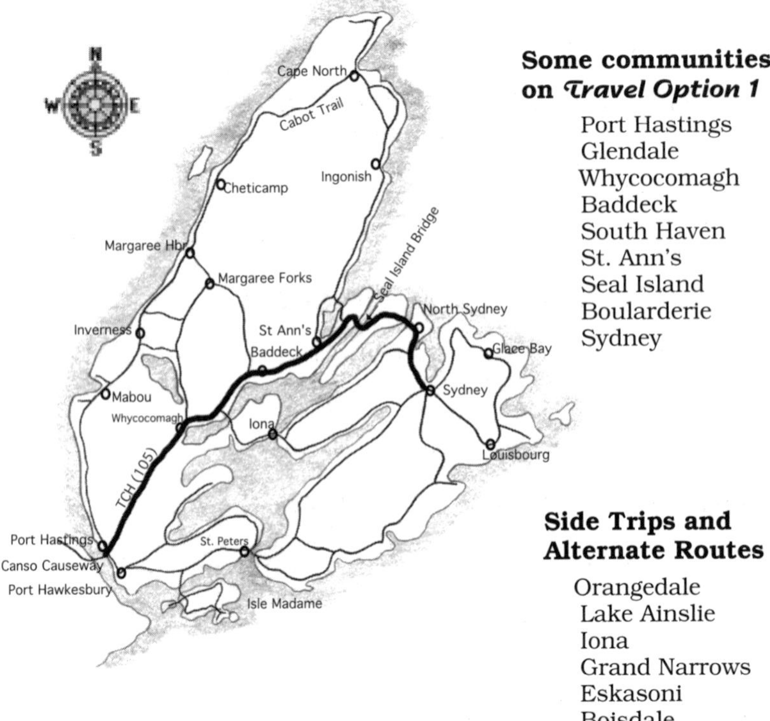

Some communities on *Travel Option 1*

- Port Hastings
- Glendale
- Whycocomagh
- Baddeck
- South Haven
- St. Ann's
- Seal Island
- Boularderie
- Sydney

Side Trips and Alternate Routes

- Orangedale
- Lake Ainslie
- Iona
- Grand Narrows
- Eskasoni
- Boisdale
- Big Bras d'Or
- Sydney Mines
- North Sydney

Special Features

- √ Canso Causeway
- √ N. S. Highland Village
- √ Alexander Graham Bell Museum
- √ hiking trails & outdoor adventures
- √ boat tours
- √ beaches and picnic parks
- √ restaurants and shopping
- √ Lake and ocean coastal drives
- √ Metropolitan Cape Breton

Don't be misled by the notion that, because this is the Trans Canada Highway, it's not scenic. On the contrary, it's a lovely drive through some very picturesque spots like Whycocomagh and Nyanza on the Bras d'Or Lakes and Kelly's Mountain with spectacular look-offs. You can stop over in Baddeck, or take a short detour into Orangedale or a side trip to Lake Ainslie.

You have two choices as to how you want to travel this Option - one is along the Trans Canada Highway (Hwy 105) via **Baddeck** all the way to Sydney, and the other is to take an alternate route through the centre of the Island via **Iona**.

The **Baddeck** alternative is a very direct way to get from the Canso Causeway to Metropolitan Cape Breton because it takes you straight through the Island from east to west, or from west to east.

The **Iona** altenative is a little more roundabout, but takes you through a very scenic, lesser-travelled segment of the Island, almost entirely along the shores of the Bras d'Or Lakes.

Julia Longacre

➵ **EN ROUTE**

Heading east toward Sydney, your journey begins in the Village of Port Hastings, just over the Canso Causeway. Once you cross the Causeway, you'll come to a rotary from which you can travel in several different directions.

You won't have to actually drive around the rotary... just take the turnoff to Highway 105, the Trans Canada Highway, which leads uphill to your left just past the Visitor Information Centre and Gift Shop.

Most of the facilities in the Port Hastings area are clustered around the rotary, but for a few of the ones listed below you'll have to drive a little south of the rotary, then backtrack.

All facilities are listed in order of appearance along the route. If any facility is 'off the beaten path', directions are given.

Port Hastings

The village of **Port Hastings**, the "gateway to the Isle", is the first community you'll see after you cross the Causeway, and the last one you'll see before you cross to the mainland. It isn't a large community, but it does have motels, restaurants, gas stations and one of the Island's main Visitor Information Centres. All the roads leading east, south and north fan out from Port Hastings.

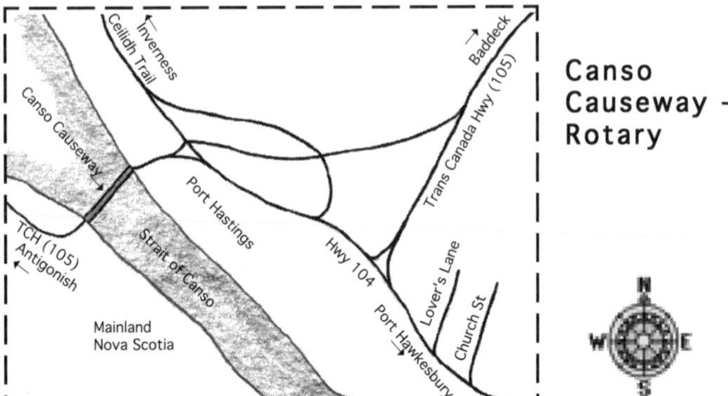

Canso Causeway - Rotary

Nova Scotia Visitor Information Centre

This should probably be your first stop once you cross the Canso Causeway. It is located on the water side of the road, just over the Causeway.

Location: Port Hastings at the rotary. **Tel:** 902-625-1717. **Season**: mid-May to mid-Oct. **Hours**: generally from 9 am to 9 pm, but sometimes closes a little earlier, depending on demand.

Glen Auld Gifts

Located: Port Hastings, next to Visitor Information Centre. **Tel:** 902-625-1649. **Owner**: G. MacLean. **Season:** mid-May to Thanksgiving. **Hours:** summer months 8:30 am to 9 pm daily; other months 9 am - 5 pm daily. **Cards**: VS, MC. **Features**: large selection of gifts, crafts and souvenirs.

Keddy's Inn and Dining Room

Location: Port Hastings. Go part way around the rotary and turn right just before the Esso Station. **Mail Addr:** Box 50, Port Hastings, B0E 2T0. **Tel**: 625-0460; toll-free 1-800-561-7666; Fax 625-1275. **Season:** year round. **Rates:** mid-range. **Cards**: most major cards. **Dng Rm Hrs:** 7 am to 11am; 5 pm to 10pm daily. **Prices**: mid-range. **Features**: licensed dining room and lounge; seniors discounts.

Port Hastings Esso - just over the Canso Causeway; 902-625-1100; open from 7 am to 11 pm daily; gas,deisel.

Smitty's Restaurant

Location: Port Hastings, at the rotary. **Owners:** M. & J. Chisholm. **Tel**: 902- 625-3346; Fax 902-625-2914. **Season**: year round. **Hours**: summer 6:30 am - 11pm; winter 7am - 10 pm daily. **Price**s: low to mid-range. **Cards:** VS, AE, debit cards. **Features:** large, bright family-style eatery; wide selection; specialty menu items for seniors, children and health conscious.

Skye Travelodge and Dining Room

Location: Port Hastings, at rotary. **Mail Add**r: Box 190, Port Hastings, N.S. B0E 2T0. **Tel:** 902-625-1300, Fax 902-625-1966, toll free 1-800-578-7878. **Season:** Year round. **Rates:** mid-range. **Cards:** most major cards. **Dng Rm Hrs:** 7 am to 10 pm daily. **Dng Rm Prices**: low to mid-range. **Features:** award-winning licensed dining room; overlooking Strait of Canso.

MacPuffin Inn, Dining Room and Gift Shop

Location: Lover's Lane, Port Hastings - first street to your left after the Skye Travelodge. **Mail Addr**: Box 558, Port Hawkesbury N.S. B0E 2V0. **Tel:** 902-625-2283; toll free 1-800-867-2212; Fax 625-1525. **Owner**: Kenzie Jones. **Season**: Jun - Oct **Rates:** from mid-range to upper end. **Cards:** most major cards. **Features:** complimentary continental breakfast; family rates; gift shop; putting green; swimming pool.

Port Hastings Museum and Archives

Location: 367 Church St, Port Hastings - second street to your left after you pass the Skye Travelodge. **Mail Addr:** Box 115, Port Hastings, N.S. B0E 2T0. **Tel:** 902-625-1295. **Season**: Jun - Oct. **Hours:** Jul & Aug - Mon to Fri 9 am to 8 pm; Sat & Sun 12 noon to 4 pm; other months - Mon to Fri 9 am to 5 pm. **Features**: genealogy records, artifacts, newspapers relating to the Strait of Canso area.

✳ For more facilities in the Port Hawkesbury area, see Travel Option 4, page 176.

➵ **EN ROUTE** - To get to the Trans Canada Highway (Hwy 105) from the Port Hastings rotary, take the road uphill to your left just past the Visitor Information Centre and Gift Shop.

Glendale

Located on the TCH (Hwy 105) between the Canso Causeway and Whycocomagh.

Glendale Concert

Location: Glendale on the TCH, on the grounds of St. Mary's Church. **Tel:** 902-625-2361 (St. Mary's Glebe). **Features:** The annual Glendale Concert is a great gathering of fiddlers and other musicians, dancers and singers.

Blues Mills

Located on the TCH, 35 km (21 mi) east of the Canso Causeway.

Mountain Brook Motel

Location: Blues Mills, on TCH (Hwy 105) 35 km (21 mi) east of Canso Causeway. **Mail Addr:** R R #1, River Denys, N.S. B0E 2Y0. **Tel:** 902-756-9094. **Owner**: M. Asaph. **Season**: Jun to mid-Oct. **Rates**: low.

Orangedale (a little detour)

Take **Exit 4** off the TCH at Iron Mines and drive about 6 km (3.6 mi) to an intersection. Keep straight for another km or so to the village of Orangedale.

In addition to the facilities listed below, you'll also find a public wharf and boat launch to the Bras d'Or Lakes, as well as a general store.

Orangedale Building Merchants

Location: Orangedale, about 7 km (4 mi) from TCH Exit 4. **Hours:** 8:30 am to 5:30 pm Mon to Sat. **Cards:** VS, MC. **Features**: hardware, general merchandise, crafts and gifts .

The Old Hotel Gallery

Location: Orangedale, about 7 km (4 mi) from TCH Exit 4. **Tel:** 902-756-2221 (shop) or 756-2927 (home). **Season**: mid-Jun to mid-Sept, or by appointment. **Hours**: 10 am to 5 pm daily, other times by chance or appointment. **Cards:** VS. **Features**: antiques, contemporary items, rocks & fossils, paintings; display of early weaving and spinning.

Orangedale Station Museum and Tearoom

A must for railway buffs or anyone interested in a unique glance into our past.

Location: Orangedale, about 7 km (4 mi) from TCH Exit 4. **Tel:** 902-756-3384. **Season**: mid-Jun to mid-Oct. **Hours**: Mon - Sat 10 am to 6 pm; Sun 1 - 6 pm. **Features**: original railway station built in1886; lots of railway memorabilia and artifacts.

Artist Adrian Syms, Sydney.

Whycocomagh

Located on the Trans Canada Highway (Hwy. 105) about 50 km (35 mi) east of Canso Causeway.

There are two parts to this very picturesque community - the **Whycoba First Nation Mi'kmaq reserve** which you will drive through on the highway, and the **village of Whycocomagh**, which is partially off the main highway.

You'll find at least six gas stations in this area, along with convenience stores, some fast food outlets, a bank in the village and a co-op grocery store on the highway, as well as the facilities listed below.

Whycoba First Nation

One of Cape Breton's five Mi'kmaq reserves.

Negemow Basket Shop

Location: Whycoba First Nation, on TCH at Whycocomagh. **Owner**: Mary Kay Goo Goo. **Season:** May to Oct. **Hours:** generally 7 am to 10 pm. **Cards:** VS, MC. **Features:** Native handcrafts and souvenirs.

Mi'kmaqs

"The earliest known inhabitants of Cape Breton were the Micmac Indians and we have little knowledge of their industry although an excavated site at Little Narrows is yielding artifacts covering a span of approximately three thousand years. We do know that they were a nomadic people who hunted the plentiful game of the forests in the winter months. In the spring and summer they moved to the shores where they fished in the coastal waters. From all accounts it appears that they were not an aggressive people and lived simple and peaceful lives which were to change dramatically after the European immigrants arrived." from The Cabot Trail, by David Street, Gage Pub, 1979.

Glenview Campground

Location: Whycocomagh - turn off TCH at Exit 5 toward Lake Ainslie; campground is short distance from the TCH. **Mail Addr:** Whycocomagh, N.S. B0E 3M0. **Tel:** 902-756-3198, o/s 902-756-2258. **Owner:** R. Jardine. **Season:** May to Oct. **Rates**: avg. **Features:** on Skye River overlooking Bras d'Or Lakes; serviced and unserviced sites; washrooms, laundromat, groceries, fireplaces, pool.

MacKeigan's Pharmacy and Rite Way Market (groceries) - Main St, Whycocomagh turn right at Exit 5. **Tel:** 902-756-2314. **Hours**: main store open from 9 am to 9 pm Mon to Fri; 9 am to 6 pm Sat; the dispensary is only open from 10 am to 6 pm Mon to Sat.

Mary Smith Bed & Breakfast

Location: Main St, Whycocomagh, turn off TCH at Exit 5 toward village then take right turn at Royal Bank sign. **Mail Addr**: Box 24, Whycocomagh, N.S. B0E 3M0; **Tel:** 902-756-2157. **Owner**: M. Smith. **Season**: mid-May to mid-Oct. **Rates**: med-low. **Features:** situated on Bras d'Or Lakes; homemade jams, jellies.

Vi's Restaurant

Location: Whycocomagh, at Exit 5 intersection. **Tel:** 902-756-2338. **Season**: year round. **Hours:** 7 am to 9:30 pm. **Cards**: VS.

➵ **EN ROUTE** - At Exit 5 on the TCH you can choose to take a Side Trip to Lake Ainslie. Details of this Side Trip are at the end of this Travel Option, page 60.

Farmer's Daughter

Location: Whycocomagh, on TCH, just east of Exit 5. **Tel:** 902-756-9042. **Owner**: J. Austen. **Season**: late Mar to late Dec. **Hours**: 9 am to 9 pm daily. **Cards:** VS, MC. **Features**: homemade soups, sandwiches; ice cream; home baking; KFC outlet; gifts and crafts; garden centre.

Fair Isle Motel

Location: Whycocomagh, on TCH, just east of Exit 5. **Mail Addr**: Box 53, Whycocomagh, N.S. B0E 3M0. **Tel:** 902-756-2291. **Owner:** M. Munro. **Season:** year round. **Rates:** mid-range. **Cards**: VS, MC, AE.

Julia Longacre

Island View Bed and Breakfast

Location: Whycocomagh, on TCH near entrance to provincial campground. **Mail Addr**: Box 96, Whycocomagh, N.S. B0E 3M0. **Tel:** 902-756-3011. **Owners:** A. & B. MacKinnon. **Season:** June - Oct. **Rates**: med-low.

Whycocomagh Provincial Park and Hiking Trail

Location: Whycocomagh, on TCH, about a half kilometer east of Exit 5. **Tel:** 902-756-2448. **Season**: mid-Jun to early Sept. **Rates:** avg. **Features:** 73 unserviced sites; pit toilets; disposal station; hiking trail.

Norma's Dining Room

Location: Whycocomagh, on TCH. **Owners**: M. & A. Abderhalden. **Tel**: 902-756-3284. **Season**: Mar to end of Oct. **Hours:** 7 am - 9 pm daily. **Prices**: mid-range. **Cards:** VS. **Features:** licensed; varied menu with Canadian and European cuisine; daily specials.

Aberdeen

Located on the Trans Canada Highway, about 54 km (32 mi) east of the Canso Causeway.

Aberdeen Motel

Location Aberdeen on the TCH. **Mail Addr:** Box 62, Whycocomagh, N.S. B0E 3M0. **Tel:** 902-756-2331; o/s 902-295-2413; Fax 902-295-1440. **Owner**: L. MacRae. **Season:** mid-May to Oct. **Rates:** med-low. **Cards:** VS, MC, AE. **Features:** conveniently located on TCH.

Another Travel Option

Alternate Route via Iona

At Aberdeen you'll come to **Exit 6** which will take you to Little Narrows and Iona.

You can choose to take this alternate route as you travel from the Canso Causeway to Sydney. It takes you across the Little Narrows ferry and along Route 223 to Iona, then from Iona through either Boisdale or Eskasoni to Sydney .

Take Exit 6 off the TCH at Aberdeen to Route 223 East. For more details of this alternate route, see page 64, at the end of this Travel Option.

NOTE: You can also choose to **just take a side trip** to Iona, which is 28 km (17 mi) from Exit 6, then return to Aberdeen and the TCH.

Bucklaw

Located on the Trans Canada Highway, about 14 km (8.5 mi) east of Whycocomagh.

Bucklaw Garage - Bucklaw; 902-756-3457; open 7 am to 7 pm daily except Wednesday.

Castle Moffett

This truly unique four-star accommodation offers its guests the old world charm of a castle with modern luxuries. The 'castle' is actually built over a brook!

Location Bucklaw on TCH, between Whycocomagh and Baddeck. **Mail Addr**: Box 678, Baddeck, N.S. B0E 1B0. **Tel:** 902-756-9070; Fax 902-756-3399. **Owners**: L. and D. Moffett. **Season:** Year round except Dec. 20 - 31. **Rates:** upper end. **Cards:** VS, MC. **Features**: deluxe suites with four-poster beds, whirlpool baths, Great Hall with fireplace; buffet breakfast included; centrally located.

Nyanza

Located on the Trans Canada Highway, 9 km (5.4 mi) west of Baddeck.

Wagmatcook - First Nations Reserve

Another of the five Mi'kmaq reserves in Cape Breton.

Mi'kmaq words for some Cape Breton **places**:

- Wagmatcook - clean waves
- Petoobok - a long dish of salt water - Bras d'Or Lakes
- Uktutuncok - highest mountain - Cape North
- Wegwaak - turning suddenly - Aspy Bay
- Edadeck - a sultry place - Baddeck*
- Abadak - place with an island near - Baddeck*

*There is some disagreement among historians as to which of these two words was actually the forerunner of the name 'Baddeck'.

Indian Bay Milling Company And Herring Choker Deli

This is a great place to stop off for a quick deli sandwich, homemade breads and salads. And if you've been craving brown rice or alfalfa sprouts, they have that too...it's a natural food store as well as a deli.

Location: Nyanza, on TCH, between Whycocomagh and Baddeck. **Owners:** L.& B. MacRae. **Tel:** 902-295-2275. **Season:** year round. **Hours:** Summer Mon to Fri 8 am - 8 pm; Sat & Sun 9 am - 8 pm; o/s hours are slightly reduced.

Don-El-Mar B & B

Location: Nyanza on TCH, next to the Herring Choker Deli (above). **Mail Addr:** R. R. #3, Baddeck, N.S. B0E 1B0. **Tel:** 902-295-1142. **Owner**: B. Plant. **Season**: mid-May to mid-Oct. **Rates:** med-low. **Features**: across from Bras d'Or Lakes with wharf for fishing; access for boating.

Trailsman Motel and Dining Room

Location: Nyanza on TCH, Hwy 105, between Whycocomagh and Baddeck. **Mail Addr:** Box 509, Baddeck, N.S. B0E 1B0. **Tel:** 902-295-2413; 1-800-304-0466; Fax 902-295-1440. **Owner:** K. MacRae. **Season:** Jun to Oct. **Rates:** mid-range **Cards:** VS, MC, AE. **Features:** on Bras d'Or Lake; licensed; outdoor pool; pedal boats; laundromat.

➵ **EN ROUTE** - At Nyanza, you'll come to Exit 7 to Margaree and Cabot Trail. See Travel Option 3, page 102, for the details of this option.

Red Barn Gift Shop and Restaurant

Location: On TCH, Hwy 105, at Exit 7. **Tel:** 295-3036. **Owner:** E. Timmons. **Season:** mid-May to mid-Oct. **Hours:** Jul & Aug - 8 am to 10 pm; other months 8 am to 8 pm. **Restr Prices**: mid-range. **Cards:** VS, MC, AE. **Features**: full menu, licenced, mini golf, wheelchair accessible.

Baddeck Inlet

Located on TCH, Hwy 105, just past Exit 7.

Baddeck Cabot Trail KOA Campground

Location: Baddeck Inlet, on TCH just east of Exit 7. **Mail Addr:** Baddeck, N.S. B0E 1B0. **Tel:** 902-295-2288; o/s 902-794-7952. **Owners:** The Flamm/Schumacher family. **Season:** mid-May to mid-Oct. **Rates:** avg. **Cards:** VS, MC. **Features:** serviced and unserviced sites, 30 & 50 amp; washrooms; laundromat; supplies.

Silver Spruce Vacation Park

Location: Baddeck Inlet on TCH, just east of Exit 7. **Mail Addr:** Box 373, Baddeck, N.S. B0E 1B0. **Tel:** 902-295-2417; 1-800-507-2228; o/s 902-295-3036. **Owner:** E. Timmons. **Season:** mid-May to mid-Oct. **Rates**: camping - avg plus; log cabins - mid-range. **Cards:** most major cards. **Features**: licenced dining room; serviced and unserviced sites- 30 & 50 amp; washrooms, laundromat, supplies, pool; lake and river fishing; log cabins.

MacIntyre's Housekeeping Cottages

These are brand new, lovely cottages with a fabulous view of the Bras d'Or Lakes.

Location: Baddeck Inlet, on TCH, 5 km (3 mi) west of Baddeck. **Mail Addr:** R. R. #3,Baddeck Inlet, N.S. B0E 1B0. **Tel:** 902-295-1133/3160. **Owners:** R. & V. McIntyre. **Season:** year round. **Rates:** med-high. **Cards:** VS, MC. **Features:** weekly rates available; fireplace in cottages; covered veranda; one cottage is wheelchair accessible; great view.

Bras d'Or Lakes Campground

Location: Baddeck Inlet on TCH, 5 km (3 mi) west of Baddeck. **Mail Addr:** Box 595, Baddeck, N.S., B0E 1B0. **Tel:** 902-295-2329; o/s 902-945-2921. **Owner:** I. Galinat. **Season:** Jun to Sept. **Rates:** avg plus. **Cards:** VS. **Features:** serviced & unserviced sites- 30 & 50 amps; laundry; showers; recreation room with video games, pool table; pool; cafe, groceries.

Pine Away Overnight Trailers

Location: Baddeck Inlet, about 2 km (1.2 mi) west of Baddeck. **Mail Addr:** Box 412, Baddeck, N.S. B0E 1B0. **Tel:** 902-295-3225; o/s 295-2079. **Owners:** A. & B. Grant.

Season: Jun to mid-Oct. **Rates:** mid-range. **Cards**:VS, MC. **Features:** centrally located near area's attractions; nature walks; all trailers have private bedroom, bath and kitchen with microwave, VCR and barbecue.

Cabot Trail Motel and Dining Room

Location: Baddeck Inlet, on TCH, about 1.5 km (1 mi) west of Baddeck. **Mail Addr:** Box 309, Baddeck, N.S. B0E 1B0. **Tel:** 902-295-2580, Fax 902-295-1303. **Owners:** G.& A. Ross. **Season:** mid-May to Oct. **Rates:** med-high. **Cards:** VS, MC. **Dng Rm Hrs:** 7:30 - 9:30 am; 5:30 -8:30 pm. **Prices:** mid-range. **Features:** overlooking Bras d'Or Lake; laundromat; licenced dining room; outdoor pool, gift shop, private beach.

Eagle Watch Boat Tours

Location: Baddeck Inlet on TCH, across from Cabot Trail Motel (above). **Mail Addr:** R. R. #1, Brookfield, N.S. B0N 1C0. **Tel:** ; 902-295-7772; o/s 902-895-6165. **Owner:** D. Ling. **Season:** mid-Jun to mid-Oct. **Hours:** 3 tours daily. **Features:** 2-hr boat tour of Baddeck Bay and Washabuck.

➳ EN ROUTE

There are three Exits to Baddeck - 8, 9 and 10. The first one, Exit 8, takes you into Baddeck via Shore Road; Exit 9, a little further east, takes you into the center of the Village, and Exit 10, takes you in from the east along Bay Road.

The facilities below are listed in order starting at Exit 8, the Shore Rd.

If you take either Exit 9 or 10 into Baddeck, just consult the map on below to get your bearings.

Baddeck

Located on the TCH (105) about mid-way between the Canso Causeway and Sydney, about 80 km (48 mi) each way, give or take a km or two.

> **Village of Baddeck**
>
> Baddeck is a bustling summer resort kind of place with a population of just over 1,000. (I suspect that number increases significantly in the summer!) You'll find just about anything you need there...for instance, gas stations both on the TCH and in the village, a bank, a hospital, shops, food stores, lots of restaurants and accommodations, and more.

Fuller's Tourist Apt.

Location: 122 Shore Rd, Baddeck. **Mail Addr:** Box 507, Baddeck, N.S. B0E 1B0. **Tel:** 902-295-3397; Fax 902-295-1551. **Owner:** Fuller family. **Season:** mid-May to mid-Oct. **Rates:** mid-range. **Cards:** VS, MC. **Features:** housekeeping; fireplace; private beach.

Sealladh Aluinn B & B

Location: 251 Shore Rd. **Mail Addr:** Box 59, Baddeck, N.S., B0E 1B0. **Tel:** 902-295-1160. **Owner:** S. Fraser. **Season:** mid-May to Oct. **Rates:** med-low. **Features:** continental breakfast; Lake view.

Restawyle Tourist Home B & B

Location: 231 Shore Rd, Baddeck. **Mail Addr:** R R #3, Baddeck, N.S. B0E 1B0. **Tel:** 902-295-3253. **Owners:** P. & P. MacAulay. **Season:** mid-May to mid Oct. (after 1996 open year round). **Rates:** med-low. **Cards:** VS. **Features:** close to Baddeck attractions; beautiful view of Lake; lots of activities like hiking, sailing, etc. close by.

Village of Baddeck

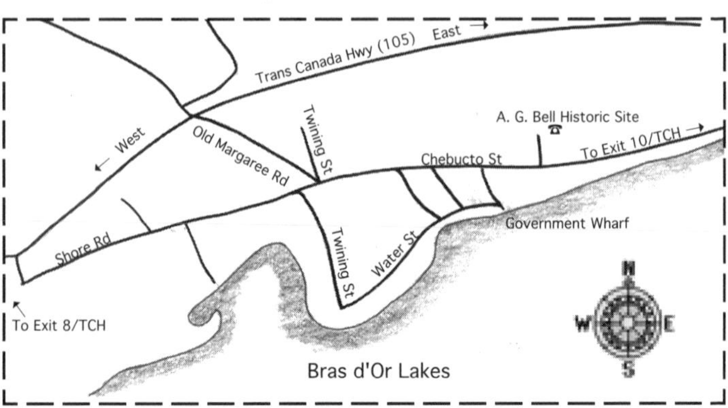

Silver Dart Lodge, MacNeil House and McCurdy's Restaurant

Location: Shore Rd, Baddeck. **Mail Addr:** Box 399, Baddeck, N.S. B0E 1B0. Tel 902-295-2340; Fax. 902-295-2484; 1-800-565-VIEW. **Owner:** W. Janes. **Season:** mid-May to mid-Oct. **Rates:** med-high to upper end. **Cards:** most major cards. **McCurdy's Restaurant Hrs.** 7 - 9:30 am; 5:30 - 9:30 pm. **Prices:** med-high. **Features:** licensed dining room with patio; live Scottish entertainment; heated outdoor pool; private beach for swimming and walking; games.

Clan Cameron B & B

Location: 282 Shore Rd, Baddeck. **Mail Addr:** Box 27, Baddeck, N.S. B0E 1B0. **Tel:** 902-295-2725. **Owner:** D. Cameron. **Season:** Year round. **Rates:** med-low. **Cards:** VS. **Features:** deck overlooking Bras d'Or Lake.

Ceilidh Country Lodge

Location: Shore Rd, Baddeck. **Mail Addr:** Box 190 Baddeck, N.S. B0E 1B0. **Tel:** 902-295-3500; Fax 902-295-3527; 1-800-565-5660.. **Owner:** MacAulay family. **Season:** May - Nov. **Rates:** mid-range. **Cards:** most major cards. **Features:** continental breakfast; overlooking the Bras d'Or Lakes.

Inverary Inn Resort - Dining Room, Gift Shop & Lakeside Cafe

Location: Shore Rd, Baddeck. **Mail Addr:** Box 190, Baddeck, N.S. B0E 1B0. **Tel:** 902-295-3500; 1-800-565-5660; Fax 902-295-3527. **Owner:** The MacAulay family. **Season:** May to Nov. **Rates:** med-high to upper end; **Cards:** most major cards. **Dng Rm Hrs**: 6:30 to 10 am; 5:30 to 9 pm. **Prices**: med-high. Cafe **Hours:** 7 am to 10 pm. **Cafe Prices:** mid-range. **Features:** licensed; indoor pool; hot tub and sauna, tennis courts, boats and other outdoor activities; kayak and zodiak rentals.

Auberge Gisele's Country Inn and Dining Room

Location: 387 Shore Rd, Baddeck. **Mail Addr:** Box 132, Baddeck, N.S. B0E 1B0. **Tel:** 902-295-2849; Fax 902-295-2033; 1-800-3040. **Owners:** H.& H. Sievers. **Season:** May to Oct. **Rates:** med-high to upper end. **Cards:** most major cards. **Dng Rm Hrs:** 7:30 - 9:30 am; 5:30 - 9:30 pm. **Prices**: upper end. **Features:** licensed Four Star dining room; sauna; whirlpool; solarium; laundromat; centrally located for touring, hiking, diving, sailing, etc.

Nova Scotia Liquor Commission - Campbell Street, off Shore Rd; 902-295-2390; open 10 am to 8 pm Mon to Thurs; 10 am to 10 pm Fri & Sat. (subject to slight variations)

Baddeck Lobster Suppers

No worries here about trying to eat your lobster politely - they expect you to make a mess!

Location: 6 Ross St, Baddeck, off Shore Rd, near MacAulay's Ford Garage. **Owners:** M. & W. MacEachern. **Tel:** 902-295-3307. **Season:** Jun to Oct. **Hours:** lunch ll:30am - 1:30 pm; dinner 4 - 9 pm. **Prices**: mid-range to upper end. **Cards:** VS, MC. **Features:** Fresh Atlantic lobster in the shell for dinner plus all-you-can-eat chowder, mussels, salad,etc. (salmon or ham alternative); lunch is lobster rolls, chowders, etc.; fully licensed; children's portions.

Island Eco-adventures

Biking, canoeing, camping, winter sports.

Location: 16 Chebucto St,Baddeck, near intersection of Chebucto St and Shore Rd. **Mail Addr:** Box 34, Baddeck, N.S. B0E 1B0. **Tel:** 902-295-3303; 1-800-707-5512. **Owner:** B. Doncaster. **Season:** year round. **Hours:** calls taken 24 hours a day. **Rates:** varied according to activity. **Cards:** MC. **Features:** hybrid bikes outfitted specially for Cabot Trail touring; mountain bikes, camping equipment; maps, canoes, cartop carriers; guided back country tours in fall; cross-country ski outfitters; agent for snowmobile outfitters.

Victoria County Memorial Hospital, Old Margaree Road, Baddeck. **Tel:** 902-295-2112. At intersection of Shore Rd, Old Margaree Rd and Chebucto St.

Lynwood Inn and Dining Room

This house, well over a century old, has been extensively renovated into a lovely inn and restaurant.

Location: 23 Shore Rd, Baddeck, at intersection of Old Mararee Rd and Chebucto St. **Mail Addr:** Box 361, Baddeck, N.S. B0E 1B0. **Tel:** 902-295-1995; Fax 902-295-3084. **Owners:** D.MacDonnell & L.DesRochers. **Season:** Rooms year round; dining room Jun - Dec. **Rates:**. upper end. **Cards:** VS, MC, Dis. **Dng Rm Hrs**: 7 - 10 am; 11:30

am - 2 pm; 5:30 - 9 pm. **Prices:** med-high. **Features:** licensed dining room with delicacies like Mussel Saffron Soup; bilingual service.

Tourist Information Centre

A good place to stop off for some brochures and information.

Location: Baddeck, at intersection of Shore Rd, Chebucto St and Old Margaree Rd. **Season:** mid-May to mid-Oct. **Hours:** generally 9 am to 9 pm, depending on demand.

Kennedy's Housekeeping Cottages

Location: 11 High St, Baddeck. At the intersection in the west end of town, take Twining St to High St. **Mail Addr:** Box 572, Baddeck, N.S. B0E 1B0. **Tel:** 902-295-2781. **Owner:** S. Kennedy. **Season**: Jun to Aug. **Rates:** mid-range.

Seaflower Gallery

Location: Chebucto St, Baddeck.**Tel:** 902-295-2386/ 1991.**Season:** year round. **Hours:** Mon. to Sat. 1 - 5 pm.; o/s open Thurs to Sat only. **Cards:** VS. **Features:** local art and art supplies, antiques and small collectibles.

The Village Kitchen

Location: Chebucto St, Baddeck **Tel:** 902-295-3200. **Owners:** T. Ashton & D. Ross. **Season:** May to Oct. **Hours:** 7 am to 8 pm, daily. **Prices:** low. **Features**: small, 'kitchen-style' eatery.

The Outdoor Store

Location: Chebucto St, Baddeck. **Tel:** 902-295-2576. **Hours**: summer - Mon to Sat 8 am to 9 pm; Sun 12 noon to 5 pm; o/s open 10 am to 6 pm Mon to Sat. **Cards:** Interac. **Features:** quality outdoor clothing and equipment; Roots outlet; kayak and bike rentals and tours; photo lab; outdoor adventure packages available.

Wong's Family Restaurant

Location: Chebucto St, Baddeck. **Tel:** 902-295-2234. **Season:** year round. Hours summer 7 am to 11 pm. **Prices**: mid-range. **Cards:** VS, MC.

Telegraph House and Dining Room

This is the oldest business presently operating in Baddeck. It's been an inn for well over a century. One of its most notable overnight guests...who else but A. G. Bell himself?

Location: Chebucto St, Baddeck. **Mail Addr:** Box 8, Baddeck, B0E 1B0. **Tel:** 902-295-1100. **Owners:** B. & M. Dunlop. **Season:** year round. **Rates:** med-high. **Cards:** VS, MC, AE. **Dng Rm Hrs:** 7 - 11 am; 11 am - 2:45 pm; 5 - 8:30 pm. **Prices**: med-high. **Features:** licensed; Victorian atmosphere.

Highwheeler Cafe

Out on the patio you can munch away on a huge deli sandwich while you watch the world go by.

Location: Chebucto St, Baddeck, just about the centre of the village. **Owners:** C. MacLeod & L. Dixon. **Tel:** 902-295-3006. **Season:** year round. **Hours:** 6 am - 10 p.m. daily in summer; o/s 7 am - 6 pm. except Sun. **Prices**: low **Cards:** VS, Debit cards. **Features:** home baked goods; deli meats and cheeses; box lunches prepared; daily specials; sidewalk patio.

Kidston Landing

Location: Chebucto St, Baddeck, in the centre of the village. **Tel:** 902-295-2868. **Owners:** P. & B. Anderson. **Season:** year round. **Hours:** Jun to Oct 9 am to 9 pm daily; o/s 9 am to 5 pm, Sundays noon to 5 pm. **Features:** pottery, pewter, music, T-shirts; casual clothes; sweaters; etc; will ship.

Blue Heron Gift Shop

Location: 507 Chebucto St, Baddeck. **Tel:** 902-295-3424. **Season:** year round. **Hours:** Mon. - Sat. 9 am to 5 pm, extra hours during summer. **Cards:** VS, MC.

Bras d'Or Yacht Club

Location: Baddeck, next to Government Wharf, Water St. **Tel:** 295-9984. **Features:** mooring, launching facilities, repairs, fuel.

Amoeba Sailing Tours

Sail on the 64-foot schooner *Amoeba* around the beautiful Bras d'Or Lakes.

Location: Baddeck Government Wharf, Water Street. **Mail Addr:** Box 673, Baddeck, N.S. B0E 1B0.**Tel:** 295-1426/ 2481. **Season:** Jun to Sept, maybe longer depending on the weather. **Sailing Times**: 11am, 2 pm,

4:30 pm & 6:30 pm. **Features:** deck seating for 43; 1 1/2 hour tours; group rates.

Loch Bhreagh Tours

Pronounced "lock bree-ah"- it means 'beautiful lake'.

Location: Baddeck, Government Wharf, Water Street. **Mail Addr:** Box 492, Baddeck, N.S. B0E 1B0. **Tel:** 902-295-2016. **Owner:** S. MacDonald. **Season**: mid-May to Oct. **Cruise Times:** 10 am; 1:30 pm and 4 pm, evening cruises by arrangement. **Prices:** generally $15 per person, but group rates are available. **Features:** 2-hour Lakes cruise aboard a 13-metre (42-foot) jet boat; shuttle to Dundee; golf packages; food service available by prior arrangement; liquor license.

Seawinds Chandlery On the Wharf

Location: on the Government wharf, Water St, Baddeck. **Tel:** 902-295-2205 **Season:** Jun to Thanksgiving. **Hours:** 9 am to 9 pm daily; after Labour Day 9 am to 5 pm. **Cards:** most major cards. **Features:** located in an old restsored wharehouse on the Baddeck wharf; carries lots of kids' things; nautical items and interesting gifts.

Rose Cottage Gallery

Location: Water St, Baddeck, near government wharf. **Tel:** 902-295-3211/3405. **Season:** Jun to early Oct. **Hours:** Jul & Aug 10 am - 8 pm; other months 10 am to 6 pm (could vary slightly). **Features:** great place for folk art buffs; some really elegant craft items and art pieces.

Kidston Island Beach

Location: Kidston Island, a short boat ride from the Baddeck Government Wharf. Boats leave from the wharf at regular intervals each day.

Baddeck Marine

Location: Water St, near Baddeck government wharf. **Tel:** 902-295-2434; Fax same. **Season:** year round. **Hours:** Jun to mid-Sept - 8:30 am to 9 pm; other months - 8:30 am to 5:30 pm. **Cards:** VS, MC. **Features:** fuel, sewage pump-out; shower and laundry services; launch; guest moorings; supplies, maintenance and marina.

Duffus House (c 1830)

(c 1830) Named for the first permanent white resident and entrepreneur of Baddeck, James Duffus.

Location: Water St, Baddeck. **Mail Addr:** Box 427 Baddeck, N.S. B0E 1B0. **Tel:** 902-295-2172l o/s 902-928-2878. **Owners:** J. & J. Langley. **Season:** mid-Jun to mid-Oct. **Rates:** med-high and upper end.. **Cards:** VS. **Features:** historic house with antiques; 1 garden suite; private dock.

Yellow Cello Pizza Cafe

Location: Chebucto St, Baddeck, east end of village near Bell Historic Site. **Owner:** W. Stephens. **Tel:** 902-295-2303. **Season:** year round. **Hours:** summer 8 am - 11 pm; winter 9 am - 10 pm. **Prices**: mid-range. **Cards:** VS & Debit Cards. **Features:** pizza, pasta, salads, soups; homemade breads; licensed; covered outdoor deck facing water.

Bell Buoy Restaurant

Location: Chebucto St, Baddeck, across from entrance to Bell Historic Site. **Tel:** 902-295-2581. **Owner:** F. MacPhail. **Season:** Jun - Oct. **Hours:** 11:30 am daily. **Prices:** mid-range to med-high. **Cards:** most major cards. **Features:** family-style restaurant; licenced; something for all tastes - seafood, meat and pasta dishes; overlooks yacht club and Baddeck Bay.

Dunlop Guest House

Location: 552 Chebucto St, Baddeck, across from the Bell Museum entrance. **Mail Addr:** 5711 Lady Hammond Rd, Halifax, N.S. B3K 2R4. **Tel:** 902-295-1100 (for bookings). **Owner:** P. Dunlop. **Season:** year round. **Rates:** mid-range. **Cards:**VS, MC, AE. **Features:** full kitchen facilities; guests must register at Telegraph House, 479 Chebucto St.

➼ **EN ROUTE** - Somewhere near the entrance to the Bell museum, Chebucto Street becomes Bay Road.

Alexander Graham Bell National Historic Site

Location: Entrance is on Chebucto St, in the east end of Baddeck. **Tel:** 902-295-2069. **Season:** Year round. **Hours:** Jul. & Aug 9 am - 8 pm; Jun & Sept 9 am - 7 pm; rest of year 9 am - 5 pm. **Admission**: low. **Cards:** Interac. **Features:** the summer of '96 will see some improvements - a new gallery exhibiting Dr. Bell's work teaching the deaf; exhibits with larger print; wheelchair ramps and accessible washrooms.

Go Fly A Kite! (at the A. G. Bell Museum)

At the Alexander Graham Bell National Historic Site in Baddeck, you'll get to see the world's largest collection of Bell memorabilia - a vacuum jacket used for artificial respiration, the original hull of his HD-4 hydrodome and a reconstruction of the hydrofoil itself, a graphophone that looks like a sewing machine. You'll find out about his work with the deaf, the flight of the Silver Dart and, of course, his invention of the telephone.

At the Bell museum kids can take part in science experiments like the ones Mr. Bell carried out with his grandchildren, visitors can have a phone conversation in a 1900-style telephone booth and...if you're so inclined, you can indeed go fly a kite!

Raj Gift Shop and Taj Restaurant

Location: Baddeck, beside the A.G.Bell Museum. **Tel:** 902-295-2534/2915. **Hours:** from Jul to Sept open from 9 am to 9 pm daily; o/s hours are from 10 am to 5 pm.

The Bay Tourist Home B & B

Location: Bay Rd, Baddeck. **Mail Addr:** Box 24, Baddeck, N.S. B0E 1B0. **Tel:** 902-295-2046. **Owners:** P.& H. Edwards. **Rates:** low. **Season:** May - Oct. **Cards:** VS. **Features:** quiet 30-acre property; light breakfast.

Broad Water Inn, Cottages and Craft Shop

A 150-year-old country inn overlooking the Bras d'Or Lakes, and log cottages nestled in the woods.

Location: Bay Rd, Baddeck, in the east end of the village, 2.2 km (1.3) east of the Bell Histsoric Site. **Mail Addr:** Box 702, Baddeck, N.S. B0E 1B0. **Tel:** 902-295-1101. **Owners:** G. Holdner & N. Kaser. **Season:** Year round. **Rates:** med-high and upper end. **Cards:** VS, MC, Dis. **Features:** beautiful country setting overlooking the Lake; substantial continen- tal breakfast; craft shop on the premises.

Breezy Brae B & B

Location: The Bay Rd (Rte. 205), Baddeck, 3 km (1.8 mi) east of village. **Mail Addr:** Box 566, Baddeck, N.S. B0E 1B0. **Tel:** 902-295- 2618 /1700. **Owners:** M. & P. Woodford. **Season:** mid-Jun to mid-Sept. **Rates:** low. **Features:** salt water swimming; substantial continental breakfast.

Bare Boat Charters

Location: Beinn Bhreagh - Baddeck, off Bay Rd. **Mail Addr:** Box 667, Baddeck, N.S. B0E 1B0. **Tel:** 902-295-3318. **Owner:** M. Harvey. **Season:** late May to early Oct. **Hours:** rentals must be booked in advance - just give them a call. **Features:** four sailing vessels ranging from 28 ft to 32 ft; fully equipped; charts of lake, lifejackets and safety equipment; day sailers have no sleeping quarters or toilet.

Bannockburn Tours

Location: Baddeck - tour van picks up passengers at motels and campgrounds in the Baddeck area - call ahead for reservations. **Mail Addr:** Box 38, Baddeck, N.S. B0E 1B0. **Tel:** 902-295-3310. **Season:** mid-May to mid-Oct or other times on request. **Hours:** Cabot Trail Tours daily from 9 am to 5 pm; shuttle service to Louisbourg on Mon, Wed & Fri. **Rates:** $49/ person for Cabot Trail tour; $35 per person to Louisbourg. **Cards:** MC. **Features:** narrated tour of Cabot Trail, lots of stops along the way, including a lunch stop; suttle service to Louisbourg.

Centre Bras d'Or Festival of the Arts

Local, national and international entertainment throughout the summer. See book insert for venues and dates. Box Office **Tel:** 902-294-3044.

Forks Baddeck and Baddeck Bridge

Take Exit 9 off the Trans Canada Highway and turn off ramp onto Old Margaree Road.

Forks Baddeck and Baddeck Bridge Area

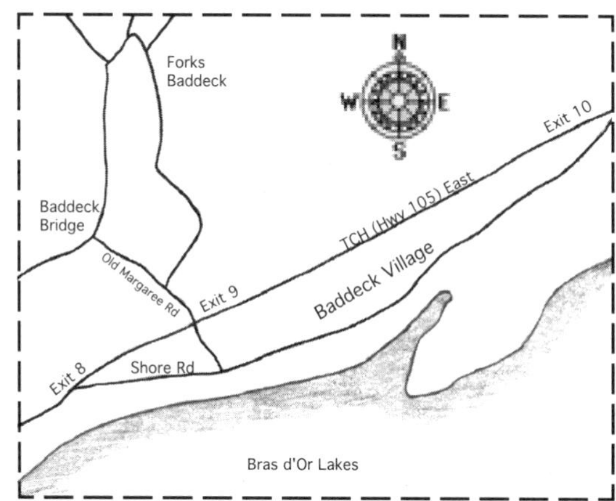

Kerr's B & B and Cottages

Location: Hillcrest Dr, Baddeck - take Exit 9 off TCH and turn onto Old Margaree Rd; take first right turn (next to RCMP) off Old Margaree Rd. **Mail Addr:** Box 731 Baddeck, N.S. B0E 1B0. **Tel:** 902-295-3476. **Owner:** S. Kerr. **Season:** year round. **Rates:** med-low. **Cards:** VS. **Features:** lake view; housekeeping cottages.

Forks Baddeck Golf Course (9-hole)

Location: take Exit 9 off TCH, turn off ramp onto Old Margaree Rd, and take first right turn off Old Margaree Road; keep on this road to the Golf Course. **Tel:** 295-2174. **Season:** opens May 11th. **Hours:** daylight to dusk. **Green fees:** daily rate $19 (plus tax); 18-holes $13. **Features:** 9-hole, slope 85; rating 57.2; canteen service,rental equipment; licenced bar; entertainment some weekends.

Auld Manse B & B

Location: Forks Baddeck. Take Exit 9 off TCH, turn off ramp onto Old Margaree Rd; take the first road to your right off Old Margaree Rd toward Forks Baddeck. Keep on the pavement until you cross two iron bridges. Take the second driveway on right past the bridges. **Mail Addr:** R. R. #1, Forks Baddeck, N.S. B0E 1B0. **Tel:** 902-295-2362; 1-800-254-7982. **Owner:** Marj Theriault. **Season:** Mar to Nov. **Rates:** low. **Cards:** VS, MC. **Features:** country setting.

Uisge Ban Falls Provincial Park and Hiking Trails

Location: Forks Baddeck - take Exit 9 off TCH, turn off ramp onto Old Margaree Rd,then take first road to your right, toward Forks Baddeck; drive until you've crossed two iron bridges. Keep right until you come to a sign for "MacPhee's Cross". Take that road and drive about 1 km to a junction. Turn left and drive into park. **Features**: trails; waterfall; lookoff sites; picnic tables; toilets of the outhouse variety.

Take a hike!

This is one of the Island's most enjoyable and user-friendly parks. There are two well-groomed **walking trails** - one goes to a beautiful waterfall and the other takes you along the North Branch of the Baddeck River.

Incidentally, "uisge ban" is Gaelic for "**white water**" and is pronounced loosely "oosh-ka ban".

M and V, B & B

Location: Baddeck Bridge. Take Exit 9 off TCH, turn off ramp onto Old Margaree Rd and keep straight on Old Margaree Rd. **Mail Addr:** Box 284, Baddeck, N.S. B0E 1B0. **Tel:** 902-295-2668. **Owners:** M. & V. Garland. **Season:** May to Oct. **Rates:** med-low. **Features:** substantial continental breakfast.

Eagle's Perch B & B

Ask for a cup of Gail's home-grown apple mint tea.

Location: Baddeck Bridge - take Exit 9 off the TCH, turn off ramp onto Old Margaree Rd and keep straight for 4 km (2.5 mi) to the Bridge. Cross bridge, turn left and drive one km. **Mail Addr:** Box 425, Baddeck, N.S. B0E 1B0. **Tel:** 902-295-2640. **Owner:** G. Holdner. **Season:** mid-May to mid-Oct. **Rates:** med-low. **Cards:** VS, MC. **Features:** lovely log home in peaceful pastoral setting; canoe rentals; close to Baddeck attractions and shopping.

Flying Squirrel B & B

Location: Baddeck Bridge - Take Exit 9 off the TCH, turn off ramp and keep straight on Old Margaree Rd for 4 km (2.5 mi); turn left toward Hunter's Mountain; drive 2 km (1.5 mi). **Mail Addr:** Box 185, Baddeck, N.S. B0E 1B0. **Tel:** 902-295-2904. **Owner:** L. Murphy. **Season:** mid May to end of Oct. **Rates:** med-low. **Features:** country setting with mountain view; very quiet.

Big Harbour

Located just off the Trans Canada Highway, about 2 km (1.2 mi) east of Baddeck. Watch for Big Harbour sign.

The Roost Bed & Breakfast

Location: Big Harbour, about 3 km (2 mi) down the Big Harbour Rd. **Mail Addr:** R. R. #2, Baddeck, N.S. B0E 1B0. **Tel:** 902-295-2722. **Owner:** L. Coleman. **Season:** mid-Jun to mid-Oct. **Rates:** med-low. **Features:** quiet location; birding - lots of eagle sightings; deck.

South Haven

Located on Trans Canada Highway (Hwy 105), about 11 km (6.5 mi) east of Baddeck.

An Seanne Mhanse B & B

Location: South Haven, on TCH. **Mail Addr:** R.R. #2, Baddeck, South Haven, N.S. B0E 1B0. **Tel:** 902-295-2538. **Owner:** L. Drinnan. **Season:** year round. **Rates:** med-low. **Features:** a 1906 Presbyterian Church Manse; centrally located for Cabot Trail, Gaelic College.

➵ EN ROUTE

Here you will come to **Exit 11** to the **Cabot Trail.** This is the Exit you would take to go around the Cabot Trail from east to west. Exit 7 at Nyanza (a few km west of Baddeck) is the way you would go if you were travelling in an easterly direction.

For details of the Cabot Trail, see Travel Option 3, page 102.

St. Anns

Located on Trans Canada Highway about 13 km (8 mi) east of Baddeck.

St. Ann's Motel

Location: South Gut St. Ann's at TCH Exit 11. **Mail Addr:** R. R. #4, Baddeck, N.S. B0E 1B0. **Tel:** 902-295-2876; o/s 902-736-8908. **Owner:** M. Marinelli. **Season:** mid-May - mid-Oct. **Rates:** med-low.. **Cards:** VS. **Features:** snack bar; restaurant next door; on shore of St. Ann's Bay.

Lobster Galley Restaurant and Gift Shop

Location: South Gut St Anns, Cabot Trail, just at the junction of TCH (105) Exit 11. **Tel:** 902-295-3100, Fax 902-929-2072 **Owner:** J.Thiele. **Season:** early May - late Oct. **Prices:** mid-range to med-high. **Cards:** all major cards. **Features:** specializes in lobster and seafood; live lobster pound; vegetarian menu; deck overlooking water.

Gaelic College of Celtic Arts & Crafts

Location: Take Exit 11 off the TCH at South Haven and drive 1 km. **Mail Addr:** Box 9, Baddeck, N.S. B0E 1B0. **Tel:** 902-295-3411, Fax 902-295-2912. **Season:** mid-May to mid-Dec. **Hours:** July/Aug. 8 am to 8 pm daily; o/s Mon. - Fri. 8 am to 5 pm. **Cards:** VS, MC. **Admission**: $2.00 covers Hall of the Clans and museum. **Restr Prices**: low

My advice...don't leave Cape Breton without stopping off at the **Gaelic College**.

This truly unique institution has been in operation since 1938 and students of Celtic tradition come from all over the world to learn everything from Scottish piping to traditional weaving to the Gaelic language itself.

As a visitor, you can watch as classes are being taught, enjoy the pipers and dancers as they practice on the parade square, sit in on a daily lunch-time 'ceilidh' or take in a Wednesday evening concert. You can even take some classes yourself if you're so inclined.

And...if you have a hankering to find your Cape Breton roots, check out the Great Hall of the Clans.

William Rogers Art Gallery

Location: Cabot Trail, adjacent to the Gaelic College. **Tel:** 902-562-2273 (home); 902-295-1040 (gallery). **Owner and Artist**: William Rogers. **Season:** late Jun to mid-Oct. **Hours:** Jul & Aug - 9 am to 5 pm daily; Sept & Oct - 10 am to 4 pm, 2 or 3 days a week (by chance or call ahead). **Cards:** VS, MC. **Features:** beautiful watercolors, most of which are painted on location in Cape Breton. Sample of artist's work below.

Artist William Rogers

St. Ann's Harbour Boat Tours

Harbour historical tours or a trip to the Bird Islands.

Location: South Haven; on the TCH, just east of Exit 11 - watch for the wharf (you can walk here from the Gaelic College - see above). **Mail Addr:** Box 33, Englishtown, N.S. B0C 1H0. **Tel:** 902-929-2563. **Owner:** D. MacAskill. **Season:** late May to late Oct. **Hours:** Bird Island Tours leave at 9 am; Harbour historical tours leave at 1:30 pm and 6 pm. **Features:** On Bird Island tour see seals, puffins, seabirds, etc; on Harbour historical tour, hear about the fascinating history of St. Ann's Bay - see the site of the very first French fortification in North America; hear about Giant MacAskill, Rev Norman MacLeod and much else.

Seal Island/Boularderie

On Trans Canada Highway, at the eastern base of Kelly's Mountain, about 35 km (21 mi) east of Baddeck.

As you're heading east from Baddeck, the Seal Island Bridge (high, isn't it?), takes you onto Boularderie Island.

Seal Island Trailer Park

Location: Seal Island, New Harris Rd - on the Baddeck side off the Seal Island Bridge. **Mail Addr:** R. R. #1, Bras d'Or, N.S. B0C 1B0. **Tel:** 902-674-2145, Fax same. **Owner:** M. Christopher. **Season:** mid-May to mid-Oct. **Rates:** avg & ave-plus. **Features:** serviced and unserviced sites; laundromat, showers, pool, beach, boat launch, fishing, playround, supplies.

Mini Dipper

Stop off for an "ice cream break" on a hot summer day - just over the bridge.

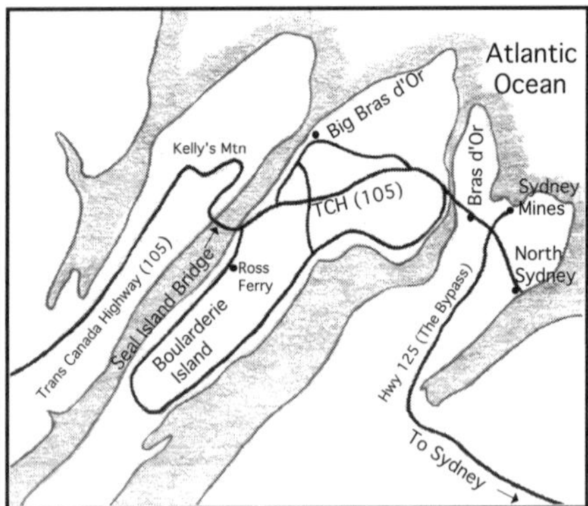

Boularderie/
Seal Island

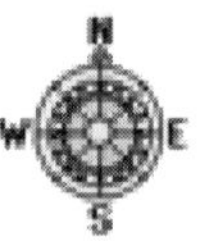

"**The Island of Boularderie** received its first inhabitant in 1820, when Donald McDonald and family arrived...In 1823, however, there was a large influx of immigrants from Gairlock and Loch Carron, in Rosshire, and each year thereafter the population was increased until Boularderie became one of the most populous districts in all Cape Breton." Patterson's History of Victoria County, originally written in 1885, published by College of Cape Breton Press in 1978.

Den of Antiquity

This requires a little detour. Turn down the Kempt Head/ Ross Ferry Rd.

Location: Boularderie - take the Kempt Head Rd, Exit 13, just east of the Seal Island Bridge. Watch for signs. **Tel:** 902-674-2505. **Owner:** J. Bonner Arnold. **Hours:** Friday to Sunday 10 am to 5 pm or so, Mon to Thurs by appointment. **Features:** friendly and knowledgeable service; good selection of collectibles and some antique furniture.

Dreamland B & B

Location: Ross Ferry. Take Kempt Head Rd, Exit 13, just east of Seal Island Bridge and drive for 16 km (10 mi). **Mail Addr:** R. R. #1, Bras d'Or, N.S. B0C 1B0. **Tel:** 902-674-2083, Fax 902-674-2991. **Owners:** M. & A. Rea. **Season:** May - Oct, or by arrangement. **Rates:** med-low. **Features:** quiet country setting overlooking Bras d'Or Lake; private beach, canoeing.

Cedar House Bakery & Restaurant

The homemade bread and desserts here are as good as (if not better than) grandma used to make, and I'm willing to stick my neck out and say their seafood chowder is the best in the world.

Location: Boularderie (Seal Island) on TCH, just east of the Seal Island Bridge. **Owners:** R. & E. MacKenzie. **Tel:** 902-674-2929. **Season:** May - Oct. **Hours:** 9 am to 9 pm. **Prices:** mid-range. **Cards:** VS, MC, AE. **Features:** great 'comfort food', homemade bread and sweets, daily specials.

Spaghetti Benders

Location: Boularderie (Seal Island) on TCH, just east of the Seal Island Bridge. **Tel:** 902-674-2600/2656. **Owners:** G., A., & N. Saker. **Season:** May to Oct. **Hours:** 9 am to 10 pm daily. **Cards:** VS. **Features:** lots of pasta and other Italian delights.

Seal Island Motel & Restaurant

Location: Boularderie (Seal Island), on TCH, about 1 km east of the Seal Island Bridge. **Mail Addr:** Box 221, Bras d'Or, N.S. B0C 1B0. **Tel:** 902-674-2418, Fax 902-674-2068. **Owner:** F. Skinner. **Season:** May to Oct. **Rates:** mid-range. **Cards:** most major cards. **Restr Hrs**: 7 am - 10 am & 4:30 pm to 9:30 pm. **Restr Prices**: mid-range. **Features:** great view; 15 min drive from Newfoundland Ferry.

Big Bras d'Or (short detour)

You'll have to venture a wee bit off the TCH to get to Big Bras d'Or.Take Exit 14, 3 km (1.8 mi) east of the Seal Island Bridge.

Gilead B & B

Location: Big Bras d'Or - take Exit 14 off TCH - first driveway on left. **Mail Addr:** R. R. #1 Bras d'Or, N.S. B0C 1B0. **Tel:** 902-674-2412. **Owners:** A. & E. Devoe. **Season:** year round. **Rates:** med-low. **Cards:** VS. **Features:** great view; birdwatching; close to Newfoundland ferry.

Bird Island Boat Tours and Mountain View by the Sea

Location: Big Bras d'Or, take Exit 14, off TCH and drive about 8 km (5 mi) **Mail Addr:** R. R. #1, Bras d'Or, N.S. B0C 1B0. **Owners:** V. & S. Van Schaick. **Season:** May to Oct. **Hours:** boat tours 10 am and 1:30 pm daily. **Accom Rates:** cabins mid-range; campground - avg. **Cards:** VS, AE. **Features:** A wonderful narrated boat ride to the Bird Islands of Ciboux and Hertford where you'll see puffins and other seabirds, grey seals, bald eagles; Coast Guard approved, licenced captains, English, French & Dutch spoken

➣ **EN ROUTE** - To continue east toward Sydney and Louisbourg from the Bird Islands Boat Tour locale, turn left from their driveway and drive about 8 km (5 mi). This will take you back onto the TCH, at Millville.

To get to Big Bras d'Or coming **from** Sydney, take Exit 16 at Millville.

The Legend of Glooscap and the Bird Islands

As the Mi'Kmaq legend goes, Glooscap, the man-god of the old Mi'kmaq religion, had a lodge in the Fairy Hole cave, which is situated at Cape Dauphin, looking out to sea. As Glooscap was returning home one evening in his canoe from his day's activities, two maidens were standing outside his cave, one on either side of the entrance. To impress them, Glooscap leapt from his canoe accidentally breaking the canoe into two pieces. The broken canoe floated out to sea and the pieces became the Bird Islands.

Meanwhile, back at the cave, Glooscap was upset that the maidens laughed at his misfortune, so he ordered them to remain there forever, standing guard over his lodge.

And to this day there they stand, two worndown stones, one on each side of the entrance to the cave.

Southside Boularderie

AnnLynn Lake Resort

Location: Southside Boularderie - heading toward Sydney on the TCH, take Exit 15 to St. James Rd (a right turn if you're heading toward Sydney), about 8 km (4.8 mi) east of the Seal Island Bridge; drive 3 km (2 mi) then turn right and drive 15 km (9 mi) almost to the end of the pavement. **Mail Addr:** R. R. #1, Bras d'Or, Box 602, N.S. B0C 1B0. **Tel:** 902-736-7319. **Owner:** The Bonnar Family. **Season:** 1996 opening late June or July; from then on open year round. **Rates:** med-high. **Cards:** most major cards. **Features:** New 2-bedroom housekeeping units sleep six; marine access to Bras d'Or Lakes; kayak and canoe rentals; fuel; canteen; eagles' nests and other delights of nature.

Bras d'Or

Located on TCH about 50 km (30 mi) east of Baddeck and 5 km (3 mi) from North Sydney. This is the end of the line for the Trans Canada Highway (105), (or the beginning if you're just setting out across the Island in a westerly direction.)

Along this stretch of highway, you'll find no less than five service stations, at least one convenience store, some fast food outlets, and a 24-hour Tim Hortons (coffee shop).

Julia Longacre

Dollie's B & B

Location: O'Toole Dr, Bras d'Or, just off TCH, 11 km (7 mi) from Seal Island Bridge, (across from Irving Station). **Mail Addr:** R. R. #1, Bras d'Or, B0C 1B0. **Tel:** 902-736-9945. **Owner:** Dollie O'Toole. **Season:** year round. **Rates:** low. **Features:** ten minutes from Newfoundland Ferry.

Farmer George's Country Fair

Everything from meat to souvenirs.

Location: On TCH at Bras d'Or. **Tel:** 902-736-8250. **Owner:** G. MacNeil. **Hours:** 10 am to 8 pm daily. **Season:** May - Oct. **Cards:** VS. **Features:** meat & fish; souvenirs; flea markets and a weekly country jamboree.

MacNeil's Motel

Location: On TCH at Bras d'Or. **Mail Addr:** Bras d'Or, N.S. B0C 1B0. **Tel:** 902-736-9106/2692. **Owners**: V. & C.MacNeil. **Season:** year round. **Rates:** med-low. **Cards:** VS, MC. **Features:** 5 km (3.5 mi)lk from Newfoundland Ferry.

Atlantic Harvest Restaurant

Location: On TCH at Bras d'Or. **Tel:** 902-736-2366. **Owner:** M. Howley. **Season:** early May to mid-Nov. **Hours:** Jul & Aug 6:30 am to 9:30 pm; other months 6:30 am to 7 pm. **Prices:** mid-range. **Cards:** VS, MC, AE. **Features:** family-style restaurant; specialties are chowder and fish and chips.

Groves Point

This will take you off the beaten path a little. At Bras d'Or on TCH (Hwy 105), take the turnoff to Groves Point.

Groves Point Provincial Park

Warm Bras d'Or Lakes water, picnic tables among the trees...a great place for a break on a hot summer afternoon.

Location: Groves Point Road, turn off at Bras d'Or and drive 5 km (3 mi) to the Park sign. **Features:** small pebble and sand beach; lots of picnic sites in the shade; warm salt Bras d'Or Lakes water; unsupervised swimming; pit toilets and change rooms.

Little Bras d'Or

Onboard Adventures

Canoe and kayak rentals and sales.

Location: At the bridge in Little Bras D'Or on TCH, turn down the Point Aconi Road. **Tel:** 902-736-8600; Fax 902-736-0858. **Season:** spring, summer & fall. **Hours**: 8 am to 5 pm daily and most evenings and weekends, weather permitting. **Rates:** hourly, half-day, day, weekend and week rates.

Arm of Gold Campground

Location: TCH at Little Bras D'Or. Take Exit 18 (George's River).then make a quick right into the campground. **Mail Addr:** Bras d'Or, N.S. B0C 1B0. **Tel:** 902-736-6671/6516. **Owner:** J. Brennick. **Season:** mid-May to mid-Oct. **Rates:** avg. **Features:** laundry; games room; showers; flush toilets; camping supplies; overlooks Bras d'Or Lake.

Annfield Manor Country Inn

Location: at Little Bras d'Or on TCH, take Exit 18 (George's River) and drive 1.5 km, watch for sign. - **Mail Addr:** R. R. 3, Bras d'Or, N.S., B0C 1B0. **Tel:** 902-736-8770. **Owner:** D. & B. Mulley. **Season:** year round. **Rates:** mid-range. **Cards:** VS, MC. **Dng Rm Hrs:** Lunch 12 noon, dinner 7:30 pm. Reservations required. **Prices:** upper end (5 course dinner). **Features:** lovely old estate with lots of character and charm.

Driftwood Tent and Trailer Park

Location: at Little Bras d'Or, take Exit 18 (George's River). and drive 2.5 km (1.5 mi). **Mail Addr:** Box 222, North Sydney, B2A 3M3. **Tel:**902-794-4519. **Owner:** R. Howatson. **Season:** Jun to late Oct. **Rates:** avg. **Features:** serviced and unserviced sites; washrooms, showers, wood, laundromat.

➼ EN ROUTE

Heading east, you'll eventually come to Exits 20E, 20 W and 21 at Bras d'Or. These are the last Exits off the Trans Canada Hwy - quite literally - until you get to Newfoundland. You have three choices at this point in your travels:

(1) keep going **straight**, which will take you directly to the Newfoundland ferry terminal (assuming you want to go to Newfoundland!) and the town of North Sydney. (see page 54 for Side Trip to North Sydney);

(2) turn right to Sydney Mines - **Exit 20W**, just past Exit 20E. (see page 54 for Side Trip to Sydney Mines);

(3) turn right at **Exit 20E** to Hwy 125, the Bypass, which will take you to Sydney, Louisbourg, Glace Bay, New Waterford, etc. See below.

Sydney

From the Trans Canada Highway (Hwy 105), at Bras d'Or, take Exit 20E to Hwy 125, the Bypass. Drive on Hwy 125 for about 20 km (12 mi). and take one of the four exits to Sydney - King's Rd, Alexandra St, George St, or Welton St (Glace Bay Highway). Note that there are no gas stations on Hwy 125.

Scotland Farms B & B

Location: 2189 Shore Rd, Point Edward - from Hwy 125 take Exit 4 or 5 to Rte 239, drive about 10 km (6 mi). **Tel:** 902-564-0074. **Owners:** S. & P. Andrews. **Season:** May to Oct. **Rates:** med-low. **Features:** working dairy farm; children welcome.

Note: For details on Sydney, see Travel Option 4, page 192.

Side Trip to

Sydney Mines & North Sydney

The two communities of **Sydney Mines** and **North Sydney** are almost inseparable in that one runs into the other somewhere along the Shore Road/Purves St. The facilities along that shore can be easily reached from either downtown Sydney MInes, or from North Sydney.

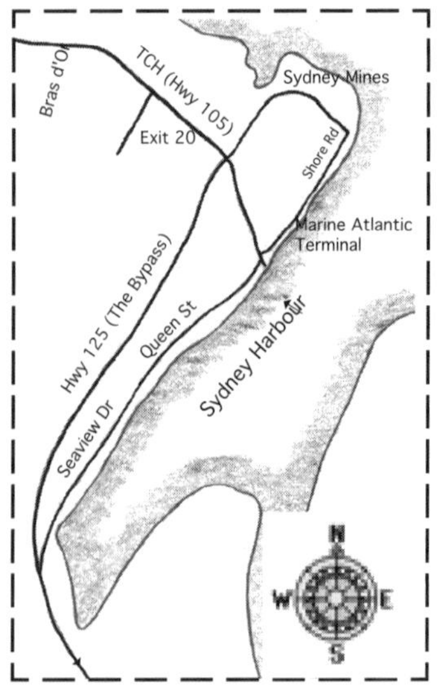

North Sydney/
Sydney Mines

Sydney Mines

From the TCH at Bras d'Or take Exit 20w and follow this road into the Town.

Coming from Sydney on Hwy 125, the By Pass, keep straight until you enter the town of Sydney Mines.

Mid-Town Bakery, 135 Main St; 902-736-1077; open 9 am to 5 pm Mon to Sat.

> ➼ **EN ROUTE** - Follow Main St until you come to the water, then turn onto Shore Rd which runs along the Harbour. It becomes Purves St as you get closer to North Sydney.

Annandale B & B

Location: 157 Shore Rd, Sydney Mines. **Mail Addr:** 157 Shore Rd, Sydney Mines, N.S. B1V 1A9. **Tel:** 902-544-1052. **Owner:** M. Sargent & S. Phillips. **Season:** year round; Dec to Mar by reservation only. **Rates:** med-low to mid-range. **Cards:** VS, MC. **Features:** Victorian house with antiques; veranda overlooking ocean; full breakfast.

Gowrie House Country Inn and Dining Room

Location: 139 Shore Rd, Sydney Mines. **Mail Addr:** 139 Shore Rd, Sydney Mines, N.S. B1V 1A6. **Tel:** 902-544-1050; Fax 902-736-0077. **Owners:** C. Matthews & K. Tutty. **Season:** Apr to Dec. **Rates:** upper end; Modified American Plan available. **Dng Rm Hrs**: one sitting per evening at 7:30pm - reservations required. **Dng Rm Prices**: upper end - four-course gourmet dinner. **Cards:** VS, MC, Interac. **Features:** Georgian house furnished with antiques; English gardens; verandas overlooking gardens and ocean; superb food; full breakfast for guests.

Garland Stubbert's B & B

Location: 117 Shore Rd, Sydney Mines. **Mail Addr:** 117 Shore Rd, Sydney Mines, N.S. B1V 1A5. **Tel:** 902-736-8466. **Owner:** G. Stubbert. **Season:** May to Oct. **Rates:** low. **Features:** large deck, with barbecues, overlooking harbour.

North Sydney

(from Sydney Mines along Shore Rd/Purves St)

Northside General Hospital, Purves Street, close to Marine Atlantic ferry terminal; **902-794-8521**.

Indian Beach

Location: Purves St, North Sydney, close to the ferry terminal. **Features**: supervised public beach, play area, washrooms, canteen, picnic tables; fire pit, running water; open till dusk.

Rollie's Wharf (Restaurant and Lounge)

Location: 411 Purves Street, North Sydney, close to the Marine Atlantic ferry terminal. **Tel:** 902-794-7774. **Season:** year round. **Hours:** Restr - 10 am to 10 pm; Lounge - 11 am to 2 am. **Prices:** mid-range to med-high. **Cards:** most major cards. **Features:** specializing in seafood and steaks.

North Sydney (from the TCH)

From the TCH, Hwy 105, keep straight at Bras d'Or (coming from the west) and you will eventually come to Exit 21 to North Sydney. Take Exit 21 then turn left at the stop sign then take a quick right and follow the signs to downtown (Commercial St).

Marine Atlantic Ferry Terminal

Ferry service from North Sydney to Port Aux Basques and Argentia, Newfoundland.

Location: North Sydney - keep straight from Bras d'Or, don't take Exit 21 and you'll find yourself at the Marine Atlantic Terminal. **Tel:** 1-800-341-7981(North America). **Season:** year-round to Port Aux Basques, late Jun to mid Sept to Argentia. **Sailing Times**: Call for the times as they change with the seasons. **Features:** on board - cafeteria, snack bar, games arcades, children's play rooms, bar, video lounges, gift shop; cabins and berths for overnight crossings; Day Cruises to Port Aux Basques; guaranteed reservations.

Dockside Ceilidhs - During the summer months you can enjoy great Cape Breton entertainment on the dock at the Marine Atlantic ferry terminal.

Best Western North Star Inn & Restaurant

Location: 39 Forrest St, North Sydney - on the hill by the Marine Atlantic Ferry Terminal. **Mail Addr:** 39 Forrest St, North Sydney, N.S. B2A 1A6. **Tel:** 902-794-8581; Fax 902-794-4628. **Owner:** G. Heading. **Season:** year round. **Rates:** med-high to upper end. **Dng Rm Hrs:** 7 am to 2 pm; 5 pm to 10 pm; lounge 4 pm to midnight. **Dng Rm Prices:** mid-range to med-high. **Cards:** most major cards. **Features:** licensed; indoor pool; close to ferry.

The Sandcastle

Gift Shop.

Location: 308 Commercial St, North Sydney, a block and a half from the Marine Atlantic terminal. **Tel:** 902-794-8400; Fax 794-1961. **Owners:** B. & M. Nicholson. **Season:** Apr to Dec. **Hours:** Mon to Sat 8 am to 6 pm - may vary a little from time to time. **Cards:** VS, debit cards. **Features:** ammonite jewellery; gold and silver jewellery; fossils; wood carvings; native crafts; kites, and more.

Nova Scotia Liquor Commission, 306 Commercial St; 902-794-4917; open 10 am to 10 pm Mon to Sat.

Heritage Home B & B

Location: 110 Queen St, North Sydney. **Mail Addr:** 110 Queen St, North Sydney, N.S. B2A 1A6. **Tel:** 902-794-4815. **Owner:** J. Moreland. **Season:** year round. **Rates:** mid-range. **Cards:** VS, MC. **Features:** Victorian home with antiques and library; situated on harbour; close to ferry; full breakfast.

Dove House B & B

Location: 108 Queen St, North Sydney. **Mail Addr:** 108 Queen St, North Sydney, N.S. B2A 1A6. **Tel:** 902-794-1055. **Owner:** H. Reashore. **Season:** mid-May to Oct. **Rates:** mid-range. **Cards:** VS, MC. **Features:** large veranda and upper deck with great view of harbour; close to ferry; full breakfast.

Alexandra Shebib's B & B

Location: 88 Queen St, North Sydney. **Mail Addr:** 88 Queen St, North Sydney, N.S. B2A 1A6. **Tel:** 902-794-4876. **Owner:** A. Shebib. **Season:** year round. **Rates:** med-low. **Features:** close to ferry; great view from all rooms; full breakfast.

➵ **EN ROUTE** - Note that Commercial St has become Queen St and Queen St turns into Seaview Dr.

Northern Yacht Club

Location: Seaview Drive. **Tel:** 902-794-2282/9121. **Features:** mooring available, marina facilities; gas and diesel available.

Farmers Outdoor Market, located on Ballast Grounds, along the shore; Friday mornings about 10 am; lots of farm fresh veggies, eggs and fruit; honey; preserves, etc.

Seaview Golf & Country Club

18-hole course overlooking Harbour.

Location: Seaview Drive, North Sydney. **Tel:** Club House 902-794-8236; Pro Shop 902-794-4111. **Season:** late Apr to late Oct. depending on weather. **Hours:** golfing starts at dawn and ends at dusk; pro shop open 8 am till dusk, except summer months when it opens at 7 am. **Green Fees:** weekdays $29; weekends and holidays $32; 'twilight rate" (after 6 pm) $17. **Features:** pro shop has full range of equipment, clothing etc; par-71; 6,120 yds; course overlooks harbour.

Gallop's Funland

Location: Seaview Dr, North Sydney. **Tel:** 902-794-7172. **Season:** Apr to Oct (depending on the weather). **Hours:** 10 am to dark. **Features:** golf driving range; mini golf; water slide; bumper cars; canteen.

Highland Motel

Location: 530 Seaview Dr, North Sydney. (Can also be easily reached also by taking Exit 3 off Hwy 125, the By-pass.) **Mail Addr:** 530 Seaview Dr, North Sydney, N.S. B2A 3N8. **Tel:** 902-794-4530. **Owner:** C. & A. Chaisson. **Season:** year round. **Rates:** med-low. **Cards:** VS, MC, DIS. **Features:** light breakfast.

North Sydney Mall

Clothing stores, card shop, donut shop, shoe store, pharmacy, grocery store, etc.

Location: 116 King Street, North Sydney; take King St. from downtown Commercial St, or take Exit 2 off Hwy 125 (the By-Pass); **Tel:** 794-4703. **Hours:** Most stores in the mall are open from 10 am to 9:30 pm, Mon to Sat; however, Shopper's Drug Mart opens at 9:30 am, and Sobey's (supermarket) opens at 8 am.

Clansman Motel & Restaurant

Location: Peppett St, North Sydney. Either take Peppett St from downtown Commercial St, or take Exit 2 off Hwy 125 (the By-Pass). **Mail Addr:** Box 216, North Sydney, N.S. B2A 3M3. **Tel:** 902-794-7226; 1-800-565-2668; Fax 902-794-4157. **Owner:** S. Allen-Simec. **Season:** year round. **Rates:** mid-range. **Cards:** most major cards. **Dng Rm Prices:** mid-range. **Dng Rm Hrs:** 7 am to 9 pm. **Features:** outdoor pool; licensed; lunch counter; close to ferry.

Travel Option 1

Julia Longacre

Side Trip to

Lake Ainslie

If you have a hankering to get off the beaten path for a while, you may want to consider a drive along beautiful Lake Ainslie. You could drive all the way around the lake, but it's a fairly long drive - about 60 km (36 mi) or so I'd say.

Either way, you'll end up back at Exit 5, TCH at Whycocomagh. From there you can continue your drive east to Baddeck and Sydney.

Although I've never been to Scotland, I think of Scotland whenever I drive along this road.. must be my Scottish ancestry surfacing.

Directons: Take Exit 5 off the Trans Canada Highway (Hwy 105) at Whycocomagh. (See page 26.)

> ➼ **EN ROUTE** - About 9 or 10 kms (6 mi) from Exit 5 you'll come to an intersection. From here you can travel up either the west side or the east side of the Lake.
>
> Facilities are listed below for both sides of the Lake.

West Side of Lake

West Lake Ainslie Cottages

Location: drive to intersection at South Lake Ainslie (see above) then up the west side of the Lake for 9 km (5.5 mi). **Mail Addr:** R. R. #3, Inverness, N.S. BOE 1NO. **Tel:** 902-258-2654; Fax 902-258-2826. **Owners:** R. & G. MacFarlane. **Season:** mid-May to mid-Nov. **Rates:** mid-range. **Cards:** VS. **Features:** licensed wildlife & fishing outfitter; housekeeping cottages; swimming; trails.

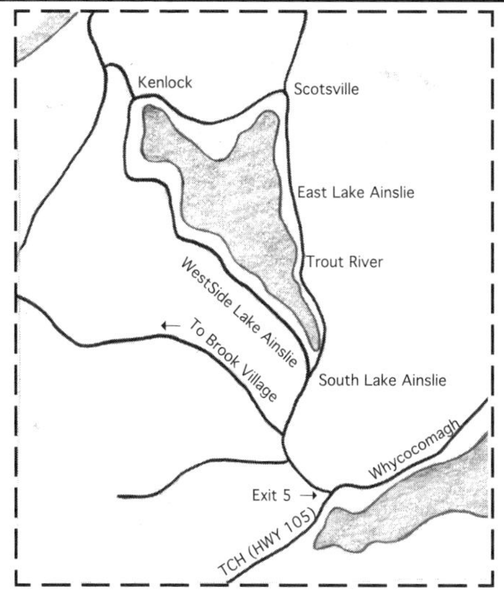

Lake Ainslie

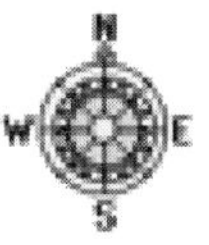

Claver House

A heritage property - a 150-year-old farmhouse in a rural lakeside setting.

Location: Cameron Rd, West Lake Ainslie. Drive up the west side of the Lake until you see Cameron Rd on your left. **Mail Addr:** R R #3, Inverness, N.S. B0E 1N0. **Tel:** 902-258-3113. **Owner:** T. Woods. **Season:** mid-Jun to Sept (1996 only, open Jul 1). **Rates:** low. **Features:** heritage farm property, overlooking Lake.

South and East Side of Lake

Ainslie Village Tent & Trailer Park

Location: South Lake Ainslie about 10 km (6 mi) from Exit 5 TCH (keep on east side of Lake). **Mail Addr:** South Lake Ainslie, N.S. B0E 3M0. **Tel:** 902-756-2333. **Owners:** S. & I. McGrath. **Season:** May to Oct. **Rates:** avg. **Cards:** VS. **Features:** serviced and unserviced sites; washrooms, disposal station; supplies; propane; pool.

MacKinnon's Campground

Location: East Lake Ainslie, about 13 km (8 mi) from Exit 5 TCH. **Mail Addr:** R. R. #1, Whycocomagh, N.S. B0E 3M0. **Tel:** 902-756-2790. **Owners:** M. & K. Gillis. **Season:** May to Oct. **Rates:** avg. **Features:** disposal station; washrooms; fireplaces; laundromat; supplies; swimming.

Trout River Provincial Picnic Park

Location: Trout River, east side of Lake Ainslie. **Features:** picnic tables, toilets, sandy beach on Lake.

Sunset Housekeeping Cottages

Location: Trout River, on the east side of Lake Ainslie, 22 km (13 mi) from Exit 5 TCH. **Mail Addr:** 157 Heathview Dr., Sydney, N.S. B1R 1S4. **Tel:** 902-258-2088; 902-562-5897/4848. **Owners:** Mombourquettes. **Season:** mid-May to end of Nov. **Rates:** med-low. **Cards:** VS. **Features:** pool and lake swimming.

East Lake Rest Cottage

Location: east side of Lake Ainslie, about 23 km (14 mi) from Exit 5 TCH. **Mail Addr:** R. R. #1 Whycocomagh, N.S. B0E3M0. **Tel:** 902-258-3621. **Owners:** A. & H. Kaech. **Season:** May to Oct. **Rates:** med-low. **Features:** housekeeping cottage; full European breakfast; swimming; French and German spoken.

Julia Longacre

MacDonald House Museum

A great collection of tools, farm machinery and other artifacts in a restored 1850's house. There's also a restored 1920's schoolhouse and a barn where square dances and concerts are held in the summer.

Location: east side of Lake Ainslie, about 24 km (14 mi) north of Exit 5 TCH. **Tel:** 902-258-3317. **Season:** mid-Jun to mid-Sept. **Hours:** for guided tours from 9 am to 5 pm daily. **Admission:** low. **Features:** public washrooms; picnic area; two hiking trails.

Scotsville School of Crafts

Location: 1 km (.6 mi) west of Scotsville, along the top of Lake Ainslie. **Tel:** 902-258-3838/2278. **Season:** year round. **Hours**: by chance or appointment. **Features**: specializing in weaving, quilting and other crafts; gift shop.

➵ **EN ROUTE** - When you get to the top of the lake, about 28 km (17 mi) from Exit 5 Whycocomagh, you will come to a junction at Scotsville. If you want to continue on around the Lake, turn left, drive across the top of the Lake, then turn south again on the west side of the Lake. This will take you back to Whycocomagh and the TCH. Or you can go back the way you came.

Alternate Route from Canso Causeway to Sydney

VIA Iona

Take a look at the map of Cape Breton on page 16. In the centre of the Island, where the larger Bras d'Or Lake meets the smaller lake, is a narrow channel of water. This channel is called the Barra Strait and the village that stands on the edge of the Barra Strait is Iona. The Iona area is a wonderful place to visit and is often missed by visitors because it's not on the main highway. This is a pity because it's a very scenic way to get from the west to the east end of the Island, or vice versa.

This alternate route takes you through places like Boisdale, Eskasoni and Grand Narrows, all along the Bras d'Or Lakes.

You will find some beautiful beaches and picnic areas along this route and the Nova Scotia Highland Village is a great place to wander back in time to visit with out Scottish pioneer ancestors.

➵ **EN ROUTE** - If you're heading east toward Sydney, take Exit 6 off the TCH at Aberdeen. (See page 27.) Drive about 1.5 km (1 mi) on Rte 223 East to the Little Narrows Ferry.

Iona and Area

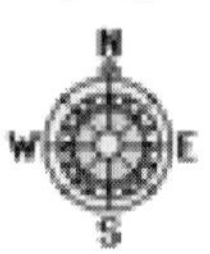

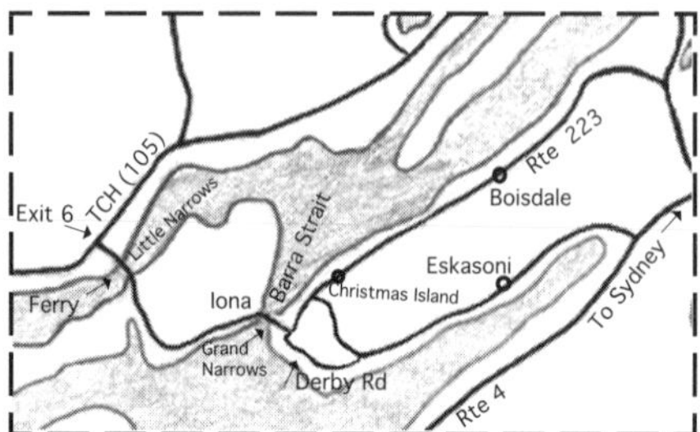

Little Narrows\ Ottawa Brook

Little Narows is located on Route 223, about 1 km (.6 mi) from the TCH Exit 6; Ottawa Brook is about 4 km (2.5 mi) from Exit 6.

Little Narrows Ferry

By name, the *Caolas Silis*, Gaelic for *Julia's Strait*

Location: Little Narrows, 1.5 km (1 mi) from Exit 6 TCH. **Facilities**: a short ferry ride across St. Patrick's Channel - quite possibly the shortest ferry ride you'll ever take. **Price**: better have lots of cash on hand...it's a whopping 25 cents to get across! **Season:** year round. **Hours:** 24 hours, daily.

Matheson's Store and Gas Bar

Location: Little Narrows,on the Iona side of the Ferry. **Tel:** 902-756-2985. **Season:** year round. **Hours:** 8 am to 9:30 pm, Mon to Sat; 1 to 8 pm Sun. **Cards:** VS, MC just for gas. **Features:** gas, convenience and some grocery items, fishing supplies.

Little Narrows Beach

Location: Little Narrows, just on the Iona side of the ferry - watch for the sign on side of road. **Features:** picnic tables, change rooms, beach.

Little Narrows Information Centre

Location: Rte 223 a short drive from the Little Narrows Ferry. **Tel:** 902-756-2413. **Season:** Jul and Aug. **Hours:** generally 9 am to 7 pm. **Features:** information; local crafts.

Iona

Located on Route 233, about 27 km (16 mi) from Exit 6 Trans Canada Highway at Aberdeen and 60 km (36 mi) south west of Sydney.

Highland Heights Inn and Dining Room

Location: Hector's Point, Iona, on Route 223. **Mail Addr:** Box 19, Iona, N.S. B0A 1L0. **Tel:** 902-725-2360, toll free 1-800-660-8122, Fax 902-725-2800. **Owners:** S. & B.MacNeil. **Season:** late May to late Oct **Rates:** mid-range. **Cards:** VS, MC, Dis. **Dng Rm Hrs:** 7:30 am - 9 pm. **Prices:** med-high. **Features:** licensed; exceptional view; traditional entertainment; laundry; mountain bikes, adjacent to Nova Scotia Highland Village (see below).

Nova Scotia Highland Village Museum

If you have even a spark of interest in Cape Breton's Scottish heritage, you'll love the Highland Village.

Location: Hector's Point, Iona, Route 223, about 28 km (16 mi) from TCH Exit 6. **Mail Addr:** Box 58, Iona, N.S. B0A 1L0. **Tel:** 902-725-2272; Fax 902-725-2227, E-Mail: nshviona@fox.nstn.ca. **Season:** full services Jun 15 - Sept 15; open with guided tours Sept 16 - Oct 8; main bldg only Oct 9 to Jun 14. **Hours:** summer - Mon - Sat 9 am - 5 pm, Sun 10 am - 6 pm; o/s - Mon to Fri 9 - 5. **Admission:** low. **Cards:** VS, MC. **Features:** "Highland Roots" - a computer assisted genogenealogical service that will help you 'dig up' your ancestors; gift shop; washrooms; special events; picnic area (see Side Bar).

Living History at the Highland Village

"Experience the lifestyle of the Highland Scots in Cape Breton. The museum presents a chronological tour of 180 years settlement on the island.

Spread over 43 acres, ten historic buildings with costumed staff give testimony to the energy, strength of character, and love of home and family of the pioneers. From a Hebridean Black House to a 1920 school, the story of the Gaels is related in their homes, artifacts, stories, songs and music."

- from N. S. Highland Village brochure

B & R Heritage Enterprises

And speaking of the Gaels...if you're interested in the Gaelic heritage of Cape Breton, stop off here.

Location: Iona, Route 223 just past the Highland Village, heading toward the Barra Strait Bridge. **Mail Addr:** Box 3, Iona, N.S. B0A 1L0; **Tel**: 902-725-2013, Fax - same. **Owners:** B. & R. McCormack. **Season:** year round. **Hours:**

Jun to Oct - open most mornings (except Sun) from 8:30 am to 1 pm. **Cards:** VS. **Features:** unique Gaelic items for sale, like CD's, books, cassettes on Gaelic language, music and culture, as well as Gaelic language and music classes. One especially interesting item - "Gaelic To Go", a 20-minute phrasebook on tape to get you started learning "the Gaelic".

Iona Esso - located next to the Barra Strait Bridge; 902-725-2040; open during the summer months from 7 am to 11 pm.

Note that this is the last place to get gas until you get to either Sydney River or Eskasoni, depending on which route you take.

MacCormack Provincial Picnic Park

Overlooks the Bras d'Or Lakes; the white gypsum cliffs adds to its charm.

Location: Iona -turn left on the Iona side of the Barra Strait Bridge and drive a short distance.

Beaches - along the road to Washabuck (watch for signs) you'll find some lovely beaches that may entice you to stop off for a swim or a picnic. It's Bras d'Or Lakes water, so it's usually pretty warm.

Grand Narrows

Located off Route 223 - just on the Sydney side of the Barra Strait Bridge.

Coming from Iona, turn right just after the bridge and drive a short distance. Turn right again. This will take you to the old ferry dock.

Coming from Sydney, watch for the turnoff at Christmas Island.

Grand Narrows Boat Charters

You may want to consider getting off the highway for a while and taking in some sights on the Lakes.

Location: Grand Narrows, at the old ferry dock. **Mail Addr:** R. R. #1 Christmas Island, N.S. B0A 1C0. **Tel:** 902-622-2743; Fax same. **Owners:** T. & E. MacNeil. **Season:** Jun to Oct. **Rates:** hourly and daily rates available. **Features:** full crew, safety equipped; fishing; scuba diving; bird watching; plan your own trip.

Grand Narrows Beach

Public beach on the Bras d'Or Lakes, located next to the old ferry dock.

➵ **EN ROUTE** - WHICH WAY FROM HERE?

You have two choices as to how you want to proceed if you're heading toward Sydney.

1. take Rte 216 East through Eskasoni (see pg 71)
2. continue on Rte 223 east through Boisdale (see below) **

There's not a lot of difference in distance and they both run along the Bras d'Or Lake. The choice is yours.

** There are no gas stations along this road until you get to Sydney River, almost 60 km [36 mi] away, so check your supply!

Christmas Island

Located about 2 km (1.2 mi) east of the Barra Strait Bridge on Route 223.

Island Wood 'en Wool

This home-based shop specializes in products made from the wool of the owners' sheep, like yarn, blankets, hides, etc. and it also carries hand-made wood products.

Location: Christmas Island, 2 km (1.2 mi) east of Barra Strait Bridge, on Route 223. **Tel:** 902-622-2552. **Owner:** G.MacKenzie. **Season:** year round. **Hours:** Jun to Aug. - Mon to Fri 9 am to 5 pm, Sat. 9 am - 4 pm, Sun 1 pm - 4 pm; rest of year - by chance or appointment. **Cards:** VS. **Features:** locally handmade wood and wool products.

Beaver Cove

Located on Route 223, between Iona and Sydney.

Beaver Cove Take Out

Location: Beaver Cove, between Sydney and Iona. **Tel:** 902-871-2180. **Season:** year round. **Hours:** 8 am to 9 pm daily. **Cards:** VS. **Features:** take-out style cafe; fast food as well as homemade chowders, soups, biscuits, etc.

Boisdale

Located on Rte 223, between Iona and Sydney.

Lakeview B &B

Location: Boisdale on Route 223. Look for the B & B sign. **Mail Addr:** R. R. #2, Christmas Island, N.S. B0A 1C0. **Tel:** 902-871-2808; cellular 565-7290. **Owner:** L. O'Handley. **Rates:** low. **Features:** hiking trails nearby, fishing and hunting guides available.

Glass Slipper Gift Shop

Interesting and unusual items made from fused glass - stained glass that's kiln fired at 1500 degrees - and that's hot!

Location: Boisdale, on Route 223. **Tel:** 902-871-2370. **Owner:** P. Romeo. **Season:** May to Dec, except 1996 when the shop won't open until June. **Hours:** Jun to Sept 9 am to 5 pm daily, other months by chance or appointment. **Features:** handpainted enamels on glass; some other local crafts.

Bras d'Or Lakes Outfitters

Catering to the outdoor enthusiasts ...hunters, fishermen or women, hikers, cyclers, etc.

Location: Boisdale, 1.6 km (1 mi) on the Iona side of the Boisdale firehall and rink, watch for the sign. **Mail Addr:** R. R. #2, Christmas Island, N.S. B0A 1C0. **Tel:** 902-871-2549 - advance reservations suggested. **Owner:** E. Rudderham. **Season:** Jun to Dec. **Features:** licensed hunting & fishing outfitter; guides for many outdoor excursions; accommodations and meals available with advance notice.

Julia Longacre

Ironville

Located on Route 223, between Iona and Sydney.

Barachois Picnic Park

A woodsy picnic park on an old farm property.

Location: Ironville, on Route 223. **Features:** walking trail; picnic tables; toilets of the outhouse variety.

➣ **EN ROUTE**- Another 10 km (6 mi) or so will take you to an intersection where Rte 223 meets up with Hwy 125, which is called "the Bypass". Turn right toward Sydney. For details of Sydney, see page 192.

➣ If you decide to take the Alternate Route through Boisdale **from** Sydney, just take Hwy 125 (the Bypass) from either Grand Lake Rd, George St, Alexandra St or Kings Rd, head west and turn off at Exit 3 to Boisdale. Then you can follow along this travel route in reverse.

Alternate Route from Iona to Sydney

VIA Eskasoni

Directions: Coming from Iona, turn right just after the Barra Strait Bridge and drive a short distance then turn right again. This will take you to the old ferry dock.

Grand Narrows/Derby Point

Bras d'Or Lakes Hideway Bed and Breakfast

This b & b is well named - it is a wonderfully private spot on a hill overlooking the Barra Strait

Location: Grand Narrows - turn onto the Derby Point Rd at Grand Narrows by the old ferry dock and drive 2 km (1.2 mi). **Mail Addr:** Grand Narrows, N.S. B0A 1C0. **Tel:** 902-622-2009. **Owners:** J. & J. Worton. **Rates:** med-low. **Season:** May - Oct; o/s by arrangement. **Cards:** VS. **Features:** patio and garden; beach access; cycling; fishing; not suitable for children.

Derby Point Beach - This is a typically appealing Bras d'Or Lake beach...secluded and peaceful, with crystal clear water. Beach shoes will come in handy here as the bottom is fairly pebbly.

Location: Derby Point Rd. - take the Derby Point Road from the old ferry dock in Grand Narrows and drive about 4 km (2.4 mi). You'll see the beach as you drive down a steep hill. Park your car along the road. **Facilities:** none really except the beach.

Eskasoni

About 2 km (1.2 mi) past the Derby Point Beach you'll come to the end of the Derby Point Rd, about 6 km (3.6 mi) altogether from Grand Narrows.

Turn right onto Route 216 East. Drive about 4 km (2.4 mi) to another junction, stay on pavement and continue on to Eskasoni, about 12 km (7 mi) away.

Eskasoni is the largest of Cape Breton's Mi'kmaq reserves.

In Eskasoni you'll find four gas stations (at least one of which is open 24 hours), convenience stores and a fast food outlet or two.

Rita Joe's Craft Shop

This shop is owned by renowned Mi'kmaq poet Rita Joe, who was awarded the Order of Canada for her poetry.

Location: Eskasoni, on main road, about the centre of the community. **Tel:** 902-379-2263. **Season:** year round. **Hours:** 9 am to 5 pm, daily. **Features**: native crafts and gifts.

The Mi'kmaqs

The Mi'kmaqs have been living in Cape Breton for at least a thousand years. Before the Europeans came, they moved around the Island, according to the season and food supply. They were a nation of hunters, trappers and fishermen.

The Mi'kmaqs played an vital role in Cape Breton's early development. They were allies of the French and acted as guides for their fur trading expeditions and often they were partners with the French in raids on British settlements. From the Mi'kmaq, the French settlers learned how to hunt and fish and survive in the wilderness.

But gradually the Mi'kmaq territory became taken up and populated by more and more settlers. In 1867 the Mi'kmaqs became wards of the federal government. Reserves were set aside for the Mi'kmaqs to live on, where they remain today.

Cape Breton has five reserves: Chapel Island (the oldest), Membertou (the only urban one), Whycoba First Nation (at Whycocomagh), Wagmatcook (at Nyanza), and Eskasoni (the largest).

➺ **EN ROUTE** - About 20 km (12 mi) from Eskasoni, you will come to the end of Route 216. At this junction turn left, toward Sydney. You are now on Rte 4. It is 18 km (9 mi) to Sydney from here.

To continue on to Sydney see page 190.

Travel Option 2

Ceilidh Trail

Canso Causeway to Margaree Harbour
Margaree Harbour to Canso Causeway
VIA Port Hood, Inverness

Some communities on *Travel Option 2*

Port Hastings
Creignish
The Judiques
Port Hood
Mabou
Inverness
Margaree Harbour

Side Trips and Alternate Routes

Port Hood Island
Lake Ainslie

Special Features

√ a western route to the Cabot Trail
√ ceilidhs and concerts
√ museums
√ beautiful beaches
√ fresh seafood
√ tuna fishing

This Travel Option takes you along the western shore of the Island through Port Hood, Mabou, Inverness and many other communities.

The western side of the Island is a wonderful drive, along warm sandy beaches and through some of the Island's most fertile farmland. The "Ceilidh Trail" is well named ('ceilidh' is a Gaelic word meaning 'party' or 'gathering')...this side of the Island is where some of our best-known fiddlers and entertainers come from: Natalie MacMaster, Buddy MacMaster, Ashley MacIsaac, The Rankins. You'll find 'ceilidhs' galore on the Ceilidh Trail.

The Ceilidh Trail meets up with the Cabot Trail at Margaree Harbour.

➵ **EN ROUTE**

If you're heading in an easterly direction, the Ceilidh Trail begins at Port Hastings, just after you cross the Canso Causeway, where you'll come to a rotary. To get to the Ceilidh Trail (Route 19), drive around the rotary to the last turnoff. Don't go too far..you wouldn't want to end up on the Causeway heading back to the mainland!

Before you begin your journey down the Ceilidh Trail, though, you might want to spend a little time in the Port Hastings area. Some of the facilities in this area are a little south of the rotary (that is, keep to your right, past the Visitor Information Centre). Just retrace your steps to get back to the rotary and the Ceilidh Trail..it's only a kilometre or so.

All facilities are listed in order of appearance along the route. If any facility is 'off the beaten path', directions are given.

Port Hastings

The village of **Port Hastings**, the "gateway to the Isle", is the first community you'll see after you cross the Causeway, and the last one you'll see before you cross to the mainland. It isn't a large community, but it does have motels, restaurants, gas stations and one of the Island's main Visitor Information Centre. All the roads leading east, south and north fan out from Port Hastings.

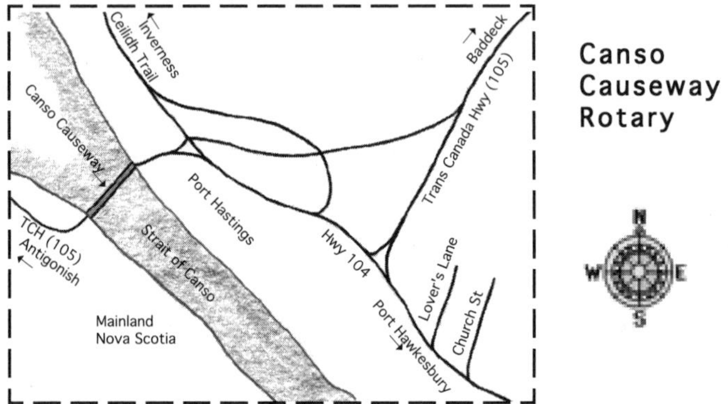

Nova Scotia Visitor Information Centre

This should probably be your first stop once you cross the Canso Causeway. It is located on the water side of the road, just over the Causeway.

Location: Port Hastings at the rotary. **Tel:** 902-625-1717. **Season**: mid-May to mid-Oct. **Hours**: generally from 9 am to 9 pm, but sometimes closes a little earlier, depending on demand.

Glen Auld Gifts

Located: Port Hastings, next to Visitor Information Centre. **Tel:** 902-625-1649. **Owner**: G. MacLean. **Season:** mid-May to Thanksgiving. **Hours:** summer months 8:30 am to 9 pm daily; other months 9 am - 5 pm daily. **Cards**: VS, MC. **Features**: large selection of gifts, crafts and souvenirs.

Keddy's Inn and Dining Room

Location: Port Hastings. Go part way around the rotary and turn right just before the Esso Station. **Mail Addr:** Box 50, Port Hastings, B0E 2T0. **Tel**: 625-0460; toll-free 1-800-561-7666; Fax 625-1275. **Season:** year round. **Rates:** mid-range. **Cards**: most major cards. **Dng Rm Hrs:** 7 am to 11am; 5 pm to 10pm daily. **Prices**: mid-range. **Features**: licensed dining room and lounge; seniors discounts.

Port Hastings Esso - just over the Canso Causeway; 902-625-1100; open from 7 am to 11 pm daily; gas,deisel.

Smitty's Restaurant

Location: Port Hastings, at the rotary. **Owners:** M. & J. Chisholm. **Tel**: 902- 625-3346; Fax 902-625-2914. **Season**: year round. **Hours**: summer 6:30 am - 11pm; winter 7am - 10 pm daily. **Price**s: low to mid-range. **Cards:** VS, AE, debit cards. **Features:** large, bright family-style eatery; wide selection; specialty menu items for seniors, children and health conscious

Skye Travelodge and Dining Room

Location: Port Hastings, next to Visitor Information Centre Gift Shop. **Mail Add**r: Box 190, Port Hastings, N.S. B0E 2T0. **Tel:** 902-625-1300, Fax 902-625-1966, toll free 1-800-578-7878. **Season:** Year round. **Rates:** mid-range. **Cards:** most major cards. **Dng Rm Hrs:** 7 am to 10 pm daily. **Dng Rm Prices**: low to mid-range. **Features:** award-winning licensed dining room; overlooking Strait of Canso.

MacPuffin Inn, Dining Room and Gift Shop

Location: Lover's Lane, Port Hastings - first street to your left after the Skye Travelodge. **Mail Addr**: Box 558, Port Hawkesbury N.S. B0E 2V0. **Tel:** 902-625-2283; toll free 1-800-867-2212; Fax 625-1525. **Owner**: Kenzie Jones. **Season**: Jun - Oct **Rates:** from mid-range to upper end. **Cards:** most major cards. **Features:** complimentary continental breakfast; family rates; gift shop; putting green; swimming pool.

Port Hastings Museum and Archives

Location: 367 Church St, Port Hastings - second street to your left after you pass the Skye Travelodge. **Mail Addr:** Box 115, Port Hastings, N.S. B0E 2T0. **Tel:** 902-625-1295. **Season**: Jun - Oct. **Hours:** Jul & Aug - Mon to Fri 9 am to 8 pm; Sat & Sun 12 noon to 4 pm; other months - Mon to Fri 9 am to 5 pm. **Features**: genealogy records, artifacts, newspapers relating to the Strait of Canso area.

✳ For more facilities in the Port Hawkesbury area, see Travel Option 4, page 176.

Troy

Located on Rte 19, The Ceilidh Trail, about a kilometre from the rotary at Port Hastings.

Marg's B & B

Location: Troy, Rte 19, the Ceilidh Trail. **Mail Addr:** R. R. #1 Port Hastings, N.S. B0E 2T0. **Tel:** 902-625-2401. **Owner:** M. Ashford. **Season:** May to Oct. **Rates:** low. **Features:** panoramic view of the Strait of Canso; hiking.

Troy Lodge Cottages

Location: Troy, on Route 19 about 4 km (2.5 mi) from rotary. **Mail Addr:** Box 399, Port Hawkesbury, N.S. B0E 2V0. **Tel:** 902-625-1684/2680. **Owner:** A. Guzdziol. **Season:** mid-Jun to Sept. **Rates:** mid-range.

Creignish

Located on Route 19, about 8 km (4.8 mi) north of the Canso Causeway. This is a Gaelic name meaning "north rock".

Creignish B & B, Campground and Environmental Shop

If you're a cyclist or an otherwise outdoorsy or nature person, you will probably love it here. The campground is unserviced on an ocean-side cliff. You can take a wild herb tour with the owner,or learn how to make things in the environmental shop.

Location: Creignish, about 10 km (6 mi) north of Causeway. **Mail Addr:** Creignish, N.S. B0E 2T0, **Tel:** 902-625-3336. **Owner:** S. Kuzminski. **Season:** May to Oct. **Rates:** B & B low; campground - avg. **Cards:** VS, MC. **Features:** ocean swimming; hiking trails; canoeing; kayaking; children's activities; campers' cookhouse; unusual craft shop.

Long Point

Located on Route 19, about 17 km (10 mi) north of the Causeway.

Craft Shop, Take-Out and Petting Zoo

Location: Long Point on Rte 19 (Ceilidh Trail).

Long Point Provincial Picnic Park

Location: Long Point, on Route 19 (Ceilidh Trail), about 20 km (12 mi) north of Canso Causeway. **Facilities:** picnic tables.

Julia Longacre

Judique

Located on Route 19, Ceilidh Trail, about 28 km (17 mi) north of the Canso Causeway and 17 km (10 mi) from Port Hood.

A & D Ultramar- Judique; 902-787-2977; Mon to Sat open 7 am to 9 pm; Sun 9 am to 9 pm; gas, diesel.

Smith's Market - Judique; 902-787-3404; open Mon to Sat 9 am to 10:30 pm; Sun 10:30 to 10:30; groceries, general merchandise.

MacLeod Highlander Farm Cottage

Location: MacLeod Settlement/ Judique. Take the MacLeod Settlement turnoff at Judique. **Mail Addr:** R. R. #2 Port Hood, N.S. B0E 2W0. **Tel:** 902-945-2971. **Owners:** A. & D. Ganz. **Season:** year round. **Rates:** mid-range. **Features**: two-bedroom housekeeping cottage; bike rentals; barbecue on deck.

Hillsdale Mohair

This is a little off the beaten path, but an interesting detour.

Location: Turn off onto the Glencoe Mills Road, which is about 6 km (4 mi) north of the stone church in Judique and follow signs. **Tel:** 902-787-2770 **Season:** year round. **Hours:** by chance or call ahead. **Features:** a herd of Angora Goats for you to see; beautiful handmade angora sweaters and other small articles of clothing, as well as yarn and fleece.

Catch of the Day

The Judique/Port Hood area is a great place to hang around if you have a certain penchant for fish ...eating it, fishing it, watching it or just talking about it. The two best places to go are to the Little Judique Harbour wharf, and the wharf at Murphy's Pond.

If you want to buy fish right off the boats, the best time to go to the wharf is between 11 a.m. and 2 p.m., especially for lobster. Lobster season on that part of the Island is May and Jun. After that you may get flounder or crab.

Tuna fishing has become quite popular in that area over the last few years. The average weight of the tuna is 900 to 1,000 pounds and if you want to see one being taken ashore (which is quite a sight!), just make your way to one of the wharves around sundown...that's when the boats come in.

I'm told there can be as many as 200 fishing boats in the Judique/Port Hood area at one time.

TO GET TO Little Judique Harbour wharf, drive through Judique toward Port Hood on Rte 19, the Ceilidh Trail, until you come to the Shore Road, a turn off to your left, 5 or 6 km (3-4 mi) past the Judique Church.

TO GET TO Murphy's Pond wharf, drive along Route 19 until you come to the Lighthouse Cottages in Port Hood. Less than a km past the Lighthouse Cottages is an intersection. Turn left and drive into the village of Port Hood, keep to your left until you pass the Court House. Take the road to your left down to the wharf. (Don't mistake this for the road to Port Hood Wharf which is before the Court House.)

C.B. Gillis B & B

Location: Hawthorne Road,(Judique) Route 19, Ceilidh Trail. **Mail Addr:** R. R. #2 Port Hood, B0E 2W0. **Tel:** 902-787-3037. Owners: C.B. and John Gillis. **Season:** Jun to Oct. **Rates:** low. **Features:** close to public beach.

Chestico Museum and Gift Shop

Location: Harbourview, on Ceilidh Trail, Route 19, 2 km (1.2 mi) south of Port Hood. **Tel:** 787-2244; o/s 787-2930. **Season:** mid-Jun to Labour Day **Hours:** generally from 9 am to 6 pm daily, but hours can vary depending on tourist traffic. **Admission**: free, donations welcome. **Features:** an old schoolhouse- turned-museum, with lots of artifacts relating to early settlers of the area; public washrooms, gift shop, and visitor information; come see the remains of a real dinosaur (lizard size) that was found in the Port Hood area (if it's not out on loan!); museum specializes in the genealogy of the Smith and MacDonald families.

Port Hood

Located on Ceilidh Trail, Route 19, between Canso Causeway and Mabou, about 45 km (27 mi) north of Canso Causeway.

Harbourview Public Beach

Location: Port Hood, on Route 19, Ceilidh Trail, just before the Lighthouse Cottages. **Facilities:** toilets; beautiful sandy beach, warm water. **Caution:** there can be undertows if the sea is high, so be careful.

Lighthouse Cottages

A beautiful setting right on the beach overlooking Port Hood Island.

Location: Port Hood, Route 19, Ceilidh Trail, about 45 km (27 mi) north of Canso Causeway. **Mail Addr:** Box 53, Judique, Nova Scotia B0E 1P0. **Tel:** 902-787-3345/2787 **Owners:** R. and C. MacDonald. **Season:** May to Oct. **Rates:** mid-range; weekly and family rates. **Cards:** VS, MC. **Features:** beautiful sandy beach, cosy looking cottages right on beach; laundromat; one cottage is barrier-free design for pysically challenged guests.

Nova Scotia Liquor Commission - Route 19, Port Hood; 902-787-3222; regular hours are Mon to Thurs & Sat 9 am to 6 pm; Fri 9 am to 10 pm; in summer open on Sat from 10 am to 10 pm.

Port Hood Boardwalk - Just across from the Liquor Commission at Port Hood on Route 19, there's a boardwalk where you can park your car and walk out along the beautiful beach. You'll have a super view of Port Hood Island from there.

➵ **EN ROUTE** - To get into the rest of the village of Port Hood, turn left off Route 19 at the intersection just past the N.S. Liquor Commission.

Sara's Visitor Centre and Craft Shop

this is an official Visitor Information Centre.

Location: on Rte 19, the Ceilidh Trail, just north of the turnoff to Port Hood village. **Tel:** 902-787-3030. **Owner:** S. Murphy. **Season:** Jun to Oct. **Hours:** Jun & Sept - 9 am to 6 pm; Jul & Aug 9 am to 8 pm; Oct. 9 am to 5 pm daily. **Cards:** VS, MC, AE. **Features:** crafts, gallery, coffee shop, information, washrooms.

Caber Feidh Restaurant

Location: Port Hood - turn off Rte 19 at the junction to the village. **Tel:** 902-787-2623. **Season:** May to Nov. **Hours:** summer 7 am to 10 pm weekdays; 7 am to 11 pm weekends; o/s a little shorter hours. **Cards:** VS.

Port Hood Co-Op - turn off Rte 19 at junction to the village; 902-787-3311; open from Mon to Wed 8 am to 5 pm; Thurs & Fri 8 am to 8 pm; Sat 8 am to 4 pm; groceries and general merchandise.

Haus Treuburg Country Inn, Dining Room and Cottages

A large Victorian house overlooking the water.

Location: Port Hood. Turn left off Route 19 at the junction to the village. **Mail Addr:** Box 92, Port Hood, N.S. B0E 2W0. **Tel:** 902-787-2116, Fax: 902-787-3216. **Owners:** G. & E. Kargoll. **Season:** May to Oct. **Rates:** inn - med-high; cottages - upper end. **Dng Rm Hrs:** 7:30 am to 9 am; 7 pm to 9 pm one sitting. **Prices:** upper end. **Cards:** VS, MC. **Features:** sandy beach, German-style breakfast, fishing tours, bike rentals, gift shop, lovely view of Port Hood Island.

Hebredean Motel

Location: Company Rd, Port Hood; take Route 19, past the Liquor Commission to the intersection. Motel is at intersection. **Mail Addr:** Box 149 Port Hood, N.S. B0E 2W0. **Tel:** 902-787-3214. **Owner:** M.C. MacDonald. **Season:** mid-Jun to end of Sept. **Rates:** mid-range. **Cards:** most major cards. **Features:** centrally located near stores, churches; across the road from public beach.

Excursion to Port Hood Island

Location: Port Hood - turn left off Route 19 at the junction to the village; keep to your left through the village until you come to the school. Turn left just past the school and drive down to the wharf. **To get across to the Island**, call Bertie Smith 787-2515 to come over and pick you up. Best to call in advance...the night before is ideal, but a hour or so may be okay. If Bertie isn't available, he may have other names for you, or you can just ask around, there are lots of boats. There's a fee for the ride, of course, but it's reasonable.

Port Hood Island is a wonderful place to spend a hot summer afternoon, or a sunny day in spring or autumn.

The history of the island, once called Smith's Island, goes back to 1786 when Captain David Smith of Massachusettes settled there with his family. Smiths have lived on the island ever since, six generations of them and in fact the only permanent residents there now are - yup! - Smiths.

There are two incredible beaches on the island, usually all but deserted. The water is wonderfully clear and warm from late July to mid-September, and you can walk along them for miles.

There are no public facilities on the island, except a small canteen in summer, so bring your own food and water. Just be careful not to overload yourself with paraphanalia because the only way to get around is on foot.

Just one word of **caution,** if there is a high sea, there can be undertows so be careful, especially with children.

Chestico Pharmacy, located in the Medical Clinic, between the school and Court House in Port Hood, on opposite side of the road; 902-787-2201; open Mon, Wed and Thurs only from 2 pm to 7 pm.

Port Hood Beach

A lovely sandy beach with warm (by our standards) water.

Location: Port Hood - turn left off Route 19, the Ceilidh Trail, at the intersection just past the N.S. Liquor Commission. Keep left through the village of Port Hood until you come to a road just before the Court House. Turn left and drive down to the beach. **Facilities:** Toilets, change rooms.

Julia Longacre

Colindale Cottages

Location: Port Hood. Drive through the village past the Court House - turn right about half a km past the Court House and drive about 4.5 km (3 mi) **Mail Addr:** R. R. #1, Port Hood, N.S. B0E 2W0. **Tel:** 902-787-2934; o/s 819-978-3348. **Owner:** A. MacPhee. **Season:** May to Oct. **Rates:** mid-range. **Features:** farm with view of the ocean; 2-bedroom housekeeping cottages.

➼ **EN ROUTE** - To get out of the village of Port Hood, back onto Route 19, drive back through the village, keep left at the Irving Station until you come to an Ultramar station. Just before the Ultramar, turn right, then left at the stop sign. Voila, you're back on the Ceilidh Trail, heading for Mabou.

Vintage Jewellery

Working Studio.

Location: East Street, Port Hood - East Street is off Rte 19 just past the second turnoff to Port Hood village; studio is the first house on the right. **Mail Addr:** R. R. #1, Port Hood, N.S. B0E 2W0. **Tel:** 902-787-2617. **Owner:** Darryl MacLeod. **Season:** year round. **Hours:** by chance or appointment. **Cards:** VS. **Features:** beautiful handmade gold, silver and gemstone jewellery; featuring Celtic designs and Cape Breton themes; watch for Darryl's jewellery in other shops around the Island.

West Mabou

Turn off Route 19, onto the West Mabou/Colindale Rd,about 12 km (7 mi) north of Port Hood. It's a beautiful drive along this road.

Mabou Pioneers Cemetery (Indian Point)

Location: drive down the West Mabou Rd for a little more than 3 km 1.8 mi), turn right and drive another km or so to Indian Point. **Features:** cemetery dedicated to the original Scottish settlers who came to the Mabou area in the early 1800's (of whom my own great- great- grandfather was one). Some of the first people who settled in the Mabou area are buried here.

Ceilidh Cottages and RV Park

There's that word again "Ceilidh" pronounced "Kay-lee" -it's Gaelic for "party or gathering". The cottages are rented by the week only.

Location: West Mabou - Cottages are about 4 km (2.5 mi.) down the West Mabou Rd, off Rte 19. **Mail Addr:** Box 94, Mabou, N.S. B0E 1X0. **Tel:** 902-945-2486/2624. **Owner:** A. Doyle. **Season:** Jun to Sept. **Rates:** cottages - by week only; RV sites - avg plus. **Cards:** VS, MC. **Features:** heated pool; tennis court; laundromat; no tenting.

West Mabou Beach

This is a spectacular beach with rolling sand dunes, beautifully warm water, and lots of room to beachcomb.

Location: West Mabou. Drive down the West Mabou Road to the end of the pavement. After a km you'll pass a cedar house and soon on your right you'll see a narrow road. Drive down this road to the beach. **Facilities:** the great outdoors!

Mabou

Called "**madawak**" by the Mi'kmaq, which means "**where the rivers meet**", Mabou is located on Route 19, the Ceilidh Trail, between Port Hood and Inverness, about 65 km (40 mi) north of the Canso Causeway. You'll find lots of gorgeous scenery, great beaches and hiking trails.

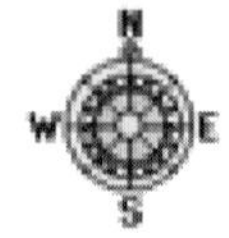

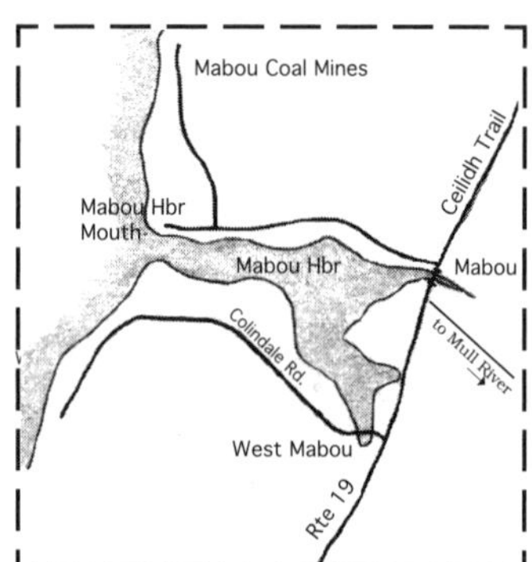

Clayton Farm B & B

This heritage house was built in 1835 and still maintains much of the original look.

Location: Mabou, on Route 19 about 15 km (9 mi) north of Port Hood, about a km before the main village of Mabou. **Mail Addr:** Box 33, Mabou, N.S. B0E 1X0. **Tel:** 902-945-2719, Fax same. **Owners:** B. & I. Smith. **Season:** May to Oct, by arrangement the rest of the year. **Rates:** med-low. **Features:** heritage property, working farm; close to ocean and activities.

Beaton's Cape Breton B & B

Location: Mabou,on Route 19, about a km south of the main village of Mabou. **Mail Addr:** Box 78, Mabou, N.S. B0E 1X0. **Tel:** 902-945-2806. **Owner:** A. Beaton. **Season:** Year round. **Rates:** med-low. **Features:** close to beaches and hiking trails; lots of entertainment in the area.

Mother of Sorrows Shrine and Gift Shop

Location: Mabou, on Ceilidh Trail. Turn onto the Rankinville Rd, just before the village of Mabou. Watch for sign. **Tel:** 902-945-2221: **Season:** shrine open year round; gift shop open from mid-April to Oct. **Hours:** mid-Apr to late May 1 to 4 pm; from late May to end of season from 9 am to 5 pm. **Cards:** VS, MC. **Features:** a small pioneer church converted to a shrine; gift shop has religious articles and souvenirs.

Duncreigan Country Inn, Dining Room and Gift Shop

A lovely new Inn with an old world feel about it; menu includes delicacies like chanterelles, lamb and Mabou cheese.

Location: Mabou, on Route 19, the Ceilidh Trail, just south of the bridge. **Mail Addr:** Box 59, Mabou, N.S. B0E 1X0. **Tel:** 902-945-2207; Fax 945-2253; 1-800-840-2207. **Owners:** E.& C. Mullendore. **Season:** accommodations, year-round; dining room, mid-Jun to mid-Oct. **Rates:** upper end. **Dng Rm Hrs:** dinner, Tue to Sun 5:30 to 8:30 pm; (breakfast for guests only). **Dng Rm Prices:** 3 courses - upper end. **Cards:** VS, MC. **Features:** complimentary continental breakfast for guests; outstanding view of harbour and Mabou highlands; mountain bikes and canoe for guests; recommended in Where to Eat in Canada.

MacMillan's Market - Mabou Village; 902-945-2000; open from 7 am to 9 pm Mon to Fri; 7 am to 6 pm Sat; 10:30 am to 8 pm Sun (closed on Sun between 12 and 1 pm); groceries and general merchandise.

Shining Waters Bakery

Location: Mabou Village, on Route 19. **Tel:** 902-945-2728. **Owner:** I. Smith. **Season:** year round. **Hours:** Mon - Thurs 6:30 am - 6 pm; Fri & Sat 6:30 am to 11 pm; Sundays in summer 8 am to 7 pm. **Cards:** VS. **Features:** home baking, light lunches, deli, full breakfasts.

Mabou Harbour

This is a beautiful drive along Mabou River with hills and rolling farmland. The turnoff is in the Village of Mabou, on Rte 19, just north of the bridge. Watch the turns on this road, there are some dandies!

Rankin's Bed & Breakfast

Location: Mabou Harbour - from the village of Mabou on Route 19, turn onto the Mabou Harbour Rd and drive about 6 km (3.5 mi). **Mail Addr:** R. R. #3, Mabou Harbour, N.S. B0E 1X0. **Tel:** 902- 945-2375. **Owners**: D. & M. Rankin. **Season:** mid-May to Oct. **Rates:** low. **Features:** property is adjacent to a wharf and lighthouse; coastal hiking trails and sandy beaches nearby.

Beinn Bhiorach Trail (MacDonald Glen)

Location: turn onto the Mabou Harbour Rd from the village of Mabou and turn right off this road onto the Mabou

Coal Mines Rd (watch for signs); drive along this road to the end and park. The trail follows the road up the hill and into the woods. **Features:** beach; coastal and woodland trail which is 16 km (10 mi) or so, but you can just walk part way and go back, or watch for a road at MacKinnon's Brook that takes you back to MacDonald Glen.

An Drochaid

That's Gaelic for "the bridge". This is a community centre for crafts, local cultural, archival material and genealogical resources (Maybe you'll find an ancestor or two in Mabou...I did!); a great stop-off for anyone interested in Celtic tradition.

Location: Mabou, Route 19, Ceilidh Trail, in the centre of the village. **Tel:** 902-945-2311, or if centre is closed, call 945-2930. **Season:** late Jun to end of Aug; open other times on request. **Hours:** generally 9 to 5, but are somewhat flexible. **Admission**: free.

The MacFarlane Woods Nature Reserve

The **MacFarlane Woods** is a protected nature reserve under the Special Places Protection Act of Nova Scotia. That means no one may carry out any activities that might disturb this very 'special place'.

The MacFarlane family settled in this area in 1820, and a descendant of that family, James St. Clair, offered the land as a nature reserve. The hardwood forest on the hilltop has never been cut and is a perfect example of the Maple, Beech and Yellow Birch trees that covered most of this area 500 years ago. **Directions:** Take the road to Mull River, just south of the Village of Mabou. Watch for signs.

Mabou Village Gallery

Location: Mabou village, Route 19, Ceilidh Trail. **Tel**: 902-945-2060, o/s 902-443-3215. **Owner:** S.Chrysler-MacDonald. **Hours:** 9 am to 6 pm. **Season:** Jul to mid-Oct. **Cards:** VS, MC. **Features:** paintings, prints and photos by Suzanne Chrysler-MacDonald; one-of-a-kind crafts.

Archie's Esso Station - Mabou, Rte 19; 902-945-2784; open 7:30 am to 9:30 pm Mon to Sat; 7:30 am to 9 pm Sun; gas, diesel.

Mull Cafe and Deli

Location: Mabou, Route 19, Ceilidh Trail, just on the outskirts of the village of Mabou. **Tel:** 902-945-2244; Fax 902-945-2154; **Owner:** C. Mullendore. **Season:** year round. **Hours:** summer 11 am to 9 pm; rest of year 11 am to 7 pm. **Prices:** mid-range. **Features:** full menu and fast food items; deli.

Mabou Service Centre - Mabou; 902-945-2229; open in summer from 7 am to 9 pm Mon to Fri; from 8 am to 9 pm Sat; from 10 am to 6 pm Sun; gas, diesel.

Glendyre Mills B & B

This is a beautiful old home in a delightful country setting, a little off the beaten path.

Location: Glendyre Mills. Just north of the Mull Cafe is a road to your right (Hwy 252). Drive down that road for 2 km (1.2 mi) then turn left onto the Smithville/ Glendyre Rd. Drive 2 km (1.2 mi) to a large yellow house **Mail Addr:** R. R. #4 Mabou, N.S. B0E 1X0. **Tel:** 902-945-2455. **Owner:** K. McIntyre. **Season:** year round. **Rates:** med-low to mid-range. **Features:** heritage property c 1848 - the site of a woolen mill; antique furnishings; beautiful gardens; farm animals.

Mabou Provincial Picnic Park

Location: Route 19, the Ceilidh Trail, 1.5 km (1 mi.) north of Mabou village, on the way to Inverness. **Facilities**: Picnic tables, lovely view of Mabou Valley.

Glenville

Located on Route 19, between Mabou and Inverness. The drive along this road is very pastoral and pleasant.

Glenora Inn & Distillery Resort and Dining Room

This is the home of "**uisge breatha**", the "water of life" which, I presume, does not refer to the water from which the whiskey is made, but rather to the whiskey itself. The distillery is North America's only producer of single malt whisky.

Location: Glenville, on Route 19, the Ceilidh Trail, just about half-way between Mabou and Inverness. **Mail Addr:** Glenville, N.S. B0E 1X0. **Tel**: 902-258-2662; Fax 902-258-3572. **Owner:** M. Young. **Season:** mid-Jun to mid-Oct; o/s by reservation only. **Rates:** mid-range to upper end. **Dng Rm Hrs:** 8 am to 9 pm; lounge 11 am to 11 pm. **Dng Rm Prices:** med-high. **Cards:** VS, MC, AE. **Features:** distillery tours; gift shop; licenced dining room.

Strathlorne

This community is about 15 km (9 mi) north of Mabou on the Ceilidh Trail.

Another Travel Option

Side Trip to Lake Ainslie

You may want to take a little detour inland along beautiful Lake Ainslie.

See page 99 at the end of this Travel Option.

Strathlorne Service Centre (Ultramar) - Strathlorne, just south of Inverness on Rte 19; **Tel:** 902-258-2095; open 7 am to 9 pm every day in summer, 8 am to 6 pm other months; gas, automotive propane.

Julia Longacre

Inverness

Located about 80 km (48 mi) north of the Canso Causeway on Route 19, the Ceilidh Trail.

In the village you'll find gas stations, several small grocery and corner stores,small cafe-style restaurants, clothing stores, a department store, banks, post office and hardware store, as well as the facilities listed below.

Cameron Stables

Here's your chance for a little outdoor adventure - a wonderful scenic trail ride along the ocean.

Location: Inverness. Just south of Inverness on Rte 19, turn off on the B.C. Banks Road (by Jingles Restaurant) and drive to the first farm on the left (#177). **Tel:** 902-258-2386. **Season:** late June to Oct. **Hours:** call ahead and book. **Price:** $12 per person per trail ride.

Gables Motel

Location: Central Avenue (the main street), Inverness on Route 19. **Mail Addr:** Box 454, Inverness, N.S. B0E 1N0. **Tel:** 902-258-2314/2412. **Owners:** J. Walker. **Rates:** low. **Season:** year round. **Cards:** VS.

Bruno's Deli - Inverness; open from 6 am to 12 pm daily; deli sandwiches and convenience items.

Inverness Miners' Museum

This museum is located in an old CN Railway Station built in 1900; you can learn all about the area's coal mining history.

Location: Inverness - Lower Railway Street. **Season:** May to mid-Oct. **Features:** archives, historical records; gift shop; information.

Inverness Beach

Location: Inverness town. Watch for the sign on the south end of main street. **Features:** a beautiful public beach with miles and miles of white sand.

Inverness Consolidated Memorial Hospital

Location: James St, Inverness - turn onto James Street from Central Ave, in the south end of the village.**Tel:** 258-2100.

Inverness Lodge By the Sea and Dining Room

Location: Central Ave, Inverness on Ceilidh Trail. **Mail Addr:** Box 69, Inverness, N.S. B0E 1N0. **Tel:** 902-258-2193; Fax 902-258-2177. **Owner:** H. Wallace. **Rates:** mid-range. **Season:** year round. **Dng Rm Hrs:** Jul to Oct - 7 am to 1 pm; 5 to 9 p m. **Prices:** mid-range. **Cards:** most major cards. **Features:** hotel and motel units; ocean swimming; lovely view of ocean from decks.

Bear Paw Gift Shop

Location: Central Ave, Inverness. **Tel:** 902-258-2528. **Season:** May to Oct. **Hours:** regular hours are 9 am to 6 pm; summer hours 9 am to 9 pm. **Cards:** VS, MC. **Features:** local and imported gifts and crafts; usually weaving in progress at the shop.

Ivan's Bakery - Central Ave, Inverness; open in summer 7 am to 12 pm Mon to Fri; 9 am to 12 pm Sat and Sun; bakery, convenience items; natural products.

Nova Scotia Liquor Commission - Central Ave, Inverness; 902- 258-2483; general hours are Mon to Thurs and Sat 10 am to 6 pm, Fri from 10 am to 10 pm; in summer same except extended hours on Sat from 10 am to 10 pm.

Inverness Raceway

For all you horse racing fans!

Located: Forest St, Inverness. Turn off Central Ave (Rte 19) in the centre of town. **Tel:** 902-258-3315. **Season:** early Jun to late Oct. **Race Times:** Wed evening at 7 pm; Sun afternoon at 2 pm. (see events insert for special events).

Scarlet Ribbons Craft Gallery

Location: Central Avenue, Inverness. **Tel:** 902-258-2231. **Season:** year round. **Features:** fresh and dried flowers; local handcrafts; souvenirs and tourist information.

Freeman Pharmacy - Central Ave, Inverness; 902-258-2400; open Mon to Sat 8:30 am to 9 pm; Sun and holidays 2 pm to 4 pm.

Inverness Beach Village

A collection of cottages and campsites on one of Cape Breton's great sandy beaches that go on forever.

Location: Inverness, at the north end of the village. **Mail Addr:** Box 617, Inverness, N.S. B0E 1N0. **Tel:** 902-258-

2653. **Owner:** Ivan MacLeod. **Season:** mid-Jun to Oct. **Rates:** cottages - mid-range. campsites - avg. **Cards:** VS, MC, DC. **Features:** sandy beach; licenced restaurant on premises (see below); campground has washrooms; serviced and unserviced sites; disposal station; laundromat; groceries.

The Casual Gourmet

Location: Inverness, at the north end of the village on the Inverness Beach Village premises (see above). **Tel:** 902-258-3839. **Season:** Jun to Oct. **Hours:** 11 am to 10 pm. **Prices:** mid-range. **Cards:** VS, MC, DC. **Features:** beachside patio; licenced; specialities include local seafood, vegetarian dishes, porridge bread; casual atmosphere.

Broad Cove

Take the Broad Cove Chapel Road, which is located about 5 km (3 mi) north of the village of Inverness, on Route 19.

MacLeod Inn B & B

Location: Broad Cove Chapel Road, turn off about 5 km (3 mi) north of Inverness (Route 19). **Mail Addr:** R.R. #1, Inverness, N.S. B0E 1N0. **Tel:** 902-258-3360. **Owner:** A. MacLeod. **Season:** May to Oct. **Rates:** med-high. **Cards:** VS, MC. **Features:** beautiful view of ocean and mountains; some rooms have jacuzzi; bicycle rentals and boat tours; ocean swimming.

Broad Cove Annual Concert

Location: Broad Cove Chapel Road about 5 km (3 mi) north of Inverness (Rte 19); on St. Margaret's church grounds. **Features**: One of Cape Breton's most popular outdoor summer concerts. If you want a taste of culture, Cape Breton style, this is it! Fiddlers. Step dancers. Gaelic songs. See insert for this year's date and time.

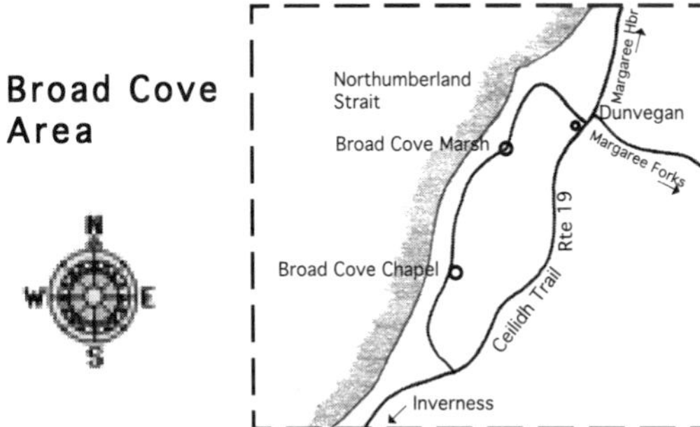

Dunvegan

A small "cross-roads" community about 13 km (8 mi) north of Inverness on the Ceilidh Trail, Route 19. (See map opposite.)

MacLeod's Beach Campsite

Location: Broad Cove Marsh Road, turn off Ceilidh Trail about 10 km (6 mi) north of Inverness. **Mail Addr:** R. R. #1, Inverness, N.S. B0E 1N0. **Tel:** 902-258-2433. **Owner:** M. MacLeod. **Rates:** avg plus. **Features:** washrooms, camping supplies, laundromat; beach swimming, toilets; disposal station.

White Barn Gifts and Crafts

Location: Dunvegan crossroads. **Tel**: 902-258-2181. **Season:** Jun to Oct. **Features:** local crafts and souvenirs.

➵ **En Route** - If you wish, you can keep straight at the Dunvegan crossroads and drive to Margaree Forks and then on to Margaree Harbour, or you can take the more direct route below, along the ocean. Turn left at the Dunvegan crossroads. See map opposite page.

Chimney Corner/Whale Cove

Located on Route 219, the Ceilidh Trail, between Dunvegan and Margaree Hbr; a lovely drive along the ocean.

Chimney Corner B & B

Rooms and one housekeeping cottage.

Location: Chimney Corner, on Route 219, the Ceilidh Trail (watch for sign). **Mail Addr:** Margaree Harbour, N.S. B0E 2B0. **Tel:** 902-235-2104. **Owners:** J. & B. Wheeler. **Rates:** B & B med-low; cottage mid-range. **Season:** mid-May to mid-Oct. **Cards:** VS, MC. **Features:** private ocean beach; evening get-togthers with substantial evening snack for B & B guests ; adult accommodation.

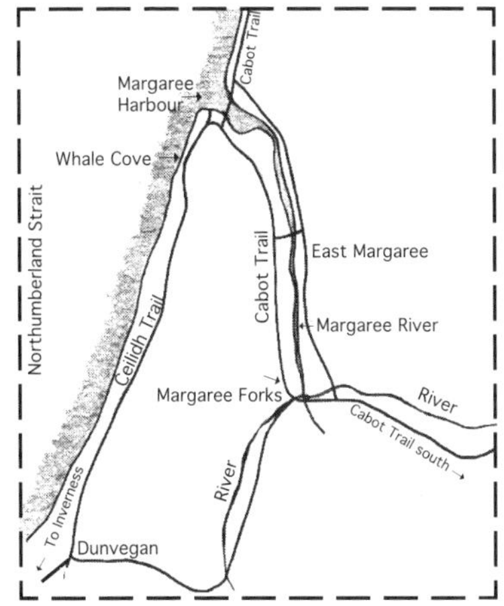

Margaree Harbour Area

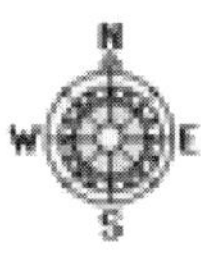

Whale Cove Summer Village

This is a "village" of cottages on a hillside overlooking Whale Cove.

Location: Whale Cove on Route 219, the Ceilidh Trail, about 4 km (2.5 mi) from Margaree Harbour. **Mail Addr:** R. R. #1, Margaree Harbour, N.S. B0E 2B0. **Tel:** 902-235-2202; Fax 235-2564. Owners: A. & A. MacKay. **Season:** May to mid-Oct. **Rates:** mid-range. **Cards:** VS, MC, AE. **Features:** beautiful sandy beach, walking trails, playground, groceries, laundromat.

Margaree Harbour

Located on Route 219, the Ceilidh Trail, about 115 km (69 mi) north of the Canso Causeway (on Ceilidh Trail), 35 km (21 mi) north of Inverness. This is a wonderful spot to spend some time swimming, picnicing, beachcombing or just taking in the supurb scenery.

Laurence's General Store and Postal Outlet

Location: Margaree Harbour Road - about 3 km (1.8 mi) north of Whale Cove on Route 219, turn left and drive about a km down that road. **Tel:** 902-235-2004. **Season:** year round. **Hours:** 8 am to 9 pm. **Features:** gas; groceries; general merchandise; postal outlet.

Margaree Boat Tours

Take a boat trip to Margaree Island wildlife reserve; deep sea fish; whale watch or have a refreshing swim off the boat.

Location: Margaree Harbour. About 3 km (1.8 mi) north of Whale Cove on Route 219, turn down the Margaree Hbr Rd. Watch for a large red barn on the water. **Owner:** Leo Burns. **Tel:** 902-235-2848. **Season:** Jun to Oct. **Features:** 40-ft. Cape Islander Lisa Mae II; deep sea fishing - all equipment supplied; safety certified each year.

Margaree Harbour Beach

A wonderful place to spend a sunny summer afternoon.

Location: Margaree Harbour - about 3 km (1.8 mi) north of Whale Cove on Route 219, turn left and drive about a km down the Margaree Harbour road to the end. Park your car at the end of the road. **Facilities**: sandy beach, picnic tables; general store close by.

Harbour View Inn B & B and chalet

Location: Margaree Harbour at the junction of the Ceilidh and Cabot Trails. **Mail Addr:** Box 52, Margaree Hbr, N.S. B0E 2B0. **Tel:** 902-235-2314. **Owner:** C. Jennex. **Season:** year round. **Rates:** med-low. **Cards:** MC. **Features:** overlooking Margaree Harbour; ocean swimming; canoeing, deep sea fishing etc close by; A-frame chalet overlooking water.

Ross House Studio

A studio and gallery of printmaker and artist Michael Armentrout.

Location: Margaree Harbour at the junction of the Ceilidh and Cabot Trails. **Mail Addr:** Box 52, Margaree Hbr, N.S. B0E 2B0. **Tel:** 902-235-2112. **Owner/Artist**: Michael Armentrout. **Season:** Jun to Oct. **Hours:** you'll find Michael in his studio most of the time, but if you want to be sure not to miss him, call ahead. **Cards:** VS, MC. **Features:** limited edition hand printed collector prints; drawings; CAPE BRETON 1997 CALENDAR - an art calendar of linocut prints by Michael and another Cape Breton artist Teena Marie Saunders. A sample of Michael's work can be seen on opposite page and on page 105; Teena Marie's work can be seen on pages 201 and 291.

The Hungry Piper Cafe and Gift Shop; The Schooner Restaurant & Lounge

Location: Margaree Harbour, at the junction of the Ceilidh and Cabot Trails. **Tel**: 902-248-2182. **Season:** Jun to Oct **Hours:** cafe -9 am to 5 pm daily; restaurant - 5 pm to midnight. **Cards:** VS, MC, AE. **Features:** piper on staff; Gaelic spoken; vegetarian menu items.

Duck Cove Inn and Dining Room

An awsome view of the Margaree River just where it empties into the Harbour.

Location: Margaree Harbour - at the junction of the Ceilidh and Cabot Trails. **Mail Addr:** Margaree Hbr, N.S. B0E 2B0. **Tel:** 902-235-2658; Fax 902-235-2592. **Owner:** G. Laurence. **Season:** Jun to mid-Oct. **Rates:** mid-range. **Cards:** VS, MC, AE. **Dng Rm Hrs:** 7:30 - 10:30 am; 12 - 2 pm; 6 - 8 pm. **Prices:** mid-range. **Features:** fishing; canoe rentals; ocean swimming.

Taylor's B & B

Location: Margaree Harbour on the Cabot Trail about 1.5 km (1 mi) south of the junction of the Ceilidh and Cabot Trails. **Mail Addr:** R. R. #1, Margaree Hbr, N.S. B0E 2B0. **Tel:** 902-235-2652. **Owners:** F. & M.Taylor. **Season:** May to Oct. **Rates:** med-low. **Features:** century-old house overlooking Margaree River and Harbour.

Artist Michael Armentrout

Mill Valley Farm B & B and cabins

Location: Margaree Harbour, Cabot Trail - about 2 km (1.2 mi) south of the junction of the Ceilidh Trail and Cabot Trail, turn onto the Scotch Hill/Mill Valley Rd, and drive about 1 km. **Mail Addr:** Margaree Hbr, N.S. B0E 2B0. **Tel:** 902-235-2834. **Owners:** S. & S.Lamont. **Season:** year round. **Rates:** B & B med-low; cabins mid-range. **Features:** French, German, Russian, Polish & English spoken; hiking trails; Olympic gym, winter activities; full complimentary breakfast for B & B guests, for cabin guests $7.50.

Margaree Harbour Craft and Gift Shop

Location: Margaree Harbour on Cabot Trail, between Margaree Hbr and Margaree Forks. **Tel:** 902-235-2824. **Season:** Jun to Oct. **Hours:** 8:30 am to 9 pm daily. **Cards:** VS, MC, AE. **Features:** specializing in woolen products; other crafts, gifts and souvenirs.

✳ For more facilities in the Margarees, see Travel Option 3, page 106.

Side Trip to

Lake Ainslie

On your travels along the Ceilidh Trail, you may want to take a little detour off the beaten path to beautiful Lake Ainslie. You can travel down either the east side of the Lake or the west side. You can go all the way around the Lake (it's about 60 km (36 mi) in all I'd say, and end up back where you started at Strathlorne. Or, you can just go part way around then go back to Strathlorn and the Ceilidh Trail.

Directons: on the Ceilidh Trail, about 5 km (3 mi) north of the Glenora Inn (between Mabou and Inverness) take the turnoff to Kenlock. After driving about 3 km (1.8 mi), you'll come to an intersection. If you keep straight you will go down the west side of Lake Ainslie; if you turn left you will travel across the top of Lake Ainslie to Scotsville, then down the east side of the Lake.

The facilities listed below are on both sides of the Lake.

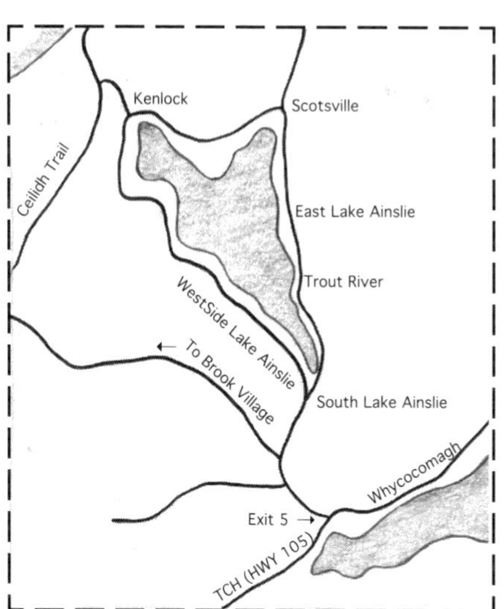

Lake Ainslie

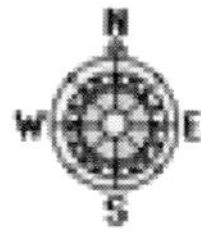

West Side of the Lake

Claver House

A heritage property...a 150-year-old farmhouse in a rural lakeside setting.

Location: Cameron Rd, West Lake Ainslie. Drive down the west side of the Lake for about 13 km (8 mi) from the junction at the top of the Lake, and watch for Cameron Rd on your right. **Mail Addr:** R R #3, Inverness, N.S. B0E 1N0. **Tel:** 902-258-3113. **Owner:** T. Woods. **Season:** mid-Jun to Sept (1996 only: open Jul 1). **Rates:** low. **Features:** heritage farm property, overlooking Lake.

West Lake Ainslie Cottages

Location: West side of Lake Ainslie. **Mail Addr:** R. R. #3, Inverness, N.S. B0E 1N0. **Tel:** 902-258-2654; Fax 902-258-2826. **Owners:** R. & G. MacFarlane. **Season:** mid-May to mid-Nov. **Rates:** mid-range. **Cards:** VS. **Features:** licensed wildife & fishing outfitter; housekeeping cottages; swimming; trails.

East, North and South Side of the Lake

Scotsville School of Crafts

Location: 1 km (.5 mi) west of Scotsville, along the top of Lake Ainslie. **Tel:** 902-258-3838/2278. **Season:** year round. **Hours**: by chance or appointment. **Features**: specializing in weaving, quilting and other crafts; gift shop.

MacDonald House Museum

A great collection of tools, farm machinery and other artifacts in a 150-year old house. There's also a restored 1920's schoolhouse and a barn where square dances and concerts are held in the summer.

Location: east side of Lake Ainslie,about 8 km (5 mi) south of Scotsville. **Tel:** 902-258-3317. **Season:** mid-Jun to mid-Sept. **Hours:** 9 am to 5 pm daily. **Admission**: low. **Features:** public washrooms; picnic area; two hiking trails.

East Lake Rest Cottage

Location: east side of Lake Ainslie. **Mail Addr:** R. R. #1 Whycocomagh, N.S. B0E3M0. **Tel:** 902-258-3621. **Owners:** A. & H. Kaech. **Season:** May to Oct. **Rates:** med-low. **Features:** housekeeping cottage; full European breakfast; swimming; French and German spoken.

Sunset Housekeeping Cottages

Location: Trout River, on the east side of Lake Ainslie, about 10 km (6 mi) south of Scotsville. **Mail Addr:** 157 Heathview Dr, Sydney, N.S. B1R 1S4. **Tel:** 902-258-2088; 902-562-5897/4848. **Owners:** Mombourquette family. **Season:** mid-May to end of Nov. **Rates:** med-low. **Cards:** VS. **Features:** pool and lake swimming.

Trout River Provincial Picnic Park

Location: Trout River, east side of Lake Ainslie. **Features:** picnic tables, toilets, sandy beach on Lake.

MacKinnon's Campground

Location: East Lake Ainslie, about 12 km (7 mi) south of Scotsville. **Mail Addr:** R. R. #1, Whycocomagh, N.S. B0E 3M0. **Tel:** 902-756-2790. **Owners:** M. & K. Gillis. **Season:** May to Oct. **Rates:** avg. **Features:** disposal station; washrooms; fireplaces; laundromat; supplies; swimming.

Ainslie Village Tent & Trailer Park

Location: South Lake Ainslie about 18 km (10 mi) south of Scotsville. **Mail Addr:** South Lake Ainslie, N.S. B0E 3M0. **Tel:** 902-756-2333. **Owners:** S. & I. McGrath. **Season:** May to Oct. **Rates:** avg. **Cards:** VS. **Features:** serviced and unserviced sites; washrooms, disposal station; supplies; propane; pool.

Travel Option 3

Cabot Trail
Nyanza to St. Ann's/South Haven
St. Ann's/South Haven to Nyanza
VIA Margarees, Cheticamp, Ingonish

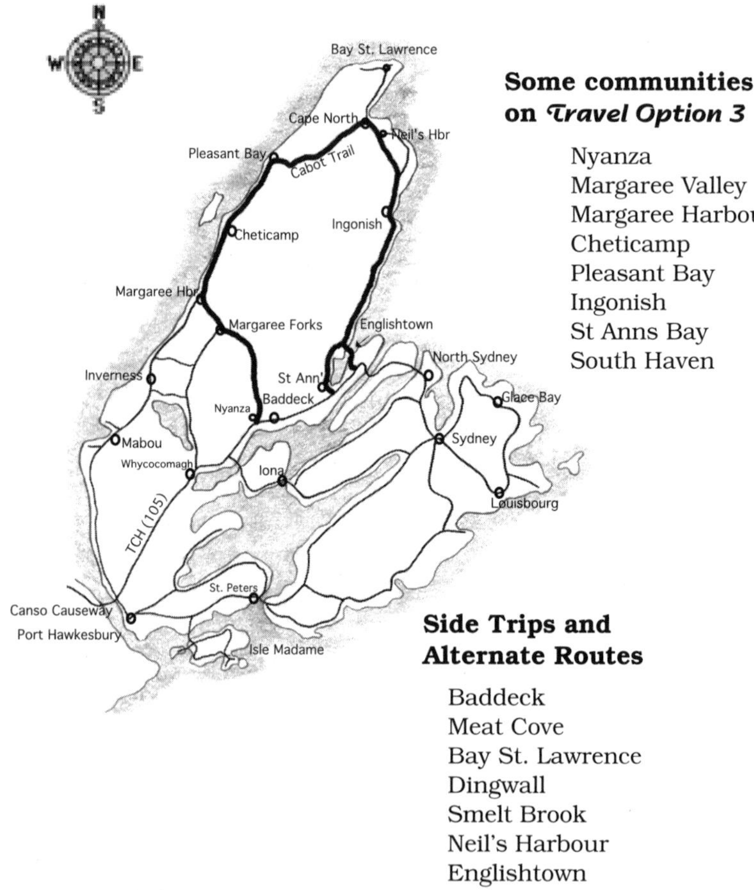

Some communities on Travel Option 3

Nyanza
Margaree Valley
Margaree Harbour
Cheticamp
Pleasant Bay
Ingonish
St Anns Bay
South Haven

Side Trips and Alternate Routes

Baddeck
Meat Cove
Bay St. Lawrence
Dingwall
Smelt Brook
Neil's Harbour
Englishtown

Special Features

- √ A. G. Bell National Historic Site
- √ Cabot Trail
- √ C. B. Highlands National Park
- √ hiking trails & outdoor adventures
- √ beaches and parks
- √ entertainment/ceilidhs
- √ accommodations/restaurants
- √ museums

This Cabot Trail Travel Option is packed with all those things that make a vacation an adventure. Mountains, beaches, hiking and biking trails, shops, intriguing history, fascinating geology, and much more.

As you can see from the map on the opposite page, The Cabot Trail is actually a loop. It winds its way from Nyanza on the Trans Canada Highway just **west** of Baddeck to St. Ann's Bay, also on the Trans Canada Highway, just **east** of Baddeck.

You can travel around the Trail in whichever direction you choose - it makes no difference. There was a time, though, back before the Trail was paved, that it **did** make a difference. Travellers were advised to go around from west to east (Cheticamp to Ingonish) so they would be driving on the inside of the road, safely away from the perilous cliffs. Now, of course, the road is wide, paved and safe, with lots of spots to pull over and get a closer look at the spectacular scenery.

A word of advice: don't be in too much of a hurry to "do the Trail". There are so many things to see and do along this route it would be a shame to miss any of them. There are over 200 km (120 mi) of spectacular beaches and parks, wonderful hiking trails, craft shops and galleries, and lots of great people willing to help make your stay memorable.

➵ **EN ROUTE**

West to East* - Take the Trans Canada Highway to Exit 7 at Nyanza, and follow the route below as it's written.

*Another great way to get to the Cabot Trail is to take the Ceilidh Trail to Margaree Harbour then pick up the Cabot Trail there. See Travel Option 2 for the Ceilidh Trail.

East to West - Take the Trans Canada Highway to Exit 11 at St. Ann's/South Haven and follow the route in reverse.

Another Travel Option

Side Trip to Baddeck

If you want to take a Side Trip to Baddeck before you set out around the Cabot Trail, you'll have to stay on the TCH for a few kilometres until you come to one of the three Exits to Baddeck (8, 9 or 10). When you've seen Baddeck, just get back on the Trans Canada Highway (105) and backtrack to the appropriate Cabot Trail exit.

See details on page 31.

All facilities are listed in order of appearance along the route. If any facility is 'off the beaten path', directions are given.

Hunter's Mountain

Hunter's Mountain Country Cottages

Location: Hunter's Mountain, 2.5 km (about 1.5 mi) north of Nyanza, Exit 7 TCH. **Mail Addr:** R. R. #3 Baddeck, N S, B0E 1B0. **Tel:** 902-295-3392; Fax same; cell phone 902-295-7170. **Season:** year round. **Rates:** mid-range. **Features:** nicely designed and decorated cottages; close to Baddeck and the Margarees; quiet country setting.

Middle River

Located on the Cabot Trail, about 9 km (5.4 mi) north of Nyanza.

The Forge Cottage - Gift Shop

Location: Middle River, on Cabot Trail.

Gas It (Service Station) - Middle River; 902-295-3221; open Mon to Fri - 7 am to 6 pm; Sat - 8:30 am to 5 pm; Sun - 10 am to 3 pm.

Sweeties Bake Shop

Location: Middle River, on Cabot Trail, 12 km (7 mi) from Nyanza. **Tel**: 902-295-2518. **Season:** year round. **Hours:** Jul & Aug - 7:30 am to 9 pm; other months 8 am to 8 pm. **Features:** convenience items, baked goods and take out.

Seven Springs Farm B & B

Location: Middle River - about 14 km (8.5 mi) from Nyanza on Cabot Trail, turn left at MacLennan's Cross, across from the Community Centre (just past Midway Motors); once you cross the river turn right (very sharp turn) and drive 3.5 km. (2.2 mi) to the 4th farm on the left. **Mail Addr:** R. R. #3, Baddeck, N.S. B0E 1B0. **Tel:** 902-295-2094; Fax same. **Owners:** K.& L. Scherzinger. **Season:** Jul to Oct 30. **Rates:** med-low. **Cards:** no. **Features:** restored 1839 farmhouse in pastoral setting; Icelandic Horse farm; 2 rooms are sitting-room suites with gas fireplace and private bath. Icelandic horses are available for guests to ride after Sept 15 - in summer they are at Cheticamp Island where they are available for trail rides along the ocean.

Artist Michael Armentrout

On pages 106 to 110, "Exit 11" should read "Exit 7"

Lake O' Law

Located on the Cabot Trail, 21 km (12.5 mi) north of Nyanza, Exit 11, Trans Canada Highway.

Lake O'Law Provincial Picnic Park

Location: Lake O'Law on Cabot Trail. **Features:** picnic tables, lake swimming and boating. **Caution**: the lake has a very strong current in places so be careful.

The Lakes Restaurant, Cottages,Campground & Gift Shop

Location: Lake O'Law, on Cabot Trail, 25 km (15 mi) north of Nyanza (TCH). **Mail Addr:** North East Margaree, N.S. B0E 2H0. **Tel:** 902-248-2360. **Owners:** the Taylors. **Season:** May to Oct. **Rates:** cottages mid-range; campsites avg. **Restaurant Hours:** Jul & Aug - 8 am to 11 pm; other months - 11 am to 7 pm. **Restr Prices**: mid-range. **Features:** lake swimming, pedal boats, canoes, mini golf, go-karts, fishing (guides available); gift shop, camping supplies, laundromat.

North East Margaree, Margaree Centre, Margaree Valley and Portree

Travelling around the Margarees is an inspiring experience, with the river, the valley, the mountains, but it can also be a tad confusing for a stranger, so I thought a simplified map might be in order.

The Margarees

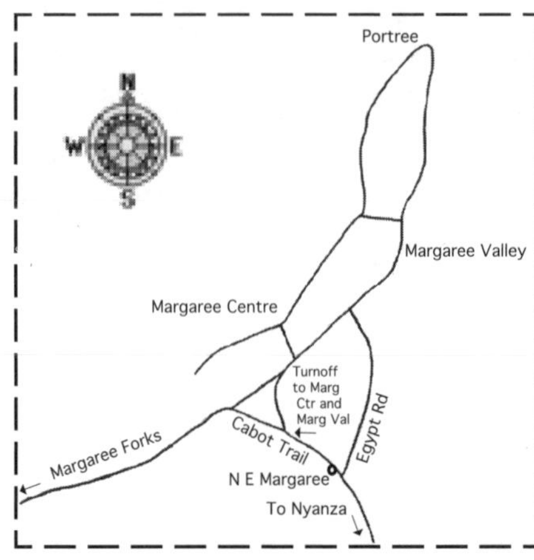

Normaway Inn and Cottages

This is a beautiful property with a charming old-world inn and new-world cottages.

Location: Margaree Valley. About 30 km (18 mi) north of Nyanza (Exit 11 TCH) on the Cabot Trail, you'll come to Egypt Road; turn there and drive about 3 km (1.8 mi.). **Mail Addr:** Box 468, Margaree Valley, N.S. B0E 2C0. **Tel:** 902-248-2987; Fax 902-248-2600; 1-800-565-9463. **Rates:** upper end - Modified American Plan available. **Season:** mid-Jun to mid-Oct or by arrangement. **Dng Rm Hrs:** 7:30 to 10:00 am; 6 to 9 pm. **Prices:** upper end (4-course gourmet dinner). **Cards:** VS, MC. **Features:** lots of ceilidhs and concerts; fireplaces/woodstoves; fishing guides and equipment; hiking trails; tennis; licenced gourmet dining; trail rides.

River Loop Hiking and Mountain Bike Trail

This is just one of several trails in this area that take you to pools of the Margaree River. It was written up by the folks at the Normaway Inn.

Location: starts at Normaway Inn (see above). **Distance**: 7 km (4.5 mi). **Time:** 1.5 hours to walk; about 45 minutes to mountain bike.

The Trail: From the Normaway Inn lobby head past the brown chalets on the gravel drive and cross a woods road, continuing onto a grassy laneway.

Follow this trail for about a km through the forest..watch the small stumps in the grass. After 2 km (1.2 mi) turn right at the paved airstrip then continue to the pavement. Turn right. Note the dirt road on the right...you'll take it coming back. Continue along the paved road and turn left after the bridge onto a dirt laneway. You'll soon see a path - follow it a short distance to the river.

To return to the Normaway Inn, retrace your steps back to the dirt road that was mentioned earlier. Follow this past a steel shed and continue onto a grassy laneway. Follow this trail through the woods to a field. Keep left, following the trail down an embankment and into another field. Cross this field, keeping to the edge, to a trail on the opposite side. Follow this trail to a paved road, turn right and continue until you come to the Normaway Inn.

Normaway Inn Fishing Outfitters

(See above for location, etc.) Outfitters for Atlantic salmon and trout in the Margaree River, Middle River, Baddeck River and Cheticamp River.

Ross' Housekeeping Motel

Location: Margaree Valley. About 30 km (18 mi) north of Nyanza (Exit 11 TCH) on the Cabot Trail, you'll come to Egypt Road; turn there and drive about 5 km (3 mi). **Mail Addr:** Margaree Valley, N.S. B0E 2C0. **Tel:** 248-2933. **Owners:** A. & B. Ross. **Season:** mid-May - mid-Nov. **Rates:** med-low. **Cards:** VS, MC. **Features:** housekeeping; fishing; hiking.

West Highland Bakery - on Cabot Trail, about a km north of Egypt Rd; 902-248-2804; bakery and convenience items.

Strathdee's Fly Shop

Location: North East Margaree. Take the turnoff to Margaree Valley/Margaree Centre, about 33 km (20 mi) north of TCH Exit 11 Nyanza; drive less than a km, then turn left. **Mail Addr:** Box 88, North East Margaree, N.S. B0E 2H0. **Tel:** 902-248-2076; Fax same. **Season:** year round. **Hours:** 10 am to 6 pm, closed on Wed. **Cards:** VS. **Features:** salmon and trout fly fishing specialists - waders, rods, flies, etc.

Margaree Salmon Museum and Gift Shop

Location: North East Margaree. Take the turnoff to Margaree Valley/Margaree Centre, about 33 km (20 mi]) north of TCH Exit 11 Nyanza; drive .5 km, then turn left. **Tel**: 902-248-2848. **Season:** mid-Jun - mid-Oct. **Hours:** 9 am - 5 pm. **Admission**: low. **Features:** memorabilia of all things related to angling on the Margaree River; public washrooms, visitor information, picnic area.

Heart of Harts B & B, Cottages and Dining Room

Location: North East Margaree. Take the turnoff to Margaree Valley/Margaree Centre, about 33 km (20 mi) north of TCH Exit 11 Nyanza, and drive .5 km. **Mail Addr:** Box 21, North East Margaree, N.S. B0E 2H0. **Tel:** 902-248-2765; Fax 902-248-2606. **Owner:** Brooks Hart. **Season:** year round. **Rates:** med-low to mid-range. **Dng Rm Hrs:** single seating 7 p.m. **Prices:** upper end for 4-course 'country gourmet' dinner. **Cards:** VS, MC. **Features:** 1880's farmhouse; salmon and trout fishing; hiking; winter sports.

Valley B & B

Location: Margaree Valley. Take the turnoff to Margaree Valley/Margaree Centre, about 33 km (20 mi) north of TCH Exit 11 Nyanza, and drive about 2 km (1.2 mi). **Mail Addr:** Margaree Vallely, N.S. B0E 2C0. **Tel:** 902-248-2651. **Owner:** A. Stepaniak. **Season:** mid-May to mid-Oct; o/s by arrangement. **Rates:** med-low. **Cards:** VS, MC.

Julia Longacre

Cranton Cottages

Location: Margaree Centre. Take the turnoff to Margaree Valley/Margaree Centre, about 33 km (20 mi) north of TCH Exit 11Nyanza; drive about 1.5 km and turn left toward Margaree Centre; drive over Cranton Bridge to cabins. **Mail Addr:** Box 59, Margaree Centre, N.S. B0E 1Z0. **Tel:** 902-248-2985. **Owners:** G.& B. Cranton. **Season:** year round. **Rates:** med-low. **Cards:** VS, MC. **Features:** housekeeping cottages; fishing and guides available; hiking; winter activities.

Alvin Ingraham's Irving Station and Store - follow directions to Cranton Cottages above then drive past it to the intersection. **Hours:** Jun to Sept - 7 am to 11 pm Mon to Thurs; 7 am to 12 pm Fri & Sat; 9 am to 11 pm Sun; hours slightly less during other months. **Tel:** 248-2629; gas and convenience items.

Brown's Bruaich na H'Aibhne B & B and Cottage

The name is Gaeilc for 'banks of the river'

Location: Margaree Centre. Follow directions to Ingraham's Irving (above), turn left and drive 2 km (1.2 mi). **Mail Addr:** Box 88, Margaree Valley, N.S. B0E 2C0. **Tel:** 248-2935; 1-800-575-2935. **Owner:** A. Brown. **Season:** year round. **Rates:** low and med-low. **Cards:** VS, MC. **Features:** rooms and one housekeeping cottage; fishing; hiking trail on premises; river swimming; winter activities.

The Margaree River

This is one of the world's most famous salmon fishing rivers, luring fishermen from all over the world. It consists of two branches, the Southwest branch which originates at Lake Ainslie, and the Northeast branch which originates at Big Intervale. The two streams meet at Margaree Forks then flow as one to Margaree Harbour and the sea.

River Trail Cottages

Location: Margaree Centre. Take the turnoff to Margaree Valley/Margaree Centre, about 33 km (20 mi) north of TCH Exit 11 Nyanza; drive about 1.5 km and turn left toward Margaree Centre; at Ingraham's Irving turn right and drive another km or so. **Mail Addr:** Box 29, Margaree Centre, N.S. B0E 1Z0. **Tel:** 902-248-2102. **Owners:** E. & C. Hart. **Season:** year round. **Rates:** mid-range. **Cards:** VS, MC, AE. **Features:** housekeeping cottages; fishing; hiking; guides available; trails to salmon pools.

Four Seasons Crafts and Collectibles

Location: Portree. Follow directions to River Trail Cottages above and drive about 3 more km (1.8 mi). **Tel:** 902-248-2342. **Season:** year round. **Hours:** Mon to Sat - 9 am to 5 pm. **Cards:** MC. **Features:** tole-painted furniture and other items; shipping can be arranged.

Portree B & B

Location: Portree. Take the turnoff to Margaree Valley/Margaree Centre, about 33 km (20 mi) north of TCH Exit 11 Nyanza; drive about 1.5 km (1 mi) and turn left to Margaree

Centre; at Ingraham's Irving turn right and drive about 7 km (4.2 mi). **Mail Addr:** R. R. #1 Margaree Valley, N.S. B0E 2C0. **Tel:** 902-248-2728. **Owner:** M. Ross. **Season:** May to Oct. **Rates:** med-low. **Cards:** VS, MC. **Features:** working farm, fishing; trails.

Big Intervale Salmon Camp

Location: Big Intervale, Margaree Valley. For specific directions to this camp, you should call ahead. **Mail Addr:** R. R. #1, Margaree Valley, N.S. B0E 2C0. **Tel:** 902-248-2275; o/s 902-454-6507. **Owner:** Bill Davidson. **Season**: mid-May to end of Oct. **Rates:** med-high. **Features:** chalet-style lodge; licenced dining room and lounge; fishing guides; packages available.

Margaree Valley Outiftters

Location: Margaree Valley, on road to Fish Hatchery (see below). **Mail Addr:** R. R. #1, Margaree Valley, N.S. B0E 2C0. **Tel:** 902-248-2375. **Owner:** D. Ross. **Season:** April to Dec - fishing and hunting season. **Features:** Complete outfitters and guides for trout and salmon fishing as well as hunting, in season.

Irving station and convenience store - Margaree Valley.

Atlantic Fisheries Visitor Interpretation Centre

Established in 1902 as the first salmon hatchery in Nova Scotia. The operation involves the spawning, incubation and rearing of juvenile Atlantic Salmon.

Location: Margaree Valley. Take the turnoff to Margaree Valley/Margaree Centre, and drive for about 5 km (3 mi) then turn at "fish hatchery" sign. Stay on the pavement until you come to the hatchery. **Features**: a very interesting display for anyone interested in salmon and/or fish farming; beautiful views of the River; public washrooms

Hart's Ultramar - located on Cabot Trail at Northeast Margaree; 902- 248-2436; open Apr to Dec 8 am to 8 pm; shorter hours in winter.

Margaree Forks

Located on the Cabot Trail, about 42 km (25 mi) north of Nyanza and 35 km (21 mi) south of Cheticamp.

Chaisson's Riverview Housekeeping Cabins

Location: East Margaree. Cross the river at Margaree Forks via Doyle's Bridge. Keep left after you cross the river. Cabins are 4 km (2.5 mi) from the Forks. **Mail Addr:** R. R. #1 Margaree Harbour, N.S. B0E 2B0. **Tel:** 902-235-2787. **Owner:** R. Chaisson. **Season:** mid-May to Oct. **Rates:** mid-range. **Cards:** VS.

Old Miller Trout Farm B & B

Location: Margaree Forks on Cabot Trail - 402 Doyles Road - just south of the Co-op store. **Mail Addr:** Box 610 Margaree Forks, N.S. B0E 1A0. **Tel:** 902-248-2080. **Owners:** P. Wood & J. Stinson. **Season:** summer of '96 - late-May to Labour day; following years mid-May to mid-Oct. **Rates:** med-low. **Features:** u-fish farm - rainbow and speckled trout; nature trails.

Harrison Hill B & B

An elegant renovated Victorian house, featuring a music room where guests can enjoy evening entertainment.

Location: Margaree Forks, on the Cabot Trail. **Mail Addr:** Box 561, Margaree Forks, N.S. B0E 2A0. **Tel:** 902-248-2226. **Owners:** M.& R. Harrison. **Season:** May to Oct. **Rates:** med-low. **Cards:** VS, MC. **Features:** music room; live theatre; gift corner; centrally located for many other Cabot Trail adventures.

Margaree Co-op (groceries and general merchandise) - located on Cabot Trail at Margaree Forks; 902-248-2543; summer hours are Mon to Wed 8 am to 6 pm; Thurs & Fri 8 am to 9 pm; Sat 9 am to 5 pm.

LeBlanc's Store - Margaree Forks; 902-248-2632; open Mon to Fri 8 am to 7 pm; Sat 8 am to 6 pm; Sun 12 noon to 6 pm; convenience items, groceries, gifts and souvenirs.

Reg's Irving - Margaree Forks; 902-248-2252; open 7 am to 8 pm daily, all year; gas, diesel and propane.

Marquerite Shoppe

Gifts and souvenirs

Location: Margaree Forks on Cabot Trail, next to Visitor Information Centre. **Owner**: B.Cranton. **Tel**: 902-248-2502. **Season**: mid-Jun to mid-Oct. **Hours**: Jul & Aug 9 am to 8 pm; other months 9 am to 6 pm. **Cards:** VS, MC.

Visitor Information Centre

Location: Margaree Forks on the Cabot Trail. **Tel:** 902-248-2803. **Season:** mid-May to mid-Oct. **Hours:** 9 am to 9 pm generally, but vary somewhat depending on demand.

Buckles Cabins, Motel and Campground

Location: Margaree Forks, on the Cabot Trail. **Mail Addr:** Margaree Forks, N.S. B0E 2A0. **Tel:** 902-248-2053. **Owners:** G. & M. Buckles. **Season:** May to Oct. **Rates:** motel med-low; cabins mid-range; campsites avg. **Features:** most units are housekeeping; campground has washrooms, showers.

Margaree Lodge and Dining Room

Location: Margaree Forks, on the Cabot Trail. **Mail Addr:** Box 550, Margaree Forks, N.S. B0E 2A0; 902-248-2193; (o/s 248-2506); Fax 902-2170. **Owner:** W. MacIsaac. **Season:** mid-Jun to mid-Oct. **Rates:** mid-range. **Dng Rm Hrs:** 7:30 - 9:30 am; 5:30 - 8:30 pm **Prices:** mid-range. **Cards:** VS, MC, AE. **Features:** outdoor pool; 9-hole golf; licenced lounge and dining room.

McDaniel B & B

Location: Margaree Forks, on the Cabot Trail, 1.6 km (1 mi) north of Margaree Forks. **Mail Addr:** Box 532 Margaree Forks, N.S. B0E 2A0. **Tel:** 902-248-2734. **Owners:** E.& N. McDaniel. **Season:** May to Oct. **Rates:** med-low. **Features:** century-old home; beautiful view of valley; salmon pools on property.

Cajun Cedar Log Cottages

Location: Margaree Forks, on Cabot Trail, between the Forks and Margaree Hbr. **Mail Addr:** Margaree Forks, N.S. B0E 2A0. **Tel:** 902-248-2494. **Owners:** J. & M. LeBlanc. **Season:** May to mid-Nov. **Rates:** mid-range. **Features:** overlooking the Margaree River.

East Margaree

Locally this is called "the French side" (of the River).

To get to East Margaree you'll have to cross the river. To do that, turn off the Cabot Trail at the East Margaree sign, about 8 km (4.8 mi) north of Margaree Forks, onto a short road that takes you over the river at three spots. It's a wonderful place to get a really good look at the renowned Margaree River. You can cross over via Doyle's Bridge at the Forks as well.

Margaree Inn B & B

Location: East Margaree. Cross the River; the Inn is on your left. **Mail Addr:** Box 19, Margaree Harbour, N.S. B0E 2B0. **Tel:** 902-235-2524/2935. **Owners:** J. & D. LeBlanc. **Season:** May to Oct. **Rates:** med-low. **Cards:** VS, MC. **Features:** 4 rooms with private baths; a renovated school located on the beautiful Margaree River.

Margaree Bicentennial Museum

Location: East Margaree. Follow directions to the Margaree Inn B & B above. At the intersection by the Inn, turn right and drive a short distance to St. Michael's Church, where Museum is located. **Tel:** 902-235-2426. **Season:** Jul 1 to Labour Day. **Hours:** Mon to Sat 8 am to 8 pm; Sun. 1 pm to 8 pm. **Features:** artifacts, records and genealogy files.

Margaree Harbour

I'm not exactly sure where Margaree Harbour begins along this road - but it doesn't really matter. The junction where the Cabot Trail meets the Ceilidh Trail is about 13 km (8 mi) north of Margaree Forks. It's a lovely drive along this road, all along the River to the Harbour.

Margaree Harbour Craft and Gift Shop

Location: Margaree Harbour on Cabot Trail, about 10 km (6 mi) north of Margaree Forks. **Tel:** 902-235-2824. **Season:** Jun to Oct. **Hours:** 8:30 am to 9 pm daily. **Cards:** VS, MC, AE. **Features:** specializing in woolen products; other crafts, gifts and souvenirs.

Mill Valley B & B and Cabins

Location: Margaree Harbour. Driving north from Margaree Forks on Cabot Trail, watch for the Scotch Hill/ Mill Valley sign, which is about 11 km (6.5 mi) north of Margaree Forks; turn and drive about 1 km down that road. **Mail Addr:** Margaree Hbr, N.S. B0E 2B0. **Tel:** 902-235-2834. **Owners:** S. & S.Lamont. **Season:** year round. **Rates:** B & B - med-low; cabins - mid-range. **Features:** French, German, Russian, Polish & English spoken; hiking trails; winter activities; full breakfast for B & B guests (breakfast is also available for cabin guests for $7.50).

Taylor's B & B

Location: Margaree Harbour on Cabot Trail, about 13 km (8 mi) north of Margaree Forks. **Mail Addr:** R. R. #1,

Margaree Hbr, N.S. B0E 2B0. **Tel:** 902-235-2652. **Owners:** F. & M.Taylor. **Season:** May to Oct. **Rates:** low. **Features:** century-old house overlooking Margaree River and Harbour.

Duck Cove Inn and Dining Room

An awsome view of the Margaree River just where it empties into the Harbour.

Location: Margaree Harbour on Cabot Trail, just at the junction of Ceilidh and Cabot Trails. **Mail Addr:** Margaree Hbr, N.S. B0E 2B0. **Tel:** 902-235-2658; Fax 902-235-2592. **Owner:** G. Laurence. **Season:** Jun to mid-Oct. **Rates:** mid-range. **Cards:** VS, MC, AE. **Dng Rm Hrs:** 7:30 - 10:30 am; 12 - 2 pm; 6 - 8 pm. **Dng Rm Prices:** mid-range: **Features:** fishing; canoe rentals; ocean swimming.

Harbour View Inn B & B and chalet

Location: Margaree Harbour at the junction of the Ceilidh and Cabot Trails. **Mail Addr:** Box 52, Margaree Hbr, N.S. B0E 2B0. **Tel:** 902-235-2314. **Owner:** C. Jennex. **Season:** year round. **Rates:** med-low. **Cards:** MC. **Features:** overlooking Margaree Harbour; ocean swimming; canoeing, deep sea fishing etc. close by; A-frame chalet overlooking water.

Ross House Studio

A studio and gallery of printmaker and artist Michael Armentrout.

Location: Margaree Harbour at the junction of the Ceilidh and Cabot Trails. **Mail Addr:** Box 52, Margaree Hbr, N.S. B0E 2B0. **Tel:** 902-235-2112. Owner/Artist: Michael Armentrout. **Season:** Jun to Oct. **Hours:** you'll find Michael in his studio most of the time, but if you want to be sure not to miss him, call ahead. **Cards:** VS, MC. **Features:** limited edition prints; drawings; Cape Breton Art Calendar by Michael and another Cape Breton artist Teena Marie Saunders. Michael and Teena's work can be seen on pages 97, 105 (Michael) and 201, 291 (Teena).

The Hungry Piper Cafe, The Schooner Restaurant & Lounge, and Gift Shop

Location: Margaree Harbour, at the junction of the Ceilidh and Cabot Trails. **Tel:** 902-248-2182. **Season:** Jun to Oct **Hours:** cafe -9 am to 5 pm daily; restaurant - 5 pm to midnight. **Cards:** VS, MC, AE. **Features:** piper on staff; Gaelic spoken; vegetarian menu items.

✳ Note: For other facilities in this area...Margaree Harbour, Whale Cove, etc, see page 95.

Belle Cote

Located just north of the long bridge at the junction of the Cabot and Ceilidh Trails.

Crossroads Restaurant

Location: Belle Cote. **Tel:** 902-235-2888. **Season:** mid-May to late Oct. **Hours:** Jul & Aug 10 am to 10 pm; other months 11 am to 7 pm, except Sat open until 11 pm. **Cards:** VS, MC. **Features:** licensed.

Lobsters and Crab

At Belle Cote Wharf you can usually buy lobsters off the boats if you're at the wharf anytime between about 10 am and early afternoon when the boats come in; lobster season is from May 1st to Jul 1st, and crab season is for a few weeks after that (there are only a few boats here that fish crab, so I'm told).

Phillip's Esso - Belle Cote; 902-235-2342; open Mon to Sat 8 am to 8 pm; Sundays in summer 8 am to 6 pm.

Belle Cote Beach
Take the road just north of Phillip's Esso...it takes you down to the wharf and a protected public beach.

Ocean Haven B & B and Cottage

Location: Belle Cote. Take the road up the mountain across from Phillip's Esso. **Mail Addr:** Box 54, Margaree Hbr, N.S. B0E 2B0. **Tel:** 902-235-2329 o/s 613-837-4954. **Owners:** J. & P. Sheehan. **Rates:** B & B med-low. **Season:** mid-Jun to mid-Oct. **Features:** ocean view, ocean swimming.

Cap Le Moine & St. Joseph du Moine

Located on the Cabot Trail...Cap Le Moine is 9 km (5.5 mi) and St. Joseph is about 12 km (7 mi) north of Margaree Hbr.

Scarecrow Theatre

Scarecrows galore - over 100 of them! Also a gift shop and takeout.

Location: Cap Le Moine, on the Cabot Trail between Margaree Hbr and Cheticamp. **Tel:** 902-235-2108. **Season:** Mid-May to Oct. **Hours:** 8:30 am to 10 pm daily.

La Bella Mona Lisa

A unique little gift shop and gallery located at St. Joseph du Moine; tel 902-224-2560.

T. R. Deveaux and Son - located at St. Joseph Du Moine; if you should need an emergency car repair, they fix radiators, brakes...things like that; 902-224-3495; they don't sell gas though; open Mon to Sat 8 am to 6 pm.

Conti's B & B

Location: 309 Bazile Rd, St. Joseph du Moine. **Mail Addr:** 309 Bazile Rd, St. Joseph du Moine, N.S. B0E 3A0. **Tel:** 902-224-2697. **Owners:** A. & J. Conti. **Season:** mid-May to mid-Oct. **Rates:** low. **Cards:** VS, MC. **Features:** wonderful views of ocean and mountains; deep sea fishing and whale watching arrangements; bilingual

Pilot Whale B & B

Location: Bazile Rd, St. Joseph du Moine. **Mail Addr:** St. Joseph du Moine, N.S. B0E 3A0. **Tel:** 902-224-2592. **Owner:** C. Power. **Season:** mid-May to end of Oct. **Rates:** med-high. **Features:** log home.

Le Theatre des Moineaux

Acadian Dinner Theatre, musical brunch and concerts.

Location: St. Joseph du Moine Parish Hall. **Tel**: 902-224-2724; Fax 902-224-1579. **Features**: Acadian food, Acadian theatre and Acadian music. See insert for this year's dates. English translation summaries are provided with French plays.

Acadian Roots

French roots in Cape Breton are long and strong: for a time in the 18th century when the rest of the Maritimes had been ceded to the British, the island remained a French enclave as Isle Royale. But when Louisbourg fell for the second time, all the French who could afford the passage...returned to France with their families. The people who remained, peasants and fishermen, gravitated over the years into two areas, centred on Isle Madame at the southern extremity and Cheticamp on the northwest coast."
...from ***A Place Apart, the Cape Breton Story***, by James B. Lamb and Warren Gordon, Stone House Publishing, Inc. 1988.

Grand Etang

Located on the Cabot Trail, 15 km (9 mi) north of Margaree Harbour and about 10 km (6 mi) south of Cheticamp.

Delaney's Coffee Bar and Kwik Way (convenience store) - Grand Etang; 902-224-1550; open from 7 am to 11 pm daily.

Lemoine Co Op (grocery store) - Grand Etang; 902-224-3335; hours are Mon to Wed from 8 am to 6 pm; Thurs & Fri from 8 am to 9 pm and Sat from 8 am to 5 pm.

Point Cross

Located on the Cabot Trail about 8 km (4.8 mi) south of Cheticamp.

Germaine's B & B

Location: Point Cross, 8 km (5 mi) south of Cheticamp on Cabot Trail. **Mail Addr:** Box 275 Cheticamp, N.S. B0E 1H0. **Tel:** 902-224-3459. **Owners:** G. & R. Doucet. **Season:** Apr to Nov, other months by arrangement. **Rates:** med-low. **Cards:** VS, MC. **Features:** close to Cheticamp; ocean view; walking trail along ocean; friendly and helpful hosts; bilingual.

Cheticamp Outfitters B & B

Location: Point Cross, about 7 km (4 mi) south of Cheticamp on Cabot Trail. **Mail Addr:** Box 448 Cheticamp, N.S. B0E 1H0. **Tel:** 902-224-2776. **Owners:** V. & G. Hache. **Season:** May to Dec, other times by arrangement. **Rates:** med-low. **Cards:** VS, MC, AE. **Features:** licensed hunting and fishing guides; hiking trails, waterfalls and beach nearby.

Flora's Gift Shop

Location: Point Cross, just south of Cheticamp on the Cabot Trail. **Tel:** 902-224-3139; Fax 902-224-1213. **Season:** May to Oct. **Hours:** shoulder season 9 am to 5 pm; summer season 8:30 am to 8 pm (hours may be slightly longer or shorter depending on demand). **Cards:** all major cards. **Features:** large selection of Cheticamp hooking plus a wide variety of other crafts and gifts; ice cream parlor; Cheticamp hooking demonstrations.

Charlie's Country Music Store

Location: just south of Cheticamp. **Tel:** 902-224-3782. **Hours:** 8 am to 10 pm daily. **Cards:** VS, MC. **Features:** very large selection of Cape Breton and Maritime music...fiddling, Acadian traditional; Irish and Scottish, etc; also carries fishing supplies and convenience items.

L'Auberge Doucet Inn

Location: 1 km south of Cheticamp. **Mail Addr:** Box 776, Cheticamp, N.S. B0E 1H0. **Tel:** 902-224-3438; 1-800-646-8668; Fax 902-224-2792. **Owners:** R. & A. Doucet. **Season:** May to Oct. **Rates:** mid-range. **Cards:** VS, MC, AE. **Features:** sundeck overlooking ocean; light snack served in evenings; continental breakfast.

Cheticamp Island

A couple of kilometres south of the village of Cheticamp, you'll come to the turnoff to Cheticamp Island. This is a beautiful spot with a sandy beach and warm water (because it's protected). You don't need to get a boat across, there's a causeway.

Seashell Cabins

Location: Cheticamp Island Rd. **Mail Addr:** Box 388, Cheticamp, N.S. B0E 1H0. **Tel:** 902-224-3569; o/s 224-1563/2705. **Owner:** M. Doucet. **Season:** mid-Jun to mid-Oct. **Rates:** med-low. **Features:** housekeeping cabins; ocean swimming.

Blue Island B & B

Location: 107 Cheticamp Island Rd. **Mail Addr:** Box 675, Cheticamp, N.S. B0E 1H0. **Tel:** 902-224-3077. **Owner:** B. Gunther. **Season:** mid-Jun to mid-Oct. **Rates:** med-low. **Features:** log house with lovely ocean view; continental breakfast.

Icelandic Riding Tours

Something a little different - a ride along the ocean on pure-bred Icelandic horses that are descendents of the Viking's horses.

Location: Cheticamp Island - watch for sign. **Tel:** 902-224-2319. **Season:** mid-Jun to mid-Sept. **Hours:** call ahead to make a reservation. **Features:** ride along the sea past working lighthouse, in view of the Cape Breton Highlands and Acadian village of Cheticamp; guided tours; for experienced riders.

Cheticamp Island Resort

Location: Cheticamp Island. **Mail Addr:** Box 160, Dominion, N.S. B0A 1E). **Tel:** 902-224-1152 or 902-849-6444. **Owner:** R. McVeigh. **Season:** Apr to Dec, other times by arrangement. **Rates:** med-high. **Cards:** VS, MC. **Features:** close to Plage St-Pierre (beach); decks with barbecue; housekeeping.

Plage St-Pierre Campground (and Beach)

Location: Cheticamp Island. Follow the pavement, watch for sign. **Mail Addr:** Box 430, Cheticamp, N.S. B0E 1H0. **Tel:** 902-224-2112. or 2642; Fax 902-224-1579. **Owners:** G. and G. Deveau. **Season:** mid-May to mid-Sept. **Rates:** campground -avg; small charge per car for a day at the beach. **Features:** campground has washrooms, disposal station, showers, serviced and unserviced sites, laundromat; beach has changing rooms, canteen, playground, mini-golf, washrooms.

Cheticamp

Located on the Cabot Trail, about 27 km (16 mi) north of Margaree Harbour.

Although traders from Jersey Island had already exploited the fishing industry on Cheticamp Island for several summers, the first permanent residents arrived in 1785. Fourteen settlers, who have since been referred to as *Les quatorze vieux* obtained a concession of 7,000 acres of land in 1790."

...from a brochure prepared by La Societé Saint-Pierre.

Cheticamp Motel

Location: Main St, Cheticamp, south end of village. **Mail Addr:** Box 698 Cheticamp, N.S. B0E 1H0. **Tel:** 902-224-2711; o/s 902-469-3380. **Owner:** E. Merry. **Season:** May to Nov. **Rates:** med-low. **Cards:** VS, MC, AE. **Features:** bilingual; breakfast served from 7:30 to 9:30 am.

The Brigadoon Restaurant

Location: Main St, Cheticamp, south end of village. **Tel:** 902-224-1551. **Season:** year round. **Hours:** Jun to Sept open from 6:30 am to 9 pm daily; other months closes at 7 pm. **Features:** family-style restaurant.

L'Escaouette

Whale Cruises and Harbour Tours.

Location: Main St, Cheticamp, south end of village. Watch for small dock and sign. **Tel:** 902-224-1959. **Owners:** N. & T. Chiasson. **Season:** late May to Oct. **Hours:** whale cruises at 9 am, 1 pm and 5 pm weather permitting; harbour cruises - during day between whale cruises, or in the evening. **Cards:** VS, MC. **Features:** comfortable boat with full canopy; bilingual guide on board; rain cheque if no whales are spotted (that sounds like a good deal!)

Cooperative Artisanale de Cheticamp

This is a craft shop, Acadian restaurant and museum, all in one.

Location: Main St, Cheticamp, south end of village. **Tel:** 902-224-2170; restaurant 902-224-3207. **Season:** May to Sept. **Hours:** May to mid-Jun and Oct - 9 am to 6 pm; mid-Jun to Sept 30 - 8 am to 9 pm daily. **Features:** craft co-op with hooked rugs, etc; Acadian museum with demonstrations in spinning, hooking and weaving; Acadian-style restaurant.

Cheticamp Co Op (groceries and general merchandise) - located in the south end of Cheticamp; 902-224-2066; open Mon to Wed 9 am to 5 pm; Thurs & Fri 9 am to 9 pm; Sat 9 am to 5 pm.

Albert's Motel

Location: Main St, Cheticamp, across from Co-op. **Mail Addr:** Box 74, Cheticamp, N.S. B0E 1H0. **Tel:** 902-224-2077 or 224-2936. **Owner:** J. Chaisson. **Season:** mid-May to mid Oct. **Rates:** med-low. **Cards:** VS, MC. **Features:** small 4-unit motel; complimentary coffee and muffins.

Sacred Heart Hospital - Cheticamp, next to St. Peter's Church; emergency 224-1500

Whale Cruisers

Location: Cheticamp, opposite St. Peter's Church. **Mail Addr:** Box 183, Cheticamp, N.S. B0E 1H0. **Tel:** 902-224-3376; 1-800-813-3376; Fax 902-224-1166. **Season:** Jul to mid-Sept. **Hours:** three cruises a day; special charters can be arranged and o/s trips by appointment. **Cards:** VS, MC. **Features:** narrated tours, interpreter aboard; see whales, sea birds, sea caves, etc.

L'Église St. Pierre (Saint Peter's Church)

The Acadian parish of Cheticamp was founded in 1785. The present day L'Eglise St. Pierre was built under the capable supervision of Père Fiset, who is buried under the sanctuary. It's a beautiful old church with frescoes and stained glass windows and its organ has been there since 1904. The stones used to build the church were hauled from Cheticamp Island, across the harbour on the ice.

Evangeline Restaurant

Location: Main St, Cheticamp. **Mail Addr:** Box 287, Cheticamp, BOE 1H0. **Tel:** 902-224-2044. **Season:** year round. **Hours:** Sun to Thurs 6:30 am to midnight; Fri open until 12:30 am; Sat open until 1:30 am. **Prices:** low to mid-range. **Cards:**VS, MC. **Features:** family dining; homemade soups and pies a specialty.

Coin des Artisans (Glenna's Crafty Corner)

Location: Main St, Cheticamp. **Tel:** 224-2900. **Season:** year round. **Hours:** Mon to Wed & Sat 10 am to 5 pm; Thurs and Fri 10 am to 9 pm. **Cards:** VS, MC. **Features:** crafts; tole painting; craft supplies; lessons.

Acadian Motel

Location: Main St, Cheticamp. **Mail Addr:** Box 11, Cheticamp, N.S. BOE 1H0. **Tel:** 902-224-2640; o/s 224-2089. **Owners:** R. & W. Aucoin. **Season:** May to Oct. **Rates:** mid-range. **Cards:** VS, MC, AE.

Quai Matthieu/The Boardwalk - located in the centre of the village - a wonderful stroll along the ocean with docks, shops, restaurants and tourist information.

Acadian Whale Cruise

Cruise aboard the *Cabot Trail II.*

Location: the wharf on the Boardwalk, Cheticamp. **Mail Addr:** Box 97, Cheticamp, N.S. BOE 1H0. **Tel:** 902-224-2793/1088. **Season:** mid-Jun to Oct. **Hours:** in summer three cruises a day 9:15 am, 1:15 pm and 5:15 pm. **Cards:**

VS, MC, AE. **Features:** 3-hr cruise to watch for whales and sea birds and learn a little about the history and geography of the area.

Dockside Treasures

Location: the Boardwalk, Cheticamp. **Tel:** 902-224-1507. **Season:** May to Oct. **Hours:** 10 am to 10 pm, daily. **Cards:** Vs, MC, AE. **Features:** gifts, crafts and souvenirs.

La Chaloupe

A restaurant and pub on the Boardwalk - great spot to really get into the Cape Breton spirit.

Location: on the Boardwalk, Cheticamp. **Tel:** 902-224-3710. **Season:** mid-May to Sept (could be open in Oct as well, depending on demand). **Hours:** restaurant open from 11:30 am to 9 pm; pub open from 1 pm to midnight or so; pub serves food. **Features:** Acadian-style fish chowder, Fricot, meat pie, and other Acadian fare; licensed; live Acadian traditional, Cape Breton and other types of music in pub from 9 to 12 pm; outdoor patio right on the Harbour.

Overnight Country Log Home

Location: Belle Marche Rd. Turn off Main St at the Post Office and drive 1.4 km (1 mi). **Mail Addr:** Box 337, Cheticamp, N.S. B0E 1H0. **Tel:** 902-224-2816. **Owner:** A. Deveaux. **Season:** Jun to Sept. **Rates:** med-low. **Features:** quiet country setting; continental breakfast; outdoor fireplace.

déjeuner de soliel B & B

Location: Belle Marche Rd. Turn off Main St at the Post Office onto the Belle Marche Rd, and follow signs. **Mail Addr:** Box 974, Cheticamp, N.S. B0E 1H0. **Tel:** 902-224-1373. **Owners:** A. & A. St. Jean. **Season:** year round. **Rates:** med-low. **Cards:** VS, MC. **Features:** quiet country setting; bilingual.

Nova Scotia Liquor Commission - located on Main St in Cheticamp, in centre of village; 902-224-2012; open Mon to Thurs 10 am to 6 pm; Fri and Sat 10 am to 10 pm. Note: hours could be extended a bit in the summer months.

Au Havre - Main St, Cheticamp; books (French and English); souvenirs; hooked mats; 902-224-3800; open Jul & Aug 9 am to 9 pm daily; other months 9 am to 5pm, Fri 9 am to 9 pm

Harbour Restaurant

Location: Main St, Cheticamp, by the Boardwalk. **Tel:** 902-224-2042. **Season:** mid-May to mid-Oct. **Hours:** 8 am to 11 pm daily. **Cards:** most major cards. **Features:** patio overlooking Harbour; full menu; offers seafood, steaks,and Acadian meals.

Frasers Motel and Cottages

Location: Main St, Cheticamp. **Mail Addr:** Box 177, Cheticamp, N.S. B0E 1H0. **Tel:** 902-224-2411. **Owner:** A. Fraser. **Season:** mid-May to mid-Oct. **Rates:** mid-range. **Features:** housekeeping cottages.

Pharmacie Acadienne - located on Main St in Cheticamp, just about the centre of the village; **Tel:** 902-224-2841; **Hours:** Mon & Thurs 9 am to 9 pm; Tue & Wed - 9 am to 5:30 pm (dispensary closed during lunch and supper hours); Sat open 9 am to 5 pm - dispensary closed at 1 pm; Sun open 2 to 4 pm - dispensary closed.

Laurence Guest House (c. 1870) B & B

Location: Main St, Cheticamp, in the centre of the village. **Mail Addr:** 15408 Main St, Cheticamp, N.S. B0E 1H0. **Tel:** 902-224-2184. **Owners:** S. LeLievre & J. Wakefield. **Season:** May to Oct, other months by arrangement. **Rates:** med-low. **Features:** heritage home in the centre of the village; bilingual; adult accommodation.

Julia Longacre

Merry's Motel

Location: Main St, Cheticamp. **Mail Addr:** Box 96, Cheticamp, N.S. B0E 1H0. **Tel:** 902-224-2456. **Owner:** G. Merry. **Season:** May to Oct. **Rates:** med-low. **Cards:** VS, MC. **Features:** complimentary continental breakfast.

Le Gabriel Restaurant and Lounge

Look for the lighthouse in the middle of the village.

Located: Main St, Cheticamp, in the centre of the village. **Tel:** 902-224-3685. **Season:** year round. **Hours:** 11 am to 10 pm during summer season; closed at 7 pm in o/s. **Cards:** all major cards. **Features:** family-style restaurant; Acadian dishes, seafood; bilingual.

Le Motif Arts Boutique

Location: Main St, Cheticamp (across from Le Gabriel). **Tel:** 902-224-1680. **Owner:** D. Bourgeois. **Season:** early May to late Oct, other months by chance. **Hours:** 10 am to 9 pm daily (other times by chance). **Features:** folk art, rugs, jewellery, folk paintings.

Laurie's Motel - Diningroom.

Location: Main St, Cheticamp. **Mail Addr:** Box 1, Cheticamp, N.S. B0E 1H0. **Tel:** 902-224-2400; 1-800-95-WHALE; Fax 902-224-2069. **Owner:** L. McKeown. **Season:** year round. **Rates:** med-high to upper end. **Dng Rm Hrs:** May to Oct 7 am to 11 am; 4:30 to 9 pm; in winter the dining room is open for breakfast only from 7 to 9 am. **Dng Rm Prices**: mid-range. **Cards:** VS, MC. **Features:** laundromat, playground, whale and nature cruises (see below).

Seaside Whale & Nature Cruises

Cruise aboard the *Love Boat.*

Location, etc: same as Laurie's Motel (above). **Season:** Jul to mid-Sept. **Hours:** 3 sailings a day. **Features:** watch for whales, seals, seabirds, etc; group rates and charters.

Ocean View Motel

Location: Main St, Cheticamp toward the north end of the village. **Mail Addr:** Box 419, Cheticamp, N.S. B0E 1H0. **Tel:** 902-224-2313. **Owner:** G.R. LeBlanc. **Season:** year round. **Rates:** mid-range. **Cards:** VS, MC. **Features:** ocean swimming; play area; picnic tables; barbecue pits; bilingual.

Le Portage Golf Club

Golf in view of the hills of the Cabot Trail.

Location: Cheticamp, in the north end of the village. **Tel:** 902-224-3338. **Season:** May to Sept. **Hours**: 7 am to dusk. **Green Fees:** adults $15 for 9 holes/$22 for 18 holes; cut rates for students and seniors. **Features:** 9-hole course but by the summer of 1997 it will be an 18-hole course; par 35; 3,183 yards; cart and club rentals.

Les Trois Pignons - (The Three Gables)

You'll recognize this building by it's wonderful red roof and, of course, the gables. It's a centre for Acadian culture as well as a source of genealogical and general information.

Location: Cheticamp, in the north end of the village. **Tel:** 902-224-2612/224-2642. **Season:** year round. **Hours:** Jul & Aug - 9 am to 6 pm daily; Jun, Sept & Oct - 9 am to 5 pm daily; other months 8:30 to 4:30 Mon to Fri only.

Les Trois Pignons

Les Trois Pignons was built in 1978 to serve the public as a cultural, information, genealogical and community centre.

At Les Trois Pignons you'll find a library with records and information on the history of the Acadians and the rug hooking industry, as well as genealogy and translation services.

In the summer months you can visit the Dr. Elizabeth LeFort Gallery where you'll see samples of her amazing tapestries as well as other rugs and hangings.

You can visit also a museum of artifacts from Marguerite Gallant's lifetime collection.

When I asked the curator here how long it took Mme. LeFort to finish one of her huge tapestries, he said eleven months. I was shocked. I had expected him to say three or four years. Apparently she works at a rate of 1 stitch a second! When you see the tapestries you'll realize how amazing that is.

Dr. Elizabeth LeFort Gallery

Location: at Les Trois Pignons (see above). **Season:** May to Oct. **Hours:** same as Les Trois Pignons.
Admission: low.
Features: more than 20 hand-hooked tapestries of "Canada's Artist in Wool"; some of her works are at the Vatican, Buckingham Palace and the White House.

Les Cabines du Portage

Location: Main St, Cheticamp, in the north end of the village. **Mail Addr:** 15660 Main St, Cheticamp, N.S. B0E 1H0. **Tel:** 902-224-2973/2822. **Owners:** G. & P. Poirier. **Season:** year round. **Rates:** mid-range. **Cards:** VS. **Features:** housekeeping; barbecues; weekly rates.

Petit Étang

(Local pronunciation sounds like 'petty de tang".)

Located on the Cabot Trail, just north of Cheticamp. This area is often referred to as Cheticamp, as the two communities run into each other.

Sunset Art Gallery

Location: Petit Étang, on Cabot Trail. **Tel:** 902-224-1831, or 224-2119; Fax 902-224-1831. **Owners**: William and Linda Roach. **Season:** mid-May to mid-Oct. **Hours:** 9 am to 6 pm daily, or by appointment. **Cards:** VS. **Features:** whimsical and colourful folk art creations of the owner William Roach and other local artists.

Le Gabion

The largest lobster trap in the world, no doubt. This one's a gift shop.

Location: Petit Étang, on Cabot Trail. **Tel:** 902-224-2492.

Étables de L'Étang - Little Pond Stables

Stop off for a short riding lesson and a trail ride along the river, ocean or mountains.

Location: Petit Étang Beach Rd. Coming from Cheticamp, take the first turnoff to your left past Le Gabion (the giant lobster trap). Drive a short distance and turn left again - watch for sign. Coming from the north, turn right onto Petit Étang Beach Rd (by Aucoin's Bakery). **Tel:** 902-224-3858. **Owner:** Helena Aucoin. **Season:** May to Oct. **Hours:** no set hours - just drop by, or call ahead to make an appointment. **Rates:** $20 per hour plus tax. **Features:** lesson before trail ride for inexperienced riders; short or long rides along the beach, Cheticamp River, golf course; short pony or horse rides for children on premises.

La Boulangerie Aucoin (Bakery) - Petit Étang; 902-224-3220; open late May to Thanksgiving from Mon to Sat 7 am to 5 pm; other months open Mon to Fri from 8 am to 5 pm; home baked breads, rolls, sweets.

Jean's Handcrafts

This is a tiny shop but it's jam-packed with Cheticamp hooking...all shapes, sizes and designs.

Location: Petit Étang. **Tel:** 902-224-2758. **Season:** May to Dec. **Hours:** 9 am to 9 pm daily to Nov, from Nov to Christmas open on Tue and Thurs only. **Cards:** VS, MC.

Park View Motel and Dining Room

Location: Petit Étang, beside the Cheticamp River. **Mail Addr:** Box 117, Cheticamp, N.S. B0E 1H0. **Tel:** 902-224-3232. **Owners:** the Chaisson family. **Season:** late-May to late Oct. **Rates:** mid-range. **Cards:** VS, MC, AE. **Dng Rm Hrs:** 7:30 am to 10 am; 5 pm to 8 pm; lounge open from 11 am to 2 am. **Features:** close to National Park; salmon fishing (guides available); close to hiking trails.

The Cape Breton Highlands National Park

Once you pass through the villages of Cheticamp and Petit Étang, you'll come to the entrance to the **Cape Breton Highlands National Park.** The drive you're about to embark on is quite possibly the most spectacular drive you'll ever take. The National Park itself is 950 sq km (366 square mi) of unspolied coastal wilderness and is a driving distance of 106 km (66 mi) from the Cheticamp entrance to the park's end at Ingonish. You'll climb four mountains, each over 1,200 feet high, and you'll encounter some of the most wonderful hiking trails, lookoffs and beaches in the country. The road through the park is, of course, part of the incredible Cabot Trail. Be sure to stop off here at the Cheticamp Information Centre before you begin your climb over the Trail.

Visitor Information Centre - C.B. Highlands Natl Park

Here you'll find lots of information and interesting things to see before you begin your trek in the Park.

Location: Cheticamp on Cabot Trail, at entrance to C. B. Highlands Natl Park. **Mail Addr:** Ingonish Beach, N.S. B0C 1L0. **Tel:** 902-224-2306, 285-2691; Fax. 902-285-2866. **Season:** year round, full summer season is late May to late Oct. **Hours:** May & Jun, Sept & Oct - 9 am to 5 pm; Jul, Aug, Sept - 8 am to 8 pm.; winter 9 am to 4 pm. **Admission**: Park Entry Permit ranges from $2 to $3. per person, with family, group and longer-stay rates. **Cards:** VS, MC . **Features:** slide show, exhibits, family corner.

Les Amis du Plein Air

A nature book store.

Location: Cheticamp on Cabot Trail, at Visitor Centre of C.B. Highlands Natl Park. **Mail Addr:** Box 472, Cheticamp, N.S. B0E 1H0. **Tel:** 902-224-3814; Fax 902-224-2445. **Season:** mid-May to mid-Oct, daily. **Hours:** Jul & Aug 8 am to 8 pm; rest of season 9 am to 5 pm. **Cards:** VS, MC. **Features:** lots of books on nature, the outdoors, hiking and exploring; calendars, souvenirs, etc.

✳ On your drive through the National Park, you'll come across many super hiking trails that are maintained by the Park authorities. You will easily spot the signs on the road.If you are at all interested in the flora and fauna of the Island, you should consider stopping off for a hike or two. Most of these trails are listed below.

L'Acadien Hiking Trail

Location: Natl Park, opposite the Visitor Centre. **Features:** 9.6 km. (6 mi.) loop; views of Cheticamp River and ocean .

Park Toll Booth - If you don't already have your permit, stop here.

Cheticamp Campground

A beautiful large campground inside the C.B. Highlands National Park.

Location: Cheticamp, just inside the C.B. Highlands Natl Park. **Mail Addr**: C.B. Highlands Natl Park, Ingonish

Beach, N.S. B0C 1L0. **Tel:** 902-224-2310, o/s 902-224-2306, 902-285-2691. **Season:** year round, hook-ups and showers mid-May to mid-Oct. **Rates:** avg plus. **Cards:** VS, MC, debit cards. **Features:** natural setting, outdoor theatre, hiking trails; serviced and unserviced sites; 2 sites are wheelchair accessible; indoor washrooms, showers, kitchen shelters with wood stoves.

Grand Falaise Picnic Park

A small picnic site, about 3 km (1.8 mi) north of the Park Entrance booth. **Features**: picnic tables, toilets.

Le Buttereau Trail

Location: Cabot Trail, across from Grand Falaise Picnic Park. **Features:** trail is 1.9 km (1.2 mi); a spot where Acadian pioneers settled many years ago.

La Bloque Picnic Site

Picnic tables right on the beach, about 9 km (5.5 mi) north of Park Entrance booth. **Features**: toilets and heaps of driftwood.

Corney Brook Campground

Location: on Cabot Trail, about 10 km (6 mi) north of Park Entrance booth at Cheticamp. **Mail Addr:** C. B. Highlands Natl Park, Ingonish Beach, N.S. B0C 1L0. **Tel:** 902-224-2306,285-2691. **Season:** mid-May to mid-Oct. **Rates:** avg. **Features:** self-registration; open tenting on ocean; unserviced sites; supervised swimming, playground, toilets, fireplaces, kitchen shelters with wood stoves.

Corney Brook Trail

Location: Cabot Trail, about 10 km (6 mi) north of Park entrance. **Features:** a woodland trail that leads you up a box canyon to a small waterfall; 8 km (5 mi) return; time 2-3 hours.

Top of French Mountain - about 15 km (9 mi) from Park Entrance booth at Cheticamp. You are 455 metres (1,492) feet above the sea here.

Skyline Trail

Location: top of French Mountain. **Features:** a spectacular view of Cabot Trail and Gulf of St. Lawrence; lots of wildlife, watch for pilot whales out at sea; 7 km (4.3 mi) loop, time 2-3 hours, elevation 1350 ft. Watch the steep cliffs!

Bog Trail

Location: French Mountain, about 20 km (12 mi) north of Park entrance. **Features:** wheelchair accessible, a .6 km (.4 mi) loop on a boardwalk; orchids and other plants.

Fishing Cove Trail and wilderness campsite

Location: French Mountain, about 22 km (13 mi) from Cheticamp. **Features:** takes you right down to the ocean - 1100 feet to the Gulf of St. Lawrence where there's a wilderness camping site, fresh and salt water; 16 km (10 mi) return; 4-5 hours.

MacKenzie Mountain - Are you ready for another mountain? This one's 335 m (1,222 feet) high with incredible lookoffs and photo opportunities. From one of the lookoffs you can see the wilderness campsite at Fishing Cove.

Pleasant Bay

Located on Cabot Trail, about 30 km (18 mi) north of Cheticamp...a truly beautiful northern coastal community. Note that when you leave Pleasant Bay you will have changed direction - you'll be heading east across the northern boundary of the Park.

Julia Longacre

Highland Fling - Shop of Interest

Location: Pleasant Bay on the Cabot Trail, at the foot of MacKenzie Mtn. **Tel**: 902-224-2990. **Owner:** W. Fraser. **Season:** mid-May to mid-Oct. **Hours:** 8 am to 8 pm daily. **Cards:** Interac. **Features:** glass, leather, pottery, collector's pieces, etc; dumping station for buses and RV's.

Cardinal Points Gifts of Distinction

Location: Pleasant Bay, on the Cabot Trail. **Tel:** 902-224-1364. **Owner:** M. Fraser. **Season:** May to Oct. **Hours:** Jul, Aug & Sept - 8 am to 8 pm; May & Oct. - 9 am to 7 pm. **Cards:** VS, MC. **Features:** gifts and crafts; tourist information; postal outlet; ice cream parlour.

The Black Whale Restaurant

Location: Pleasant Bay, on Cabot Trail. **Tel:** 902-224-2185. **Owner:** B. Atwell. **Features:** Wild Bill's Oyster Bar, seafood.

Old Fisherman's Chowder Shop, Coffee Shop and Gift Shop

Location: Pleasant Bay, on Cabot Trail. **Tel:** 902-224-3572. **Season:** mid-Jun to end of Sept. **Hours:** chowder shop open from 10 am to 5 pm; gift shop open generally from 8 am to 6 pm (can vary a little at times). **Cards:** VS, MC. **Features:** seafood chowder; gifts and souvenirs.

Salty Mariner's Inn, Motel and Tin Pan Galley Restaurant

Location: Pleasant Bay on the Cabot Trail. **Mail Addr:** Pleasant Bay, B0E 2P0. **Tel:** 902-224-1400. **Owners:** L. & V. Arsenault. **Season:** May to Oct; o/s by arrangement. **Rates:** mid-range and med-high. **Cards:** VS, MC, AE. **Dng Rm Hrs:** 8 am to 10 p.m. **Prices**: mid-range. **Features:** licenced; panoramic view of ocean; breakfast for inn guests; swimming, whale and dolphin watching; day care.

Highland Coastal Tours & Charters

3-hour coastal tour aboard the 48-ft. Northumberland *Sonya Maria I.*

Location: Pleasant Bay, on Cabot Trail. Turn down the Harbour Rd/Red River Rd, then make a quick left and drive down to the wharf. **Tel:** 902-224-1825, Fax same. **Owner:** W. Fraser. **Season:** mid-Jun to mid-Sept; other times on request. **Hours:** three sailings daily, 9:30 am, 1:30 pm, 6:00 pm. **Features:** coastal tour to watch for whales, seabirds, seals; interpreter aboard.

Reed Timmons Folk Art Studio

Location: Pleasant Bay, at junction of Cabot Trail and Harbour Rd/Red River Rd. **Tel:** 902-224-3575. **Season:** Jun to Oct, other months by chance or appointment. **Hours:** 10 am to 8 pm generally, but sometimes the hours vary. **Features:** folk carvings by Reed Timmons - specializing in whales, gulls, fishermen, animals.

Pleasant Bay Gas Bar - Pleasant Bay, on the Cabot Trail; 902-224-2076; open daily from 8 am to 10 pm, May to Oct; gas, diesel, snack bar, convenience items; accepts most major credit cards.

Windswept B & B

Location: Pleasant Bay - 2 km (1.2 mi) down the Red River Rd. **Mail Addr**: Pleasant Bay, N.S. B0E 2P0. **Tel**: 902-224-1424. **Owner**: T. Thompson. **Season**: Jun to Sept. **Rates**: med-low. **Cards**: VS, MC. **Features**: beautiful setting between ocean and mountains; full breakfast.

Rusty Anchor Restaurant

Location: Pleasant Bay. **Tel:** 902-224-1313. **Season:** May to Oct. **Hours:** Jul & Aug 8 am to 10 pm; other months 11 am to 9 pm (breakfast on weekends only in the shoulder months). **Prices**: mid-range to med-high. **Cards**: VS, MC, direct payment. **Features**: oysters, mussels, lobster and crab; salad bar; children's menu.

Whale and Seal Cruise

Location: Pleasant Bay, on Cabot Trail - turn down the Harbour Rd/Red River Rd, then make a quick left and drive down to the wharf. **Owner:** Capt. Mark Timmons. **Tel:** 902-224-1315/2597. **Season:** Jun to mid-Sept. **Hours:** Jun - one trip a day usually at 2 pm; July to Sept -3 trips daily 9:30 am, 1 pm & 5 pm. **Cards:** VS, MC. **Features:** 11-m (35 ft) Cape Islander *Bay Venture*; see humpback, fin, minke and pilot whales, seals, eagles, sea caves, waterfalls.

Mountain View Motel and Restaurant

Location: Pleasant Bay, on Cabot Trail. **Mail Addr:** Pleasant Bay, N.S. B0E 2P0; 902- 224-3100. **Owners:** L. & B.Mattie. **Season:** mid-May to mid-Oct. **Rates:** med-high. **Dng Rm Hrs:** 7 am to 10 pm. **Prices**: mid-range. **Cards:** most major cards. **Features:** motel units and cottages; licenced; outdoor pool; tennis court.

MacIntosh Brook Campground

Hiking trail and picnic park

Location: on Cabot Trail, about 3 km (1.8 mi) east of Pleasant Bay. **Mail Addr:** C.B. Highlands Natl Park, Ingonish Beach, N.S. B0C 1L0. **Tel:** 902-224-2306, 285-2691. **Season:** mid-May to mid-Oct. **Rates:** avg. **Features:** self-registration; 10 unserviced sites; toilets; kitchen shelters & wood stoves. **Hiking Trail**: Starts at campground and ends at a waterfall; 2.8 km (2.75 mi) return; time 50 min.

Lone Sheiling

Cottage and hiking trail

Location: on Cabot Trail, about 6 km (3.6 mi) east of Pleasant Bay. **Features**: a replica of a Scottish shepherd's hut; a short trail along the edge of a valley where you'll find **very** old trees, rare ferns and many varieties of wildflowers. Trail is an .8 km (.5 mi) loop; washrooms halfway around.

North Mountain

Yes, another mountain, and this one is every bit as high as the others - 445 m (1,460 ft). to be exact - but this one is inland. The views are breathtaking; the geology of this area is fascinating. Those green-coloured rocks you may notice close to the top of the mountain are a mere 1.5 billion years old! North Mountain is about 13 km (8 mi) east of Pleasant Bay.

Big Intervale

Located on the Cabot Trail, just at the base of North Mountain.

Big Intervale Campground and Picnic Park

Location: on the Cabot Trail, as you come down off North Mtn. **Features:** open, unserviced campsites on the shore of the South Branch of the North Aspy River; pit toilets, kitchen shelters with wood stoves; fireplaces; self-registration.

Beulach Ban Falls and Aspy Trail

Location: on Cabot Trail. Across from Big Intervale Campground, take the road by the park warden's residence and drive 2 km 1.2 mi) to the falls. You can stop off for a picnic or walk all or part of the beautiful Aspy Trail. Trail starts at the falls and is 9.6 km. (6 mi.) return; it runs along the valley then climbs to an elevation of 1500 feet.

MacKinnon's Farm

Maple syrup, organic strawberries, oysters - you can even fish for your own rainbow and speckled trout. This farmhouse was built in 1870 and is one of the very few homes left in Big Intervale, once a thriving community..

Location: Big Intervale, watch for roadside stand. **Tel:** 902-383-2611. **Season:** strawberries available from mid-July to mid-Aug; oysters and maple products and U-fish are around all summer; pony rides available sometimes as well.

Keep an Eye Out

Kenneth MacKinnon of MacKinnon's Farm (above) told me I should mention two things about this area.

Number one - the ***rabbits!*** He says the current rabbit population is unbelievable and you could see a hundred or more on your travels along this part of the trail. Kids will be especially interested in this prospect. Of course, the rabbit population is cyclical and this is a peak time...in a few years there may be next to none.

The **second** thing he told me about is the ***moose*!** If you've ever seen a moose up close you'll know what I mean when I say they are **awsome.** If you've never seen one, you're in for a special treat. Mr. MacKinnon says in the fall he has seen as many as 15 moose along the highway on the top of North Mountain. Now that would be a sight! Dusk is the best time.

Cape North

Located on the northern tip of the Cabot Trail, 70 km (42 mi) from Cheticamp, 30 km (18 mi) northeast of Pleasant Bay. You'll find a grocery store, fast food outlets, bakery and convenience store.

Arts North

This shop carries high quality crafts like pottery, jewellery, canvas mats, handpainted silks, etc. Also, it's a showcase for emerging Cape Breton artists and craftspeople to show and sell their work.

Location: Cape North, on the Cabot Trail. **Tel:** 902-383-2911. **Season:** Jun to Oct. **Hours:** Jul & Aug 9 am - 6 or 7 pm; shoulder season 10 am to 5 pm. **Cards:** VS, MC. **Features:** quality juried Cape Breton crafts; shipping available.

MacLeod's Ultramar - on the Cabot Trail at Cape North, just at the turnoff to Bay St. Lawrence; 902-383-2747; open from mid-May to Sept - 8 am to 7 pm; other months from 8 am to 5 pm.

Oakwood Manor Bed & Breakfast

A pleasant old home in a pastsoral setting, a little off the beaten path, but worth the short drive.

Location: At Cape North, turn onto Bay St. Lawrence Road and drive about a km to the Northside Road. Drive a short distance down the Northside Road. **Mail Addr:** Box 19, Dingwall, N.S. B0C 1G0. **Tel:** 902-383-2317. **Owners:** S.& H. McEvoy. **Season:** May to Oct. **Rates:** med-low. **Features:** lovely location; full breakfast.

Morrison's Pioneer Restaurant

Many years ago, the building that houses this restaurant was a general store and community gathering place.

Location: Cape North, at the turnoff to Bay St. Lawrence. **Tel:** 902-383-2051; Fax 902-383-2890. **Season:** mid-May to Thanksgiving. **Hours:** Jul & Aug 7:30 am to 9:30 pm; shoulder months 8 am to 8 pm. **Prices**: mid-range. **Cards:** VS, MC, AE. **Features:** family dining; seafood a specialty; licensed.

North Highlands Community Museum

Location: Cape North at turnoff to Bay St. Lawrence. **Season:** mid-Jun to mid-Oct. **Hours:** 9 am to 7 pm. **Admission**: free. **Features:** artifacts and historical records of the Scottish pioneers who first settled this area; picnic area.

MacDonald's Motel and Cabins

Location: Cape North, Cabot Trail. **Mail Addr:** R. R. #1, Dingwall, N.S. B0C 1G0. **Tel:** 902-383-2054, Fax 902-383-2200. **Owner:** Mrs. A. J. Morrison. **Season:** Jun to mid-Oct. **Rates:** med-low. **Cards:** VS, MC. **Features:** housekeeping.

Food Town and Bakery - Cape North; open late Jun to Sept 8 am to 8 pm; rest of year 9 am to 5:30 pm; carries ice cream, groceries, bakery, coffee.

Side Trip to

Bay St Lawrence & Meat Cove

At Cape North you'll come to the turnoff to **Bay St. Lawrence** and **Meat Cove**. This is an area that I think is one of Cape Breton's hidden treasures. It's well worth taking the time to explore.

It takes you along the beautiful and very historic **Aspy Bay**, out to the extreme northern tip of the Island.

When you're finished exploring, just make your way back to Cape North and continue along the Cabot Trail.

Julia Longacre

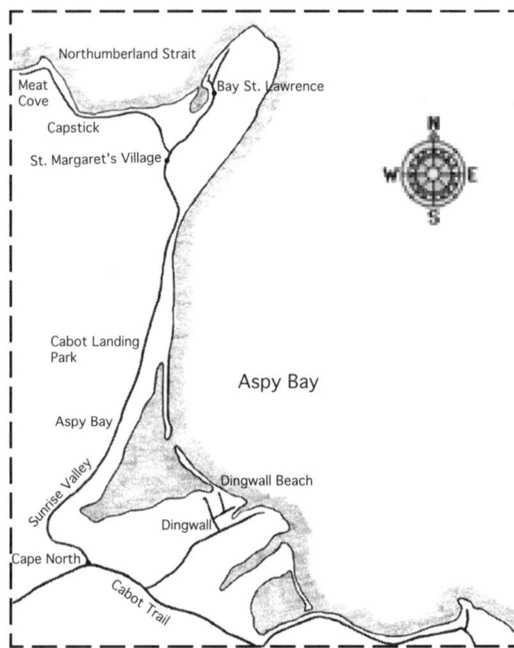

Bay St. Lawrence/ Meat Cove Area

The Aspy Steamers

Before the Cabot Trail was constructed, communities in the north of the Island depended on the sea for their contact with the outside world.

"Early schooners, trading vessels and eventually steamships plied these waters to provide essential supplies, transport and leisure travel for the local populace and to bring visitors to the north country. In the process, they perpetuated the attraction, adventure and romance of the sea.

The most famous vessels were the three Aspy's: Aspy I (1911-24), Aspy II (1926-30) and Aspy III (1930-64). They became household names as they helped to reduce isolation and to introduce the ways and goods of the industrial age to the communities north of Smokey Mountain. They also brought visitors to this beautiful area and eventually stimulated tourism, economic development and participation in the material, educational and cultural advances of the 20th century." from ***The Cabot Trail 1932-1992***, a commemorative booklet marking the 60th anniversary of the Trail.

Cabot's Landing Provincial Park

If you have a penchant for picnics on the beach, this park is the place for you. It's a wonderful spot surrounded by mountains,ocean...and history.

Location: About 10 km (6 mi) from Cape North on the Bay St. Lawrence Road. **Features:** the alleged site of John Cabot's landing on this continent 500 years ago; a beautiful walk along a barrier beach with a fresh water pond on one side, Aspy Bay on the other; picnic tables, toilets, sandy beach.

Capstick, Meat Cove

About 15 km (9 mi) from Cape North you'll come to a turnoff to Capstick and Meat Cove (the most northerly inhabited spot on the Island). It's a wonderfully scenic drive, unpaved from Capstick on.

Meat Cove Campground

This is truly a wonderful camping spot, situated on the most northerly inhabited spot on the Island, where you can sit outside your tent and watch the whales and seals cavorting offshore. The McLellan family have lived and fished in Meat Cove for six generations.

Location: Meat Cove, about 12 km (8 mi) from turnoff at St. Margaret's Village. **Mail Addr:** Meat Cove, N.S. B0C 1E0. **Tel:** 902-383-2379. **Owner:** K. McLellan. **Season:** Jun - Oct. **Rates:** avg. **Features:** unserviced sites; toilets, showers, fire pits; whale watching from campground; hiking & mountain biking trails, swimming; fresh lobster available.

St. Margaret's Village

Located on the Bay St. Lawrence Rd about 15 km (9 mi) from Cape North.

Highlands By the Sea B & B

Location: St. Margaret's Village. **Mail Addr:** St. Margaret's Village, N.S. B0C 1R0. **Tel:** 902-383-2537. **Owners:** S.& R. MacDonald. **Season:** mid-Jun - Oct. **Rates:** low. **Cards:** VS **Features:** swimming, deep sea fishing; bird watching; whale cruises; mountain bikes.

Buck's B & B

Location: St. Margaret's Village. **Mail Addr:** Box 17 St. Margaret's Village, N.S. B0C 1R0. **Tel:** 902-383-2075/ 2579; Fax 902-383-2995. **Owner:** W. Buchanan. **Season:** May - Oct., o/s by arrangement. **Rates:** low.

Bay St. Lawrence

Located about 16 km (10 mi) from Cape North on the Cabot Trail. Photographers and artists have a field day in this delightfully picturesque seaside community, especially when the fishing boats are in the harbour.

And, if you're there at the right time when the boats are coming in, you'll be able to buy fresh seafood, which varies according to the season. Boats usually return home in late morning or early afternoon.

Burton's General Store, Bay St. Lawrence. Turn onto Cove Rd, before the wharf; 902-383-2856/2666; open from 9 am to 9 pm daily.

Burton's Sunset Oasis Motel

Newly built motel with full housekeeping and a truly spectacular view of the mountains and sea.

Location: Bay St. Lawrence. Turn right onto Cove Road, before the wharf. **Mail Addr:** Bay St. Lawrence, N.S. B0C 1G0. **Tel:** 902-383-2666/2856; Fax 902-383-2669. **Owners:** M. & D. Burton. **Season:** year round. **Rates:** upper end. **Cards:** VS, MC. **Features:** great view, full housekeeping; store with some groceries, etc; laundromat; private beach, hiking trails, peaceful and private.

Jumping Mouse Camping

A hillside campground with a magnificent view of the ocean.

Location: Bay St. Lawrence, turn right onto a narrow road just past the wharf. **Mail Addr:** St. Margaret Village, N.S. B0C 1R0. **Tel:** 902-383-2914. **Owner:** M. Gahlinger. **Season:** May to Oct. **Rates:** avg. **Features:** unserviced sites; shower, toilets, firewood, nature trail, small shelter; sail charter by appointment; ocean swimming, privacy.

Whale Watch

Take a tour aboard the *Bonnie Susan*, a 32-ft. Cape Island fishing boat.

Location: Bay St. Lawrence wharf. **Mail Addr:** Capstick, N.S. B0C 1E0. **Tel:** 902-383-2981, o/s 902-429-0325. **Owner:** Capt. Dennis Cox. **Season:** Jun - Sept. **Hours:** Jul & Aug three daily sailings 10:15 am, 1:30 pm, 4:30 pm; limited outings in Jun & Sept. **Features:** frequent sightings of whales, seals, dolphins, seabirds, moose and bear; shipwrecks, sea caves and waterfalls.

Island Whale Watch & Nature Tours

Location: Bay St. Lawrence Wharf. **Tel:** 902-383-2379. **Owner:** Capt. K. McLellan. **Season:** July - Oct. **Hours:** 3 regular trips daily: 10:30 am, 1:30 pm and 4:30 pm; also available for special charters. **Features:** 10-m (32-ft) Cape Islander *Rhonda-Eileen*; travel along uninhabited coastline - Money Point to Lowland Cove; hear whales through on-board 'hydrophone', an underwater microphone that picks up and magnifies the many different voices of the whales and dolphins.

➵ **EN ROUTE**: To get back to the Cape North and the Cabot Trail, drive back the same way you came, about 16 km (10 mi). Turn at Cape North toward Ingonish and continue your journey along the Cabot Trail.

The Wonders of Nature

"Just past the big red fire hall in Cape North you'll see what looks like a castle made of plaster. In fact, this is gypsum quarried from this area. Long ago (350 million years), this area was a shallow sea in the middle of all the continents. Salts precipitated out of the seawater and formed gypsum deposits. During the ice age, rivers under the glaciers washed away some of this soft gypsum, creating valleys, like the one next to this hillside." from ***A Nature and Hiking Guide to Cape Breton's Cabot Trail***, by David Lawley, Nimbus Pub. 1994.

Side Trip to

Dingwall

Turn off the Cabot Trail about a km or so south of Cape North.

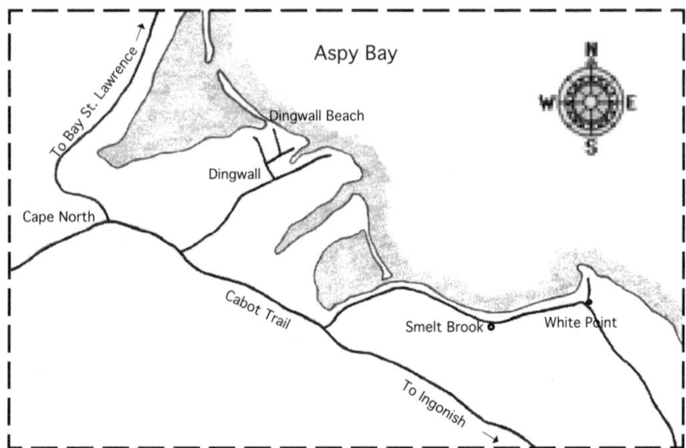

Dingwall

Dingwall Beach

A beautiful beach on the wide open Atlantic, take a hike or a swim,soak up the sun, have a picnic, or just enjoy the view.

Location: Dingwall. After you turn off onto the Dingwall Road from Cape North, drive 2 km (1.2 mi) then turn onto the Mountain View Rd. After a short distance turn right onto the road leading to the wharf. When you come to a “white” road (it’s gypsum) turn and follow it to the end. **Features:** if you walk left along the beach it will take you to a narrow channel. Across the channel is the beach at Cabot’s Landing Park. See map above.

The Inlet B & B

Well-named for its truly lovely setting on an inlet of Dingwall Harbour.

Location: Dingwall, 2.5 km (1.5 mi.) off the Cabot Trail. **Mail Addr:** Box 18, Dingwall, N.S. B0C 1G0. **Tel:** 902-383-2112. **Owners:** M.& B. Fitzgerald. **Rates:** med-low. **Season:** May to Oct; other months by arrangement.

Features: swimming; whale and bird watching; boat tours arranged; winter activities.

The Markland Coastal Resort and Restaurant

A 70-acre coastal retreat

Location: Dingwall, about 5 km (3 mi) from Cabot Trail. **Mail Addr:** Dingwall, N.S. B0C 1G0. **Tel:** 902-383-2246; 1-800-872-6084; Fax 902-383-2092. **Owner:** C. MacLean. **Season:** mid-May to Oct. **Rates:** upper end. **Cards:** VS, MC, AE. **Dng Rm Hrs:** 7:30-9:30 am, 5:30 - 9:30 pm. **Prices:** upper end. **Features:** licensed gourmet restaurant; outdoor pool, play area, bicycles and canoes available; glorious sandy beach for exploring. (ask about the ship The August which went down just off the coast there in the 1700's)

Julia Longacre

EN ROUTE - to get back to the Cabot Trail from Dingwall, just drive back the way you came to South Harbour.

South Harbour

Located on the **Cabot Trail** just south of the Dingwall turnoff.

Hide Away Campground

Camp overlooking beautiful Aspy Bay. If you're an oyster fan, you can sit down and feed on oysters on the half-shell here too.

Location: South Harbour. Turn off the Cabot Trail onto the Shore Road, just about a km south of the Dingwall turnoff. Campground is about 2 km (1.5 mi) down the Shore Rd. **Mail Addr:** R. R. #2, Dingwall, N.S. B0C 1G0. **Tel:** 902-383-2116; o/s 902-383-2701. **Owners:** A. & S. Dunphy. **Season:** Jun - Oct. **Rates:** avg. **Features:** 5 sites with electricity, other unserviced; showers; toilets; fireplaces; swimming; hiking; playground; outdoor kitchen shelter and disposal station; oysters (on the half-shell); close to one of Cape Breton's most beautiful beaches.

Tartans and Treasures

Location: South Harbour, Cabot Trail, about 3 km (1.8 mi) from Cape North. **Owners:** R. & N. Connors. **Tel:** 902-383-2005/2421. **Season:** May to Oct. **Hours:** sunrise to sunset. **Cards:** VS, MC, AE. **Features:** tartan clothing and accessories; Inuit art; model ships; woolen blankets, etc; public washrooms; picnic tables; information.

Danena's Restaurant and Take Out

Location: South Harbour, about 3 km (1.8 mi) south of Cape North. **Tel:** 902-383-2118. **Owner**: L. Cook. **Season**: May to Oct. **Hours:** dng room - 11 am to 9 pm; take-out - 11 am to 10 pm. **Prices:** low to mid-range. **Cards**: VS. **Features:** dining room and take out.

Country Crafts

Location: South Harbour, about 4 km (2.4 mi) south of Cape North. **Tel:** 902-383-2933. **Owner**: P. Courtney. **Season**: May to early Oct. **Hours**: Jul & Aug 9 am to 6 pm; shoulder months 11 am to 4 pm. **Cards**: VS, MC. **Features:** hand-knit sweaters; quilts; pottery and other crafts.

Another Travel Option

Alternate Route via Smelt Brook/White Point

There's an alternate way to get from South Harbour to Neil's Harbour or vice versa. It takes you off the beaten path a wee bit, along the ocean through the communities of Smelt Brook and White Point and is less than a km longer than if you stay on the Cabot Trail.

Directions: if your're heading **south** on the Cabot Trail, take the White Point Rd at South Hbr.

If you're heading **north** turn off the Cabot Trail at Neil's Hrb.

If you choose not to take this Alternate Route just go to page 148.

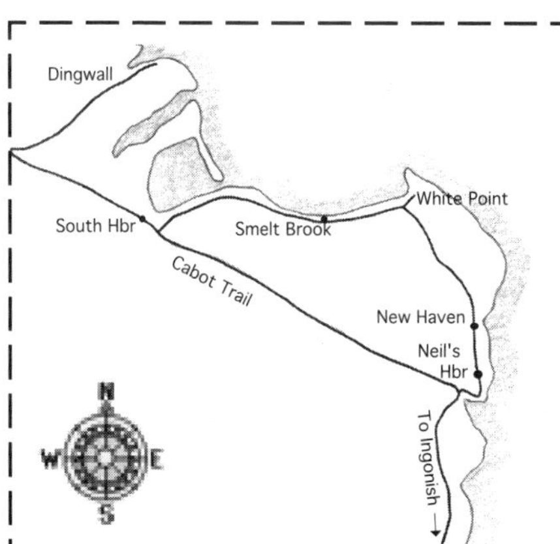

Scenic Route South Hbr to Neil's Hbr

Smelt Brook

Located on the scenic drive between South Harbour and Neil's Harbour.

Smelt Brook Pottery

Working studio and shop where you'll find a super selection of useful and beautiful stoneware pottery.

Location: Smelt Brook, on the scenic drive from South Hbr to Neil's Hbr. Watch for sign. **Mail Addr:** R. R. #2, Dingwall, N.S. B0C 1G0. **Tel:** 902-383-2732; Fax same. **Owner:** D. & L. Doyon. **Season:** year round. **Hours:** from mid-May to late Nov studio is open generally from 9 am to 5 pm daily; other months by appointment. **Cards:** VS, MC. **Features:** lots and lots of 'pots'...something for any occassion; custom orders filled; will ship.

SeaSpray Cycle Center

You may want to consider parking your car for awhile and seeing the sights from a mountain bike.

Location, etc: same as Smelt Brook Pottery, above. **Season:** mid-May to mid-Oct. **Hours:** 9 am to 5 pm daily. **Cards:** VS, MC. **Features:** mountain bikes for on- or off-road touring; guided day trips and back country explorations; rentals include racks, bags and helmets; full repair shop on premises.

Julia Longacre

White Point

Located on the scenic drive between South Hbr and Neil's Hbr. Take the White Point turnoff about 5 km (3 mi) from Smelt Brook.

Two Tittle B & B

Location: White Point - 2119 White Point Rd. **Mail Addr:** R. R. #2 Dingwall, N.S. B0C 1T0. **Tel:** 902-383-2817. **Owners:** C. & M. Dunphy. **Season:** year round. **Rates:** med-low. **Features:** see whales and eagles from deck overlooking Aspy Bay; hiking trails and beach.

White Point Whale & Scenic Tour

Location, etc. - same as Two Tittle B & B above. **Season:** mid-May to mid Oct. **Features:** 2 1/2 hour coastal tour in beautiful Aspy Bay; 3 cruises daily.

New Haven/Neil's Harbour

Located on the south east end of the scenic drive between South Hbr and Neil's Hbr.

Little Cove B & B

Watch the sun rise over the ocean.

Location: New Haven/Neil's Harbour, just across from the New Haven wharf. **Mail Addr:** Box 118, Neil's Hbr, N.S. B0C 1N0. **Tel:** 902-336-2484. **Owners:** N. & R. Warren. **Season:** year round. **Rates:** med-low. **Cards:** VS. **Features:** wonderful ocean view; walking trail along the beach.

Neil's Harbour Co-Op (groceries and general merchandise); 902-336-2827; open Mon, Tue, Wed & Fri from 9 am to 6 pm; Thurs from 9 am to 8 pm; Sat from 9 am to 5 pm.

Sea Swell Ventures

Deep sea fishing charters and coastal whale-watching tours.

Location: Lighthouse Rd, Neil's Hbr Wharf. **Tel:** 902-336-2212; cell phone 902-563-6455. **Owner:** Greg Organ. **Season:** Jun to Oct. **Cards:** VS. **Features:** see the National Park from the water.

Fresh Fish and Seafood -There are two wharves in this area...one at New Haven and one at Neil's Hbr (Lighthouse Rd). As in many small fishing communities in Cape Breton, you can generally buy lobsters, crab, etc. off the fishing boats as they come in from their day of fishing. The best time is late morning and early afternoon. Lobster season is from May 15 to Jul 15 and crab season is from about the third week of May until the quotas are reached.

Chowder House

Location: Lighthouse Rd, Neil's Hbr. **Tel**: 902-336-2463. **Season**: mid-Jun to early Oct. **Hours**: 11 am to 8 or 9 pm. **Cards**: VS. **Features**: chowder, lobster and crab dinners.

> **En Route** - Neil's Hbr is the end of the Side Trip. Keep going on the Cabot Trail from here.

Neil Brook Picnic Site

Location: Cabot Trail, just south of the Neil's Hbr turnoff. **Features**: a waterside spot with picnic tables.

Buchanan Memorial Hospital, located on the Cabot Trail, just south of the Neil's Hbr turnoff; **902-336-2200.**

Jigging Cove Lake Trail

Location: On Cabot Trail, about 4 km (2.4 mi) south of the Buchanan Hospital. **Features:** 4.8 km (3 mi.) loop, time 1 hr; a relaxing walk around the lake that hooks up with the Coastal Trail. (see below).

Black Brook Beach

A glorious sandy beach, with sometimes very wild surf.

Location: Black Brook, about 8 km (4.8 mi) south of Neil's Hbr. **Features:** great swimming and body surfing; washrooms; picnic tables; lots of parking. **Caution:** Read and heed signs...beach is not supervised.

Jack Pine Trail and Coastal Trail

Location: Black Brook Beach, watch for signs. **Features:** 2.8 km. (1.7 mi.) loop. **Coastal Trail** - It's easy to run out of superlatives when talking about hiking trails in the Highlands, but this one really is special. **Features:** 11 km (6.6 mi.) return.

Black Brook Picnic Park

Location: Black Brook, on the Cabot Trail less than a km south of Black Brook Beach. **Features:** picnic tables and washrooms.

Green Cove Trail and Lakie's Head Look-off

Location: Cabot Trail, just south of the Black Brook Picnic Park. **Features:** perfect spots for just stretching your legs and taking in some of that envigorating salt sea air; great spots for coastal plant life and sea birds; telescope at Lakie's Head through which observers have seen almost every kind of whale.

The Ingonishes

There are almost as many Ingonishes as there are Margarees...and it's not really clear to me where one Ingonish ends and another begins. However, I don't think it will affect your enjoyment of this area.

In addition to the facilities listed below, you'll find gas stations, convenience stores and fast food outlets scattered throughout the Ingonishes.

North Ingonish

Located on the Cabot Trail about 15 km (9 mi) south of Neil's Hbr.

Warren Lake Beach and Hiking Trail

A fresh-water beach (just for a change) where you can picnic, hike and swim.

Location: about 15 km (9 mi) south of Neil's Harbour. Watch for the sign. **Features:** lovely fresh-water sandy beach; picnic tables; toilets. **Hike**: starts at picnic area and takes you around the lake - 8.5 km. (5.3 mi.) loop, time 2-3 hrs.

Mary Ann Falls

This is yet another spot where you can pull over, have a picnic, take a little walk and enjoy the natural beauty of the Island. The falls adds that little touch of excitement to a summer afternoon picnic.

Location: Warren Lake Beach turnoff (see above) then take a quick right and drive about 7 km (4 mi) to the falls.

Broad Cove Campground

A wonderful family campground with great facilities.

Location: about 16 km (9.5 mi) south of Neil's Harbour. **Mail Addr:** C B Highlands Natl Park, Ingonish Beach, N.S. B0C 1L0. 902-285-2524, o/s 902-285-2691. **Season:** mid-May to mid-Oct. **Rates:** avg and avg plus. **Features:** serviced and unserviced sites (2 wheelchair accessible); washrooms; kitchen shelters with wood stoves; beautiful ocean beach with a sandy fresh water lake beside it; hiking trails; campfire rings. Park policy: "No camper will ever be turned away."

Last summer while my family and I camped at Broad Cove, we met a family from New Hampshire, David and Anita Stolper and their daughter Lilly. For seven or eight years the Stolpers have been coming to Cape Breton to spend a good part of their holidays at Broad Cove. Lilly and my daughter Kate became instant friends. David taught my son Daniel to ride the waves on a "boogie board". And they showed us a trail to a waterfall we'd never been to before. They told us, too, about the exotic places around the world they've lived.

It occurred to me, after they left, how lucky we are in Cape Breton to have the beauty that surrounds us to keep people like the Stolpers coming back year after year.

Dino's Camping Trailer Park and variety store

Location: North Ingonish, on Cabot Trail. **Mail Addr:** Box 64, Ingonish, N.S. B0C 1K0. **Tel:** 902-285-2614. **Owners:** T. & E. Hardy. **Season:** Jun - Oct. **Rates:** avg. **Features:** close to beaches and other attractions; open campground with serviced sites; washrooms; showers; laundromat; groceries and bakery.

Bear Cove B & B

Location: North Ingonish, on Cabot Trail. **Mail Addr:** Box 41, North Ingonish, B0C 1K0. **Tel:** 902-285-2699. **Owners:** J. & G. Brown. **Season:** Jun to mid-Oct. **Rates:** med-low. **Features:** close to golfing, swimming, hiking.

Sleepy Hollow Cottages

Location: North Ingonish. Turn off onto Snow Road. **Mail Addr:** Box 175, Ingonish, N.S. B0C 1K0. **Tel:** 902-285-2227. **Owners:** P. & G. Brown. **Season:** mid-Jun to Sept 30. **Rates:** med-high. **Cards:** VS, MC. **Features:** housekeeping cottages; direct access to beach; private island for guests to explore; housekeeping.

Whale Island Boat Charters

Location: North Ingonish, Cabot Trail. **Tel:** 902-285-2338; Fax same; 1-800-565-3808. **Owner:** J. Donovan. **Season:** May - Nov. **Features:** deep-sea fishing; whale watching; shark charters; diving charters; fishing equipment supplied.

Rocky Bay Cottages

Location: North Ingonish, Cabot Trail. **Mail Addr:** Box 164, North Ingonish, N.S. B0C 1K0. **Tel:** 902-285-2020. **Owner:** T. Hardy. **Season:** Jun to mid-Oct. **Rates:** mid-range. **Features:** housekeeping; view of ocean.

The Point

Cottages by the sea. If ever there was an ideal spot for holiday accommodations, this is it. The Point dates back to 1935, just three years after the completion of the Cabot Trail.

Location: North Ingonish, Wharf Road. **Mail Addr:** Box 67, Ingonish, N.S., B0C 1K0. **Tel:** 902-285-2804; Fax same. **Rates:** mid-range. **Season:** late May to late Oct. **Cards:** VS. **Features:** housekeeping cottages; fireplaces or wood stoves; swimming; fishing and boat tours; lobster & crab from fishermen in season.

The Spruces Art Gallery

A fine collection of artist Vernon Amos' paintings. See next page for a sample of his work.

Location: North Ingonish, near the Wharf Road. **Tel:** 902-285-2983. **Owners:** V. and J. Amos. **Season:** Jun to Sept. **Hours:** 10 am to 6 pm daily, o/s by appointment. **Cards:** VS. **Features:** landscapes and seascapes, many of Cape Breton; water color reproductions.

Lynn's Craft Shop & Art Gallery

Paintings and prints by well-known artist Christopher Gorey. See page 155 for a sample of his work.

Location: North Ingonish, near the Wharf Road. **Tel:** 902-285-2735. **Owner:** L. Gorey. **Season:** mid-May to mid-Oct. **Hours:** Jul & Aug - 9 am to 8 pm; other months - 9 am to 5 pm. **Cards:** VS, MC., AE. **Features:** pottery, iron work, candles, paintings and prints.

Sea Breeze Cottages and Motel

Location: North Ingonish, about 20 km (12 mi) south of Neil's Harbour, **Mail Addr:** Box 63, Ingonish, N.S. B0C 1K0. **Tel:** 902-285-2879; Fax same. **Owner:** B. Williams. **Season:** year round. **Rates:** motel & cottages mid-range; chalet upper end. **Cards:** VS, MC. **Features:** sundecks; chalets with fireplaces; ocean swimming; mini golf; beautiful view.

Artist Vernon Amos, see page 151.

Driftwood Lodge

Rooms, apartments, cottage and a 6-bedroom farmhouse. **Location:** North Ingonish, 8 km (5 mi.) north of Ingonish Beach **Mail Addr:** Box 27, Ingonish, N.S. B0C 1K0. **Tel:** 902-285-2558. **Owners:** S. Kulig & W. Tacreiter. **Season:** Jun to Oct. **Rates:** low to mid-range. **Cards:** VS. **Features:** great view of ocean and mountains; swimming; close to restaurants, laundromat.

Brookside Drive-In and Laundromat, North Ingonish; open from May to Oct; Hours 8 am - 9 pm.

IGA - groceries and general merchandise; North Ingonish.

Coastal Waters Restaurant

Location: North Ingonish. **Tel:** 902-285-2526; Fax 902-285-2339. **Owner:** F. Warren. **Season:** May to Oct. **Hours:** 8 am to 9 pm daily. **Prices:** mid-range. **Cards:** VS, MC. **Features:** family restaurant; children's menu.

Ingonish

Located on the Cabot Trail about 22 km (13 mi) south of Neil's Hbr.

Glengorm Resort, Restaurant and Gift Shop

Location: Ingonish, about 6 km (3.6 mi) north of Park Entrance at Ingonish Beach. **Mail Addr:** Box 39, Ingonish, N.S. B0C 1K0. **Tel:** 902- 285-2049; Fax 902-285-2395. **Owner:** R. P. Meisner. **Season:** Jun to Oct. **Rates:** mid-range to med-high. **Dng Rm Hrs:** 7:30 - 9 am; 6 - 8 pm. **Dng Rm Prices:** mid-range. **Cards:** most major. **Features:** outdoor pool; ocean swimming; licensed; gift shop.

Ingonish Chalets

Beautiful log cabins and motel suites, situated in the heart of Ingonish.

Location: Ingonish Centre, about 6 km (3.6 mi) north of Park Entrance at Ingonish Beach. **Mail Addr:** Box 196, Ingonish Beach, N.S. B0C 1L0. **Tel:**902-285-2008; Fax same **Owners:** R. & J. Humphries. **Season:** year round. **Rates:** suites mid-range; chalets upper end. **Cards:** VS, MC, AE. **Features:** housekeeping cottages; some chalets have wood stoves; private path to beach; hiking trails; close to golf course; tennis courts; fishing; whale watching;

Deervale Cottages

Location: Ingonish Centre, about 4 km (2.4 mi) north of Park Entrance. **Mail Addr:** R. R. #1, Ingonish Beach, N.S. B0C 1L0. **Tel:** 902-285-2212. **Owners:** L. & J. Morrissey. **Season:** Jun - Oct. **Rates:** mid-range. **Cards:** VS. **Features:** housekeeping; close to beaches and activities.

Ingonish Beach

Located on Cabot Trail at the eastern entrance to (or exit from) the C.B. Highlands Natl Park.

North Bay Beach

An absolutely glorious sandy beach with clear, 'crisp' ocean water.

Location: Ingonish Beach, about 3 km (1.8 mi) north of the Park Entrance. **Facilities:** picnic area among the trees; indoor washrooms and change rooms; long sandy beach for exploring.

Franey Trail

Mountain climb with supurb view at top.

Location: Ingonish Beach about 2 km (1.5 mi) north of Park Entrance. **Features:** 6.4 km. (4 mi.) loop, time 2.5 hours. You will climb about a thousand feet in just 3 km. The view at the top is spectacular - open sea, Cape Smokey, Franey Mountain, the Clyburn Valley. Watch for moose. Park officials suggest you take the trail to the top, then descend the mountain by the fire tower access road.

Clyburn Brook Picnic Park and Clyburn Valley Trail

Location: about a km north of the Park Entrance. Trail is 9.2 km (5.7 mi) return; time 2-3 hours; takes you through the Clyburn Valley where you'll come across the remnants of gold mining days at Clyburn and the remains of what was once a hotel, if you can believe it! **Picnic Park:** (just on the other side of the brook before you start on the trail) has picnic tables, toilets and kitchen shelters with wood stoves and wood. On a crisp fallish day, it's fun to take the time to build a fire and cook the old fashioned way.

Ingonish Campground

Location: Ingonish Beach, less than a km north of the Park Entrance. **Mail Addr:** C B Highlands Natl Park, Ingonish Beach, N.S. B0C 1L0. **Tel:** 902-285-2329, o/s 902-285-2691. **Season:** Jul & Aug. **Rates:** avg. **Features:** beach swimming; Park policy "no camper will ever be turned away"; open and wooded unserviced campsites; flush toilets; washrooms with showers; kitchen shelters with wood stoves; fireplaces.

Keltic Lodge, Dining Room and Gift Shop

A deluxe resort hotel and cottages.

Location: Ingonish Beach, Middle Head Peninsula, just north of Park Entrance. **Mail Addr:** Ingonish Beach, N.S. B0C 1L0. **Tel:** 902-285-2880; Fax 902-285-2859; 1-800-565-0444. **Season:** Jun to mid-Oct. **Rates:** upper end, Modified American Plan available. **Dng Rm Hrs:** 7 to 9:30 am; 12 to 2 pm; 6 to 9 pm. **Dng Rm Prices:** upper end. **Cards:** all major cards. **Features:** deluxe accommodations in a spectacular setting high on cliffs of Middle Head Peninsula; 18-hole golf course; tennis; swimming pool; hiking; lounge with evening entertainment; room service; laundry; gift shop; dinner dress code.

Middle Head Trail

If you can't quite afford to *stay* at Keltic Lodge, you can do the next best thing...take a hike around the peninsula, it's a super trail. **Location:** on Keltic Lodge property (see above). **Features:** 4 km (2.5 mi) return; time 1 - 1.5 hours; the tip of the peninsula is closed during nesting season to give the common and arctic terns some privacy!

'Afternoon Watch', 21" x 14 " watercolour by Christopher Gorey, Ingonish. (See page 151.)

Atlantic Restaurant

A family-style restaurant operated in conjunction with Keltic Lodge.

Location: Take turnoff for Keltic Lodge, just north of the Park entrance, Ingonish Beach. Tel: 902-285-2880. **Hours:** Daily 8 am to 7 pm. **Season:** June 1 to mid-Oct. **Prices**: med-high. **Cards:** most major cards. **Features:** casual atmosphere; seafood specials; great view overlooking ocean.

The Highlands Links Golf Course

Rated in Canada's top 40 golf courses and given a 4-star rating from Golf Digest in 1995. Great vista overlooking ocean and mountains.

Location: Ingonish Beach,on Keltic Lodge property, just north of the Park Entrance. **Tel:** 902-285-2600; o/s 902-285-2270. **Season:** late May to mid-Oct. **Hours:** 6 am to 9 pm daily. **Green Fees**: $38, o/s $32. **Cards:** VS, MC. **Features:** 18 holes, par 72, slope rating 139.

Ingonish Beach

A great family beach.

Location: Ingonish Beach on Cabot Trail. Take the Keltic Lodge turnoff just north of the Park Entrance then keep to your right after you turn off. **Features:** picnic area, washrooms, telephones, canteen, hiking trail, lake and ocean swimming.

C. B. Highlands National Park Visitor Information Centre

This is the exit from the National Park if you're heading south.

Location: Ingonish Beach at eastern border of C B Highlands Natl Park. **Tel:** 902-285-2535, o/s 285-2691, Fax 902-285-2866. **Season:** year round, full summer season is late May to late Oct. **Hours:** May & Jun, Sept & Oct - 9 am to 5 pm; Jul, Aug, Sept - 8 am to 8 pm; winter 9 am to 4 pm.

Les Amis du Plein Air

A nature bookstore.

Location: Ingonish Beach on Cabot Trail, at Visitor Information Centre of C.B. Highlands Natl Park. **Tel:** 902-224-3814; Fax 902-224-2445. **Season:** mid-May to mid-Oct, daily. **Hours:** Jul & Aug 8 am - 8 pm; rest of season 9 am - 5 pm. **Cards:** VS, MC. **Features:** lots of books on nature, the outdoors, hiking and exploring; calendars; souvenirs.

The Island Inn B & B and Dining Room

Location: Ingonish Beach, just south of the National Park entrance. **Mail Addr:** Box 116, Ingonish Beach, N.S. B0C 1L0. **Tel:** 902-285-2404, 1-800-533-7015; o/s 902-285-2684. **Owners:** P & P.MacKinnon. **Season:** rooms year round, dining room mid-Jun to Sept. **Rates:** mid-range. **Dng Rm Hrs:** dinner from 4:30 pm to 9 pm. **Prices:** mid-range to med-high. **Cards:** VS, MC, AE. **Features:** licensed; lobster suppers Jun to Aug.

Highland Reflections Gift Shop

Location: at Island Inn B & B, above. **Season:** Jun to mid-Sept. **Hours:** generally, 9 am to 6 pm daily, may vary at times. **Features:** wood carvings; stained glass; and other local crafts.

Cape Breton Highlands Bungalows

Location: Ingonish Beach, just south of the National Park entrance. **Mail Addr:** Box 151, Ingonish Beach, N.S. B0C 1L0. **Tel:** 902-285-2000, o/s 902-285-2743. **Owner:** P. Donovan. **Season:** Jun - mid-Oct. **Rates:** mid-range. **Cards:** VS, MC. **Features:** good family housekeeping accommodation; lake swimming; playground; pedal boats and canoes; laundromat.

Atlantic Whale-Watching Tours

Location: Ingonish Beach. About 6 km (3.6 mi) south of the Park entrance, you'll come to a junction by the Skyline Cabins. Turn there, then take the first right and drive about a km or so. **Mail Addr:** Ingonish Beach, N.S. B0C 1L0. **Tel:** 285-2320. **Owner:** M. J. Whitty. **Season:** Jul - mid-Oct. **Hours:** three trips daily. **Features:** 39-foot Cape Islander; sightings of pilot and minke whales, seals, bald eagles, seabirds.

Skyline Cabins

Location: Ingonish Beach, about 6 km (3.6 mi). south of the Park Entrance. **Mail Addr:** Box 26, Ingonish Beach, N.S. B0C 1L0; o/s Box 133, Staten Island, NY. 10305. **Tel:** 902-285-2055. **Owner:** Joyce Marra. **Season:** Jun 1 - mid-Oct. **Rates:** med-low. **Cards:** VS, MC. **Features:** housekeeping.

Kate's Korner - fast food and bakery; Ingonish Beach; 902-285-2898; open daily at 7 am.

Nova Scotia Liquor Commission - Ingonish Beach; in summer open weekdays from 10 am to 9 pm; Fri & Sat 10 am to 10 pm; closes at 6 (except on Fri) other months.

Ingonish Ferry/Ingonish Harbour

Located on the Cabot Trail at the base of Cape Smokey.

Muddy Rudder Seafood Shack

Enjoy fresh seafood in the open air.

Location: Ingonish Ferry about a km north of ski lodge.

Ski Cape Smokey

"Come ski with the eagles" or in summer, just ride with them. Ski Cape Smokey is a ski hill in winter, scenic rides and other recreation in summer.

Location: Ingonish Ferry, on Cabot Trai, just north of Cape Smokey. **Mail Addr:** Box 123, Ingonish Beach, N.S. B0C 1L0. **Tel:** 902-285-2778. **Season:** year round. **Cards:** VS, MC. **Features:** ski hill elevation of 1,000 ft; lounge and restaurant; summer operation provides scenic rides to top of the mountain...the view is indescribable!

Coastal Whale Watching Boat Tours

Location: Ingonish Harbour at base of Cape Smokey - watch for wharf and Boat Tour sign. **Mail Addr:** Box 8, Ingonish Hbr, N.S. B0C 1L0. **Tel:** 902-285-2714. **Owner:**

Capt. P. Donovan. **Season:** Jun to end of Sept. **Cards:** VS, MC. **Features:** two and one-half hour trip; watch for whales, dolphins, sea birds, off the coast of the Cabot Trail.

Sea Visions Whale Watch

"See whales by sail" - aboard the 57-ft schooner William Moir.

Location: Ingonish Ferry, at base of Smokey. Watch for sign. **Tel:** 902-285-2628/2058. **Owner:** P. MacKinnon. **Season:** early Jun to mid-Sept. **Sailing Times**: 10 am, 1:30 pm and 4:30 pm daily. **Cards:** VS, MC. **Features:** two and one-half hour sail up and down coast or wherever the whales are; also see puffins, eagles, seals, etc.

Knotty Pine Cottages and Tourist Home

Location: Ingonish Ferry, near the base of Cape Smokey. **Mail Addr:** R. R. #1, Ingonish Ferry, N.S. B0C 1L0. **Tel:** 902-285-2058; 1-800-455-2058. **Owners:** R. & P. MacKinnon. **Season:** year round. **Rates:** med-low to med-high. **Cards:** VS, MC. **Features:** housekeeping; patio decks overlooking ocean; some cottages with fireplace, whirpool.

Smokey View Cottages

Location: Ingonish Ferry, 2.5 km (1.5 mi) north of Cape Smokey. **Mail Addr:** Box 238, Ingonish Beach, N.S. B0C 1L0. **Tel:** 902-285-2662. **Owner:** W. MacDougall. **Season:** year round. **Rates:** summer med-high. **Cards:** VS, MC. **Features:** spacious housekeeping cottages; close to local attractions.

'On top of old Smokey'

Cape Smokey Park and Hiking Trail

Location: On the Cabot Trail, smack dab on top of Smokey. **Hiking Trail**: If you're up for a super hike along the mountain, find the trail sign, by the parking area. Trail is 8 km.(5 mi); you'll see for miles from the lookoffs. **Hours:** closes at 9 pm. **Features:** picnic tables; lookoffs.

What happened to the trees?

In the late 1960's a forest fire devastated this forest. As you can see, it's been trying hard to recover ever since ...not an easy task in a place like this. The good news is that blueberries love to grow there (late summer) as do mayflowers, our provincial flower (spring).

Wreck Cove

Located on Cabot Trail, about 10 km (6 mi) south of Cape Smokey. The name 'Wreck Cove' refers, I think,to ship wrecks, not your state of mind after coming down Smokey.

Wreck Cove General Store

Gas, groceries, and big wonderful lobster sandwiches!

Location: Wreck Cove on Cabot Trail. **Tel**: 902-929-2900. **Season:** year round. **Hours:** 7 am to 9 pm. **Cards:** all major cards. **Features:** live lobster tank - you can buy lobster live or cooked; lobster sandwiches; snack bar; gas; picnic shelter and outside picnic tables; fishing and camping supplies.

Birch Plain/ Breton Cove/North Shore

Located on Cabot Trail, between Cape Smokey and the Englishtown Ferry.

The Silver Gull Gift Shop

Location: Birch Plain on the Cabot Trail, about 12 km (7 mi) or so south of Cape Smokey. **Tel:** 902-929-2523. **Owner:** L. MacQuarrie. **Season:** Jul to Oct. **Hours:** 9 am to 6 pm. **Features:** a lovely collection of gifts and craft items; Cheticamp hooking; quilts; model schooners; china; jewellery, etc.

Kerr's Eat & Sleep

Location: Breton Cove, Cabot Trail, about 20 km (12 mi) south of Cape Smokey. **Mail Addr:** R. R. #1, Englishtown, N.S. B0C 1H0. **Tel:** 902-929-2114. **Owner:** J. Kerr. **Rates:** pay what you can! **Season:** year round. **Features:** camping sites available; walking trail; cross-country ski trail; excellent view of ocean and woods.

Now here's something you won't find everyday on your travels...a bed and breakfast with no set rates. Owner Jean Kerr says, "We have no rates and no prices. If guests would like to make a donation to replace or add to our home, we will have more to offer on your next trip by." Really!

Plaster Provincial Picnic Park

Location: North Shore on the Cabot Trail, about 15 km (9 mi) north of the Englishtown Ferry. **Features:** a little woodsy stop-over with a short trail down the bank to St. Ann's Bay.

Indian Brook

Located on the Cabot Trail about 45 km (27 mi) south of Ingonish and 12 km (7 mi) from the Englishtown Ferry.

Knotstalgia

Nautical items for use "indoor, outdoor, inshore and offshore".

Location: Indian Brook on the Cabot Trail. **Tel:** 902-2432, Fax 902-929-2067. **Owner:** G. Mason. **Hours:** summer 9 am - 7 pm; fall 9 am - 5 pm; o/s by chance or appointment. **Season:** May to Oct. **Cards:** VS. **Features:** mats, trivets, rope ladders, etc. made of manila; also lead-free pewter items made by a local artisan Jim Thompkins (Piper Pewter).

Leather Works by John C. Roberts

Quality leather goods, made on the premises. John will let you watch how it's done if the timing is right.

Location: Indian Brook on the Cabot Trail. **Tel:** 902-929-2414. **Owner:** J. Roberts. **Hours:** 9 am to 5 pm but often open till 6 or 7 in Jul & Aug; o/s by chance or appointment. **Season:** May to Oct. **Cards:** VS, MC. **Features:** belts and wallets, moulded leather vases and 18th & 19th century leather fire bucket reproductions; other Cape Breton crafts.

Piper's Old Manse Guest House (B & B)

Location: Indian Brook on Cabot Trail, about 10 km (6 mi) north of the Englishtown Ferry. **Mail Addr:** R. R. #1, Englishtown, N.S. B0C 1H0. **Tel:** 902-929-2233; Fax 902-929-2067. **Owners:** J. & L. Piché. **Season:** mid-May to mid-Oct. **Rates:** low. **Cards:** VS, MC.

Piper's Campground, Restaurant and Gift Shop

Location: Indian Brook on Cabot Trail, about 5 km (3 mi) north of Englishtown Ferry. **Mail Addr:** Indian Brook, N.S.

B0C 1H0. **Tel:** 902-929-2233, Fax 929-2067. **Owner:** J. Piché. **Season:** mid-May to mid-Oct. **Rates:** avg. **Cards:** VS, MC. **Hours:** (gift shop/restaurant) 8 am to 10 pm. **Restr Prices:** mid-range. **Features:** oceanside camping; serviced and unserviced sites; laundromat, washrooms, supplies; heated saltwater pool; family-style restaurant.

Indian Brook Service Station; 902- 929-2278; open in summer from 7:30 am to 8 pm daily.

Try something a little different...

Canoe Trip to Indian Brook Falls

There are many wonderful waterways for canoeing in Cape Breton. This particular canoe trip is a condensed exerpt from a book called *Canoe Cape Breton* written back in the 1970's. I chose this one because my husband and I made the trip many years ago and I still remember how much fun it was.

Location: Indian Brook bridge - on Cabot Trail, about 10 km (6 mi) north of the Englishtown Ferry; at the bridge, make your way down the bank to the shore. **Time**: about 2 1/2 hours up and about 15 minutes down! **Precautions**: depending on the time of year and amount of rainfall, Indian Brook can range from quite fast to very fast and you may encounter white-water, and "chutes". **Distance:** I'd say it's about 1.5 km or so to the Great Falls.

The Voyage: The first part of the trip is a combination of pushing, dragging and carrying the canoe, with short ventures paddling in backwater pools and fast water. You'll see two small falls on the way up.

"There can be no clear-cut directions for the trip upstream, for conditions will change with the season and rain-fall, and your run "downhill" will be based upon your observations while proceeding upward."

Have fun!

➵ **EN ROUTE** (if you're heading south on the Cabot Trail)

Just **south** of Indian Brook you'll come to an intersection, where you may, or may not, choose to part company with the Cabot Trail.

If you take Route 312, straight ahead, you will come to the Englishtown Ferry.

If you turn right and stay on the Cabot Trail you will drive around St. Ann's Bay.

The Englishtown Ferry route is shorter and a lovely drive along the causeway (Route 312). You may, however, encounter a wait at the ferry, especially in summer months. You can spend the time exploring the lovely beaches along the causeway.

The drive around St. Ann's Bay is a delight with lots of scenery, history, artisans' shops and outdoor activities.

The choice is yours! Both options will take you to the Trans Canada Highway, just at the base of Kelly's Mountain.

Below is the St. Ann's Loop alternative, which is the continuation of the Cabot Trail to the end.

The alternative Englishtown Ferry route is on page 169.

St. Ann's Loop

Just south of Indian Brook, after you cross the Barachois Bridge heading south, turn right toward St. Anns. This will keep you on the Cabot Trail until it ends at the Trans Canada Highway.

The St. Ann's Bay region has a fascinating history. In the early sixteen hundreds it was the site of the first Jesuit Mission in the New World. In 1820 a Scottish ship heading to the United States from Pictou, was forced to take shelter in St. Ann's Bay because of a storm. The travellers were so taken with the Bay, they stayed . Fishing, farming and shipbuilding thrived there for many years. The leader of those first Scottish settlers was a man named Rev. Norman MacLeod, who at the age of seventy decided to take 130 adventurers from St. Ann's Bay and head for Waipu, New Zealand. They sailed on a ship called the "Margaret" which they built themselves. Today there remains a very strong tie between the people of St. Ann's and the people of Waipu.

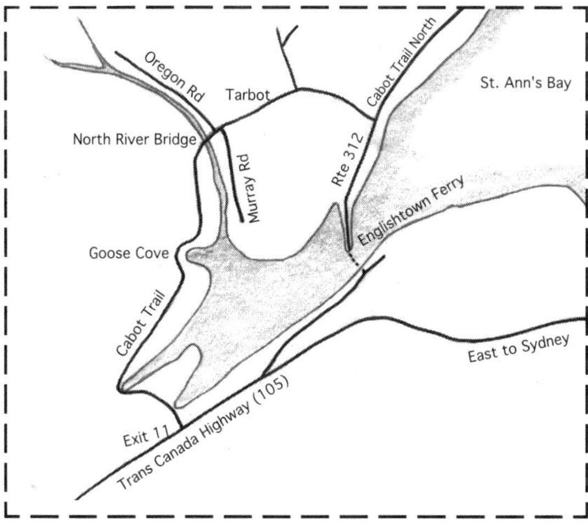

St. Ann's Bay and Englishtown Ferry Region

Tarbotvale and Tarbot

Located on the St. Ann's Loop - Tarbotvale is about 2 km (1.2 mi) and Tarbot is about 4 km (2.4 mi) from the turnoff at the Barachois Bridge.

Greer's B & B

A very pleasant woodland retreat, high on a mountain, looking over the Cabot Trail.

Location: Tarbotvale, St. Ann's Loop. At Tarbotvale watch for Greer's sign, turn off and drive along the road, across the iron bridge and up the hill. **Mail Addr:** Tarbotvale R. R. #4, Baddeck, N.S. B0E 1B0. **Tel:** 902-929-2115. **Owners:** A. & B. Greer. **Season:** Jun to Sept. **Rates:** med-low. **Cards:** VS, MC. **Features:** lovely mountain view; special diet needs considered; hiking, birdwatching, swimming in a real old fashioned "swimming hole".

Wild Things

Location: Tarbot, St. Ann's Loop, Cabot Trail . **Tel:** 902-929-2021. **Season:** mid-Jun to mid-Oct. **Hours:** 9 am - 5 pm. **Features:** One-of-a-kind wood carvings and turnings, fossils, Mexican jewellery.

Sew Inclined

Location: Tarbot, St. Ann's Loop, Cabot Trail - about 6 km (3.5 mi) from Barachois Bridge turnoff. **Tel:** 902-929-2050/2782/2259. **Season:** shop May - Dec; from home Jan - Apr. **Hours:** Jun to Oct - 9 am to 5 pm daily; other months Mon to Fri only. **Cards:** VS. **Features:** unique one-of-a-kind vests, hats, etc.; "The Musician's Shirt" - historical 18th century workman's shirt.

Iron Art & Photography

Location: Tarbot, St. Ann's Loop, Cabot Trail. **Tel:** 902-929-2821/2318. **Owners:** G. & C. Kennedy. **Season:** Jun to Oct. **Hours:** open most days , weekends only in Oct. **Cards:** VS. **Features:** award-winning photography by Carol Kennedy; fanciful and useful metal objects for home and garden; oil paintings, water colours and drawings by Gordon Kennedy.

North River and North River Bridge

Located on St. Ann's Loop, Cabot Trail.

North River Kayak Tours & Boat Rentals

Location: North River, St. Ann's Loop. Turn down the Murray Road just by the North River Bridge and drive about 3 km (1.8 mi); watch for the sign. **Owner:** Angelo Spinazzola. **Tel:** 902-567-2322; Fax same. **Season:** mid-May to mid-Oct. **Hours:** call ahead, 24-hours in advance is preferred. **Cards:** VS. **Features:** North River and St. Ann's Bay offer some of the most fascinating scenery on the Island, especially from the water; lunch provided; Angelo, who is also a musician, will probably share some of his music and stories with you.

Stephen's B & B

Location: North River Bridge, St. Ann's Loop, 279 Murray Road. Turn down Murray Road at the Bridge. **Mail Addr:** R. R. #4 Baddeck, N.S. B0E 1B0. **Tel:** 902-929-2860. **Owners:** M. & B. Stephen. **Season:** mid-May to mid-Oct. **Rates:** med-low. **Features:** beautiful view of North River from a restored country home.

School on the Hill

Location: North River Bridge, St. Ann's Loop- shop entrance is on the Oregon Road, by the North River Bridge. **Owner:** J. Grose. **Tel:** 902-929-2024. **Season:** Jun 1 - mid-Oct. **Hours:** Jun, Sept, Oct - daily 8:30 am to 6 pm; Jul & Aug - every day 8:30 am to 7 pm. **Cards:** VS, MC. **Features:** shop is a converted school house with lots of local and Nova Scotia crafts.

North River Provincial Picnic Park and Hiking Trail

The trail here is a wonderful long (by my standards) woodland and riverside hike to a waterfall. The first few kilometres of the trail was, in the mid-1800's, a settlement of Scottish pioneers. If you keep a sharp eye out, you can spot the occassional stone fence or foundation remnant along the way.

Location: North River Bridge, St. Ann's Loop. Turn onto the Oregon Road at the North River Bridge and drive about 3.5 km (2 mi) to the picnic park. Drive into the park to the end of the road and park. There's a sign marking the trail. **Facilities:** picnic tables and toilets; salmon and trout pools; hiking trail is 9 km. (5.5 mi.) each way with a 32-metre (100-ft.) waterfall at end of trail.

Goose Cove

Located on the St. Ann's Loop, Cabot Trail, about 12 km (7 mi) from Exit 11, TCH.

Goose Cove Pottery

You're invited to watch Carole MacDonald as she creates her earthenware, stoneware and porcelain pieces.

Location: Goose Cove, St. Ann's Loop, Cabot Trail. **Tel**: 902-929-2293. **Season:** shop open mid-Jun to Labour Day. **Hours:** 9 am to 5 pm daily. **Cards:** VS, MC. **Features:** a working craft studio; functional dinnerware; colorful "majolica" earthenware; one-of-a-kind Raku pieces.

St Ann's, North Gut St. Ann's and South Gut St. Ann's

This area of the St. Ann's Loop stretches from Goose Cove south to Exit 11 on the Trans Canada Highway at South Haven.

McGovern's of Hummingbird Hill B & B

Location: St. Ann's, on the Cabot Trail, about 9 km (5.5 mi) north of Exit 11 TCH. **Mail Addr:** R. R. #4 Baddeck,N.S. BOE 1B0. **Tel:** 902-929-2880. **Owners:** J. McGovern. **Season:** year round. **Rates:** med-low. **Features:** beautiful view of St. Ann's Harbour.

MacLeod Pioneer Cemetry

Location: St. Ann's Loop, Cabot Trail, about 5 km (3 mi) north of the TCH, Exit 11.

St. Ann's Provincial Picnic Park

Location: St. Ann's Loop, about 2 km (1.2 mi) north of the TCH, Exit 11. **Facilities**: picnic tables among the trees; views of the water along short walking trail by the highway.

William Rogers Art Gallery

Location: St. Ann's Loop, Cabot Trail, adjacent to the Gaelic College,1 km north of the TCH, Exit 11. **Tel:** 902-562-2273 (home); 902-295-1040 (gallery). **Season:** late Jun to mid-Oct. **Hours:** Jul & Aug - 9 am to 5 pm daily; Sept & Oct - 10 am to 4 pm, 2 or 3 days a week (by chance or call ahead). **Cards:** VS, MC. **Features:** beautiful watercolors, most of which are painted on location in Cape Breton. See page 45 for a sample.

The Gaelic College of Celtic Arts and Crafts

Location: South Gut St. Ann's, Cabot Trail, 1 km north of the TCH, Exit 11. **Mail Addr:** P.O. Box 9, Baddeck, N.S. B0E 1B0. **Tel:** 902-295-3411, Fax 902-295-2912. **Hours:** July/Aug 8 am to 8 pm, daily; other months Mon - Fri 8 am to 5 pm. **Season:** mid-May to mid-Dec. **Cards:** VS, MC. **Prices**: $2.00 admission, covers Hall of the Clans and museum. **Restaurant Prices**: low.

My advice...don't leave Cape Breton without stopping off at the Gaelic College.

This truly unique institution has been in operation since 1938 and students of Celtic tradition come from all over the world to learn everything from Scottish piping to traditional weaving to the Gaelic language itself.

As a visitor, you can watch as classes are being taught, enjoy the pipers and dancers as they practice on the parade square, sit in on a daily lunch-time ceilidh ("kay-lee", a gaelic word meaning party) featuring the College instructors, or take in a Wednesday evening concert.

And...if you have a hankering to find your Cape Breton roots, the Great Hall of the Clans is the place to look.

Lobster Galley Restaurant and Gift Shop

Location: St. Ann's, Cabot Trail, just at the junction of TCH Exit 11 and the Cabot Trail. **Tel:** 902-295-3100, Fax 902-929-2072 **Owner:** J.Thiele. **Season:** early May - late Oct. **Prices**: mid-range to med-high. **Cards:** all major cards. **Features:** specializes in lobster and seafood; live lobster pound, vegetarian menu; deck overlooking St. Ann's Harbour.

St. Ann's Motel and Diner

Location: St. Ann's, Cabot Trail, just at the junction of TCH Exit 11 and the Cabot Trail. **Mail Addr:** R. R. #4, Baddeck, N.S. B0E 1B0. **Tel:** 902-295-2876; o/s 902-736-8908. **Owner:** M. Marinelli. **Season:** mid-May to mid-Oct. **Rates:** med-low. **Cards:** VS. **Features:** overlooking St. Ann's Harbour.

EN ROUTE - This is Exit 11, where the TCH (Hwy 105) and the Cabot Trail meet.

➳ If you've been travelling south on the Cabot Trail, you've come to the end. If you want to go to Sydney from here, pick up Travel Option 1 at South Haven on page 43.

⇜ If you've just come from the Sydney area and are just starting your trip around the trail, Exit 11 is the place to start. Just follow along this Travel Option in reverse.

Julia Longacre

Alternate Route from Indian Brook to TCH and Vice Versa

VIA Englishtown

EN ROUTE
➛ Heading south on the Cabot Trail- at the Barrachois Bridge, keep going straight through the intersection onto Rte 312 south.

← Heading north from the TCH, take Exit 12 off the TCH at the western base of Kelly's Mountain.

Jersey Cove and Englishtown

Located on Route 312, about 50 km (35 mi) south of Ingonish.

St. Ann's Bay Campark

Location: Jersey Cove, on Cabot Trail, about 2.5 km (1.5 mi) north of ferry. **Mail Addr:** Englishtown, N.S. B0C 1H0. **Tel:** 902-929-2582. **Owners:** F. & A. Gentile. **Season:** mid-May to mid-Sept. **Rates:** avg. **Features:** ocean swimming; washrooms; laundromat, canteen; serviced and unserviced sites.

Chapel Art Gallery and Book Room

Location: Jersey Cove, Route 312, about 2 km (1.2 mi) north of ferry. **Tel:** 902-929-2324.

Cabot Trail Outdoor Adventures

Location: Jersey Cove, Route 312. **Tel:** 902-929-2546. **Features:** guided sea-kayaking trips along east coast of Cabot Trail; hiking and sea-kayaking weekends; short trips and lessons.

Sea Shanty Antique & Craft Shop

An intresting little shop in an authentic old fishing shanty.

Location: Jersey Cove, Route 312, 1.5 km (1 mi) north of the Englishtown Ferry, on the causeway. **Tel:** 902-929-2992. **Owner:** M. Smith. **Season:** Jun to Sept. **Hours:** daily 9 am- 6 pm. **Cards:** VS, MC. **Features:** antiques, collectibles; great location to bird watch, especially for shore birds.

Englishtown Ferry

Location: Englishtown, on Route 312, about 52 km (31 mi) south of Ingonish and 5 km (3 mi) from TCH Exit 12. **Fee:** ~~50 cents~~ 1.75 - the best bargain on the Island (except for the Little Narrows ferry which is only 25 cents!). **Features:** Takes you on a very short boat ride across St. Ann's Bay... a mere two minutes on a good day, so don't plan on catching up on any sleep during the crossing.

Note: You will probably encounter a lineup in the summer months.

If you're not in any great hurry to get to where you're going, you should consider pulling over on the caueway leading to the ferry and spending some time there. It's a super place for spotting bald eagles, sandpipers, ruddy turnstone, arctic tern, and others, and it is a lovely place for a swim...keep a km or so away from where the ferry runs. and if the wind and waves are high, be cautious of undertows.

Giant MacAskill gravesite - located just on the Englishtown side of the ferry dock. If you know the story of the 7 ft. 9 in. **Giant Angus MacAskill**, who came from Englishtown, you may want to stop off here where he's buried. If you don't know about Cape Breton's "gentle giant", drop into the museum just up the road.

"The Gentle Giant"

Angus MacAskill was born in the Hebrides Islands, off the coast of Scotland in 1825. His parents and his nine brothers and three sisters were all of average size. As a grown man Angus stood 7' 9" tall and weighed 170 kg (425 lbs), but in spite of his size, he was perfectly proportioned.

In 1849, when Angus was 24, he joined the circus and travelled around the world.

After a serious accident, he returned to Englishtown, became a businessman, and died in 1863 at the age of 38.

Englishtown Old General Store

A restored 1930's building with general store, museum with artifacts from the very early French settlement at Englishtown, and a marine museum.

Location: Englishtown, about a km or so from the ferry. **Tel:** 902-929-2400. **Season:** Jun to Oct. **Hours:** generally 9:30 am to 7:30 pm; may vary at times.

Englishtown Ridge Campground

High on a hill overlooking St. Ann's Bay.

Location: Englishtown, on Route 312, between Exit 12 TCH and the Englishtown ferry. **Mail Addr:** Box 161, Bras d'Or, B0C 1B0. **Tel:** 902-929-2598; o/s 902-674-2373. **Owner:** L. Serroul. **Season:** mid-May to Oct. **Rates:** avg plus. **Cards:** VS. **Features:** serviced and unserviced sites, some wheelchair accessible; pool; playground; sauna; licensed lounge and cafe; laundromat; showers; store.

Sale-A-Craft Flea Market - located at Englishtown, a few km from the ferry; open on weekends.

Giant MacAskill Museum

A great collection of articles belonging to Angus MacAskill, the Cape Breton giant who stood 7 ft 9 in tall and who travelled all over the world with the Barnum & Bailey Circus. He died in 1863.

Location: Englishtown, on Route 312, between TCH Exit 12 and the Englishtown Ferry. **Tel:** 902-929-2106. **Season:** mid-May to early Oct. **Hours:** daily 9 am to 6 pm. **Admission**: low. **Features:** clothing, furniture and other personal articles belonging to Giant MacAskill.

➼ **EN ROUTE**

At the end of Rte 312 you'll come to the TCH (105), Exit 12.

If you're heading toward Sydney, turn left onto the TCH and pick up Travel Option 1 on page 46.

Travel Option 4

Canso Causeway to Sydney
Sydney to Canso Causeway
VIA St. Peter's/Isle Madame

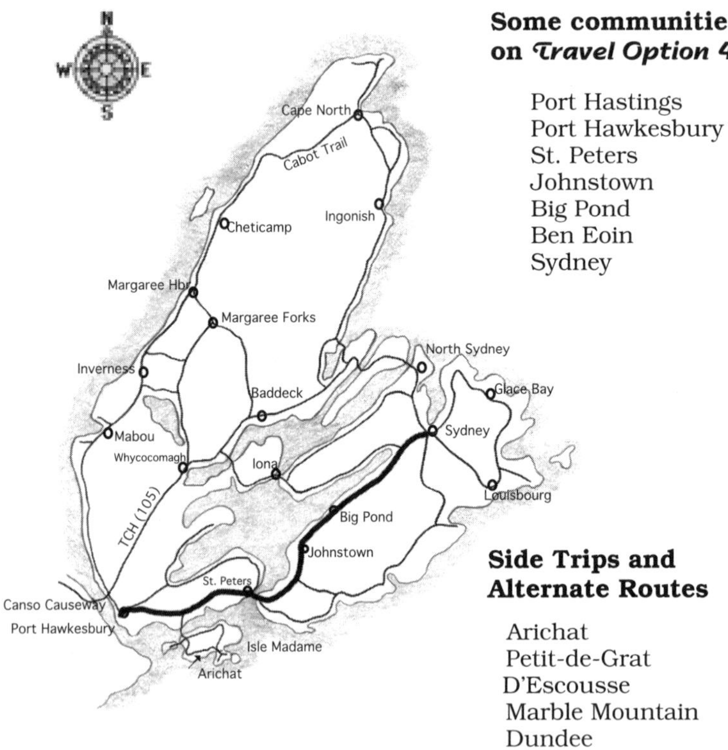

Some communities on Travel Option 4

Port Hastings
Port Hawkesbury
St. Peters
Johnstown
Big Pond
Ben Eoin
Sydney

Side Trips and Alternate Routes

Arichat
Petit-de-Grat
D'Escousse
Marble Mountain
Dundee

Special Features

- √ Canso Causeway
- √ St. Peter's Canal
- √ Acadian communities
- √ beaches, parks and picnic sites
- √ concerts and festivals
- √ shopping, restaurants
- √ Bras d'Or Lakes ocean drives
- √ museums

If you look at the map of Cape Breton you'll see that Travel Option 4 takes you pretty much straight across the Island along the south-eastern shore of the Bras d'Or Lakes.

The drive between Port Hawkesbury and St. Peters on Hwy 104 is a limited access highway. It's not scenic, but it **is** fast and once you get to St. Peters you'll start to follow the Lakes closely. You'll find lots of lookoffs and roadside vistas to enjoy. Photo opportunities, picnic spots and warm Bras d'Or swims will greet you all along the way.

If, on your travels along Travel Option 4, you choose to take a an **Alternate Route** through **Dundee** and perhaps **Marble Mountain** (page208), you will be treated to yet another side of the Lakes - one that is less travelled, peaceful and exceptionally beautiful.

You can also choose to take a **Side Trip** around **Isle Madame** (page 215), which will take you away from the Bras d'Or Lakes and show you the much more rugged and unpredictable territory of the mighty Atlantic Ocean.

EN ROUTE

For the eastward traveller, Travel Option 4 begins at Port Hastings, just over the Canso Causeway. Once you cross the Causeway, you'll come to a rotary from which you can travel in several different directions.

If you're driving straight through on Travel Option 4, you won't have to actually go around the rotary. Just keep to your right, past the Nova Scotia Visitor Information Centre, toward Port Hawkesbury.

However, some of the facilities in Port Hastings are at various spots around the rotary, so don't miss them.

I suggest as well that you stop off at the Visitor Information Centre as the staff there will have lots of brochures and information for you.

All facilities are listed in order of appearance along the route. If any are a little 'off the beaten path', directions are given.

Port Hastings

The village of **Port Hastings**, the "gateway to the Isle", is the first community you'll see after you cross the Causeway, and the last one you'll see before you cross to the mainland. It isn't a large community, but it does have motels, restaurants, gas stations and one of the Island's main Visitor Information Centre. All the roads leading east, south and north fan out from Port Hastings.

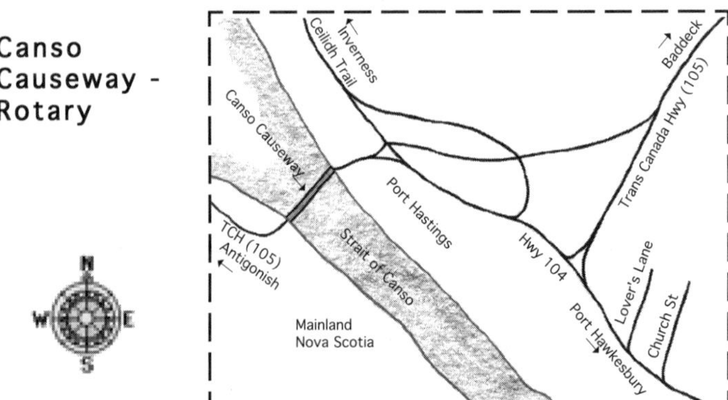

Canso Causeway - Rotary

Nova Scotia Visitor Information Centre

This should probably be your first stop once you cross the Canso Causeway. It is located on the water side of the road, just over the Causeway.

Location: Port Hastings at the rotary. **Tel:** 902-625-1717. **Season**: mid-May to mid-Oct. **Hours**: generally from 9 am to 9 pm, but sometimes closes a little earlier, depending on demand.

Glen Auld Gifts

Located: Port Hastings, next to Visitor Information Centre. **Tel:** 902-625-1649. **Owner**: G. MacLean. **Season:** mid-May to Thanksgiving. **Hours:** summer months 8:30 am to 9 pm daily; other months 9 am - 5 pm daily. **Cards**: VS, MC. **Features**: large selection of gifts, crafts and souvenirs.

Keddy's Inn and Dining Room

Location: Port Hastings. Go part way around the rotary and turn right just before the Esso Station. **Mail Addr:** Box 50, Port Hastings, B0E 2T0. **Tel**: 625-0460; toll-free 1-800-561-7666; Fax 625-1275. **Season:** year round. **Rates:** mid-range. **Cards**: most major cards. **Dng Rm Hrs:** 7 am to

11am; 5 pm to 10pm daily. **Prices**: mid-range. **Features**: licensed dining room and lounge; seniors discounts.

Port Hastings Esso - just over the Canso Causeway; 902-625-1100; open from 7 am to 11 pm daily; gas,deisel.

Smitty's Restaurant

Location: Port Hastings, at the rotary. **Owners:** M. & J. Chisholm. **Tel**: 902- 625-3346; Fax 902-625-2914. **Season**: year round. **Hours**: summer 6:30 am - 11pm; winter 7am - 10 pm daily. **Prices**: low to mid-range. **Cards:** VS, AE, debit cards. **Features:** large, bright family-style eatery; wide selection; specialty menu items for seniors, children and health conscious

.

Skye Travelodge and Dining Room

Location: Port Hastings, at the rotary. **Mail Addr**: Box 190, Port Hastings, N.S. B0E 2T0. **Tel:** 902-625-1300, Fax 902-625-1966, toll free 1-800-578-7878. **Season:** Year round. **Rates:** mid-range. **Cards:** most major cards. **Dng Rm Hrs:** 7 am to 10 pm daily. **Dng Rm Prices**: low to mid-range. **Features:** award-winning licensed dining room; overlooking Strait of Canso.

Artist Thorn Morrow, Sydney. See page 258.

MacPuffin Inn, Dining Room and Gift Shop

Location: Lover's Lane, Port Hastings - first street to your left after the Skye Travelodge. **Mail Addr**: Box 558, Port Hawkesbury N.S. B0E 2V0. **Tel:** 902-625-2283; toll free 1-800-867-2212; Fax 625-1525. **Owner**: Kenzie Jones. **Season**: Jun - Oct **Rates:** from mid-range to upper end. **Cards:** most major cards. **Features:** complimentary continental breakfast; family rates; gift shop; putting green; swimming pool.

Port Hastings Museum and Archives

Location: 367 Church St, Port Hastings - second street to your left after you pass the Skye Travelodge. **Mail Addr:** Box 115, Port Hastings, N.S. B0E 2T0. **Tel:** 902-625-1295. **Season**: Jun - Oct. **Hours:** Jul & Aug - Mon to Fri 9 am to 8 pm; Sat & Sun 12 noon to 4 pm; other months - Mon to Fri 9 am to 5 pm. **Features**: genealogy records, artifacts, newspapers relating to the Strait of Canso area.

MacPuffin Motel, Dining Room & Gift Shop

Location: Port Hastings, about 3 km (1.8 mi) from the rotary on Rte 104. **Mail Addr:** Box 558, Port Hawkesbury, N.S. B0E 2V0. **Tel:** 902-625-0621; Fax 902-625-1525; 1-800-867-2212. **Owner:** K. Jones. **Season:** May - Dec. **Rates:** rooms mid-range; suites upper end. **Cards:** most major cards. **Dng Rm Hrs:** 7 am - 10 am; 6pm - 9 pm. **Prices**: mid-range. **Features:** Licensed; air purified rooms available; laundromat; gift shop; indoor pool.

Port Hawkesbury Motel and Dining Room

Location: Port Hastings - 3 km (1.8 mi) from the rotary on Rte 104. **Mail Addr:** Box 549, Port Hawkesbury, N.S. B0E 2V0. **Tel:** 902-625-2480. **Owner:** M. Adams. **Season:** year round. **Rates:** mid-range. **Cards:** VS, MC, AE. **Dng Rm Hrs:** 6 am to 9 pm. **Dng Rm Prices:** mid-range.

➛ **EN ROUTE** - About 6 km (3.5 mi) from the Canso Causeway on Rte 104 (straight past the Visitor Information Centre) you'll come to the turnoff to Granville Street. This will take you to the 'down-town' part of Port Hawkesbury.

Downtown Port Hawkesbury (Granville St)

Turn down Granville Street off Rte 104 (see above) and drive along the water to the business district of the Town.

Harbourview B & B

Location: 209 Granville St, Port Hawkesbury. **Mail Addr:** 209 Granville St, Port Hawkesbury, N.S. B0E 2V0. **Tel:** 902-625-3224. **Owner:** M. Pase. **Season:** mid-May to mid-Oct.

Rates: med-low. **Cards:** VS. **Features:** restored heritage property; located on Strait of Canso; smoke-free property; full breakfast.

The Creamery

On the waterfront.

Location: Granville St, Port Hawkesbury. Farmers market, craft market, ceilidhs, concerts, and much more...see below.

The Waterfront

Granville St, Port Hawkesbury.

The citizens of Port Hawkesbury have been busy these last couple of years, and things are really starting to take shape there on the waterfront. On Granville St you'll find **The Creamery** (see below), a centre for lots and lots of activities. For instance...from Jun to Oct a farmers' market and craft fair every Sat from 9 am to 3 pm; Tuesday evening Ceilidhs (fiddling, stepdancing, etc) at 7 pm, July to Sept; and outdoor concerts every Sun night from Jul to Sept; boat and scuba diving tours; deck for picnics and relaxing; ice cream parlour and lunch counter; Pub for special events (weekly schedule posted); dinner theatre. See book insert for dates of events.

At the Waterfront, too, you'll find a Pirate Ship playground, horse and buggy rides during the Farmer's Market; and a train ride that will take you from Port Hawkesbury to the Railway Museum in Orangedale.

And a little farther down the street, there'll be a boat builder for you to watch, an art gallery and gift shop (below) and a cafe.

For more information on the Waterfront activities call **902-625-3224** during business hours.

Customs House Gallery & Gifts

See local marine artist J. Franklin Wright's originals and prints, as well as other local art work and crafts.

Location: on the Waterfront, Granville St, Port Hawkesbury. **Tel:** 902-625-2747. **Owner:** B. MacKinnon. **Season:** year round (opening 1996 on July 1). **Hours:** 9 am to 8 pm daily. **Cards:** VS, MC, Interac. **Features:** original art, sculpture, wrought iron; pottery; handcrafted gifts and souvenirs; information on where you can find other artists and craftspeople on the Island.

Reeves Street, Port Hawkesbury

Located along Rte 104, about 7 km (4 mi) from the Canso Causeway, Reeves St is actually part of Rte 104.

Along here you'll find several service stations and quite a few fast food restaurants like Subway, Dairy Queen ,Tim Hortons, KFC and others. You'll also find three small shopping plazas... the Causeway Shopping Centre and the Island Gateway Plaza, both on your left, and a little further up on your right is the Chediac Plaza.

In these plazas you'll find an assortment of grocery stores, convenience stores,department stores, banks etc.

The following are some of the facilities you'll find in the Reeves St area.

MacKeigan's Pharmacy, Causeway Shopping Centre, Reeves St, Port Hawkesbury; **Tel:** 902-625-1113; **Hours:** Mon to Fri open 9 am to 9 pm; Sat 9 am to 6 pm.

Nova Scotia Liquor Commission, Causeway Shopping Centre, Reeves St, Port Hawkesbury; **Tel:** 902-625-2010; regular hours are Mon to Wed 10 am to 6 pm; Thurs to Sat 10 am to 10 pm; in summer hours are extended a bit so you might want to call ahead.

Some Restaurants on Reeves St

- Papa's Pub & Eatery, Island Gateway Plaza; 902-625-3270
- Rose Garden Restr, Island Gateway Plaza; 902-625-5600.
- Louis' Family Restr, Reeves St; 902-625-0111
- Billy Joe's Place, Reeves St.

Auberge Wandlyn Inn and Dining Room

Location: 689 Reeves Street, Port Hawkesbury, N.S. B0E 2V0. **Mail Addr:** Box 759, Port Hawkesbury, N.S. B0E 2V0. **Tel:** 902-625-0320; Fax 902-625-3876; 1-800-561-0000 (cntrl & easternCanada); 1-800-561-0006 (USA). **Season:** year round. **Rates:** med-high to upper end. **Cards:** major cards. **Dng Rm Hrs:** 7 am - 9:30 pm. **Prices**: mid-range. **Features:** licensed; outdoor and indoor pool.

➻ **EN ROUTE**

At the east end of Reeves St, Port Hawkesbury, there is a junction.

Turn left off Reeves St if you're heading east toward St. Peters.

If you're coming **from** St. Peters, turn left **onto** Reeves St.

Port Hawkesbury Centre

Location: on Rte 104. Turn left at the east end of Reeves St. **Tel:** 902-625-0382; **Hours:** Mon to Wed 10 am to 6 pm; Thurs & Fri 10 am to 9 pm; Sat 10 am to 5 pm. **Features:** clothing stores, jeweller, Walmart, supermarket, bookstore etc.

Shoppers Drug Mart, located in Port Hawkesbury Centre (above); **Tel:** 902-625-1801. **Hours**: Mon to Fri 9 am to 9 pm; Sat 9 am to 6 pm; Sun and holidays 1 pm to 5 pm.

More Travel Options

If you're heading east, you have **three** choices now as to how you'll travel to St. Peters from Port Hawkesbury:

Opt (a)- you can drive **directly** to St. Peters on Hwy 104 (details are below);
Opt (b) - you can take an alternative route via **Isle Madame** (details are at the end of Travel Option 4, page 215)
Opt (c) - you can take a detour through beautiful **Dundee**. (details are at the end of Travel Option 4, page 208)

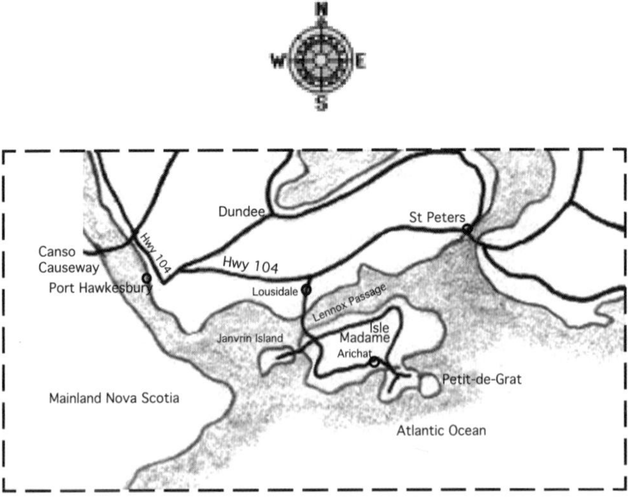

Port Hawkesbury, St. Peters, Isle Madame

Port Hawkesbury to St. Peters
The DIRECT ROUTE ↔ Hwy 104

Directions: Just past the Port Hawkesbury Centre, is a turnoff ramp to St. Peters. Turn here onto Hwy 104, which is a limited access highway with no facilities on it except the hospital below. Follow Hwy 104 until you get to St. Peters.

Coming west from St. Peters, just drive on Hwy 104 to the end and follow the signs.

The Strait Richmond Hospital at Evanston; **902-625-3100**, about 12 km (7 mi) or so from Port Hawkesbury.

St. Peter's

Located about 43 km (25.5 mi) east of Port Hawkesbury and 85 km (51 mi) west of Sydney.

St. Peters is a busy little village in which the main business street is actually part of the highway. You'll find convenience and grocery stores, post office and service stations (open until at least 10 pm in summer months) as well as the facilities listed below.

Glad Tidings (Christmas shop)

Location: St. Peters, as you come into the village from the west. **Tel:** 902-535-2248. **Season:** May to Dec 24. **Hours**: Mon, Tue, Wed & Sat - 9 am to 5 pm; Thurs & Fri - 9 am to 9 pm; Sun - 9 am to 7 pm. **Cards:** VS, MC, Interac. **Features:** a great place to find gifts for those Christmasy friends back home.

Wallace MacAskill Museum and Gift Shop

St. Peters is the birthplace of renowned marine photographer Wallace R. MacAskill.

Location: St. Peters. **Season:** Jul- Sept. **Hours:** 10 am - 6 pm. **Features:** restored original residence of W. MacAskill; display of his hand-tinted photographs; artifacts relating to his sailing hobby and his life

Presents of Mine Crafts and Gifts

A lovely selection of gift and souvenir items.

Location: Main St, St. Peters. **Tel:** 902-535-3199; Fax same. **Owner:** Fran Doyle. **Season:** year round. **Cards:** VS, MC, Interac.

Lynn's Flowers & Gifts

Location: Main St, St. Peter's. **Owner:** C. MacPhail. **Tel:** 902-535-2377, fax 902-535-2084. **Season:** year round. **Hours**: 9 am - 5 pm, Mon - Sat. **Cards:** VS, AE.

Parker's Restaurant and Coffee Shop

Location: Main St, St Peter's. **Tel:** 902-535-2405. **Season:** year round. **Hours:** weekdays - May to Oct 7 am to 10 pm; weekends - 7 am to 11 pm; coffee shop open from 6 am to midndight. (restaurant hours may be slightly longer in summer) **Cards:** VS, MC, AE. **Features:** family-style restaurant.

Lawton's Drugs - Main St, St. Peters; 902-535-2203; open Mon to Wed 9 am to 8 pm; Thurs & Fri 9 am to 9 pm; Sat 9 am to 5 pm; Sun 1 pm to 3 pm; extended summer hours are Sun from 12 noon to 5 pm.

River Tillard Hiking Trail

An old railway bed converted to a super nature trail along the shores of St. Peters Bay.

Location: St. Peters. In the centre of the village, turn down Pepperell St toward the water (right if you're heading toward Sydney); trail begins a couple of hundred yards down Pepperell St (turn right onto the trail) **Features:** wonderful oceanside hike with views of lighthouse, Isle Madame; trail is 2 km (1.2 mi) to an old railway trestle at River Tillard; beaches and picnic tables; watch for blue herons, eagles and osprey.

> ➵ **EN ROUTE** - If you're heading west and want to take the Alternate Route through Dundee and Marble Mountain (page 208), turn off here at the Irving station.

MacDonald's Hotel and Dining Room

An older style hotel with continental breakfast.

Location: 9383 Pepperell St, St. Peters - turn at the Irving Station in the centre of the village. **Mail Addr**: Box 70, St. Peters, N.S. B0E 3B0. **Tel:** 902-535-2997; 535-2996. **Season:** Apr - Dec. **Rates:** low. **Cards:** most major cards. **Dng Rm Hrs:** 8 - 10 am; 11 am - 3 pm; 4:30 - 10 pm.

Nova Scotia Liquor Commission; St. Peters, 902-535-2117; open Mon to Thurs & Sat 10 am to 6 pm; Fri 10 am to 9 pm; extended summer hours - open Sat until 9 pm.

MacDonnell Pharmacy - Main St, St. Peters, close to Canal; 902-535-3196; **emergency number** when store is closed **902-535-2173**; open Mon & Tue from 9am to 6 pm; Wed, Thurs & Fri from 9 am to 8 pm; Sat from 9 am to 5 pm; closed Sun.

Country Lane Crafts

Location: Main St, St. Peter's, near Canal. **Tel:** 902-535-3126, fax 902-535-3089. **Owners:** A. & M. Touesnard. **Season:** year round **Hours:** Mon - Wed & Sat 10 am to 5 pm; Thurs & Fri 10 am to 8 pm; Sun 1 to 4 pm. **Cards:** VS, MC, AE. **Features:** usually someone is working on a craft in the store so you can watch...maybe even learn how it's done.

Bras d'Or Lakes Inn and Restaurant

A large family-style restuarant.

Location: St. Peter's, by the Canal. **Mail Addr:** St. Peters, N.S. B0E 3B0. **Tel:** 902-535-2200; Fax 902-535-2784; 1-800-818-5885. **Season:** year round. **Rates:** mid-range. **Cards:** VS, MC, AE. **Dng Rm Hrs:** 7 am to 9 pm **Restr Prices:** mid-range. **Features:** lovely view of the lake; licensed.

St. Peters Marina

Location: St. Peters, at the Canal. **Mail Addr:** St. Peters, N.S. B0E 3B0. **Tel:** 902-535-2729. **Features:** floating finger docks for 15 - 20 boats; gas, diesel, water and power; washrooms with showers; laundry facilities; club room; picnic area.

Julia Longacre

St. Peter's Canal

The only functioning tidal lock system in Nova Scotia.

Location: St. Peters, east end of Village. **Tel:** 902-535-2118. **Season:** Canal is accessible year round. **Features:** interpretive exhibit outside; picnic facilities; mooring for boats; washrooms; wheelchair accessible.

Nicolas Denys Museum

Location: St. Peters, next to Canal, take road up along the canal on St. Peter's side. **Tel:** 535-2379. **Season:** Jun - Sept. **Hours:** 9 am - 5 pm daily. **Admission**: adults 50 cents, children 25 cents. **Features:** building is reminiscent of the original 1650 trading post built here by Nicolas Denys of France; washrooms, picnic area.

St. Peter's Canal

The area around the Canal at St. Peters has a long and fascinating history.

Before the builders of the canal blasted and dug away the solid granite isthmus that once separated the Altantic Ocean and the Bras d'Or Lakes, ocean-going ships had to be hauled overland from the Ocean to the Lake.

As early as 1520, Portugese fishermen used the isthmus as a seasonal fishing station. And before that the Mi'kmaqs used the isthmus to portage their canoes.

Its history is linked, too, with the activities at Fortress Louisbourg in the 1700's, providing the first line of defence to the fort via the "French Road", which ran eastward through the woods.

Nicolas Denys was one of Cape Breton's first true entrepreneurs. Apparently in 1677 he pursuaded the French government to give him the right to exact a duty from all persons who took coal or gypsum from Cape Breton...a tidy income, I'm sure, in itself; but in addition he was also granted permission to require all traders of fur to buy a license from him.

Battery Provincial Park

Location: St. Peters, on the Canal; take the road up along the Canal, on the Sydney side. **Tel:** 902-535-3094. **Season:** mid-Jun to early Sept. **Rates:** avg. **Features:** picnic area;

unserviced sites; toilets, disposal station; cold water taps; fire grills; wood; beach; frontage on Canal.

Campbell's Dairy Freeze - Route 4 near the St. Peter's Canal - fast food, ice cream.

St. Peter's R.V. Campground

Location: St. Peters. About a km east of the St. Peters Canal, turn onto Rte 247 (next to the Dept. of Transport building). Campground is just after you turn onto Rte 247. **Mail Addr:** Box 226, St. Peters, N.S. B0E 3B0. **Tel:** 535-3333; Fax 535-2202. **Owners:** R. & L. Wambolt. **Season:** Jun to Sept. **Rates:** avg. **Cards:** VS, Good Sam. **Features:** serviced and unserviced sites overlooking Bras d'Or Lakes; washrooms; laundromat; camp cabins, fire pits; playground; heated pool.

Joyce's Motel and Cottages

Location: St. Peters, 1.6 km. (1 mi.) east of village on Rte 4. **Mail Addr:** Box 193, St. Peter's N.S. B0E 3B0. **Tel:** 902-535-2404; o/s 902-535-2231. **Owners:** M.& R. Robertson. **Season:** mid-May to Oct. **Rates:** mid-range. **Cards:** VS, MC. **Features:** overlooking Bras d'Or Lakes; pool; launching dock; laundromat, playground; fishing; boat rental.

Chapel Island

Located on Route 4, about 9 km (5.4 mi) east of St. Peters.

Chapel Island Mi'kmaq Reserve

Location: Chapel Island, Rte 4, 11 km (6.5 mi) east of St. Peters, the oldest of Cape Breton's five Mi'Kmaq reserves.

St. Anne's Mission

Each summer the community of Chapel Island hosts the **St. Anne's Mission**, a cultural and spiritual celebration for the Mi'Kmaq nation. This is the site where the Mi'kmaq were first introduced to Christianity and where Abbé Maillard, a well-known French missionary, preached his first sermon. The Mission is a blending of the Mi'kmaqs' Christian beliefs and their traditional spirituality.

The Mission is usually held during the last week of July. Visitors are welcome.

Indian Lake Handcrafts

Location: Chapel Island, Rte 4. **Tel:** 902-535-3299. **Owner:** J. Doucette. **Season:** year round. **Hours:** opens in morning at no set time, but stays open until 11 every night. **Features:** Indian handcrafts and other gift and convenience items.

Soldier's Cove/Johnstown

Located on Rte 4, between St. Peters and Sydney; Soldier's Cove is 10 km (6 mi) east of St. Peters and Johnstown is about 27 km (16 mi) east of St. Peters. Soldier's Cove was once called 'Laugh at the Yankies' by some soldiers who settled there after fighting in the War of 1812.

Soldier's Cove Gas & Variety, located at Soldiers Cove, on Rte 4; 902-535-2272; open 7 am to 9 pm daily.

Johnstown Market

Located on Rte 4 between St. Peters and Sydney, about 28 km (17 mi) east of St. Peters. This is a converted school where you'll find a collection of shops and activities of particular interest to travellers...it's worth the stop-off. There's a craft shop, chowder house, catamaran sailing tours, information centre, a credit union, public beach, picnic area, washrooms, and across the road a shrine and walking trail.

Turnstone Gallery and Fine Crafts

Location: Johnstown Market, on Route 4. **Tel:** 902-535-3444. **Season:** Jul and Aug. **Hours:** Mon - Sat 9 am to 6 pm; Sun 12 noon to 5 pm. **Cards:** VS, MC. **Features:** a lovely collection of Atlantic Canada handcrafts.

Super Natural Sailing Tours

Catamaran sailing on the Bras d'Or Lakes. In case you don't know, a 'catamaran' is a vessel (in this case a sailing vessel) with two hulls.

Location: Johnstown Market, Route 4. **Mail Addr:** R. R. #1, St. Peters, N.S. B0E 3B0. **Tel:** 902-535-3371; 1-800-903-3371; Fax 902-535-2209. **Owners:** J. & J. Fennell **Season:** May to Oct. **Cards:** VS, Interac. **Features:** guided sailing adventure on a 50-foot wooden catamaran the "Bras d'Or Sea", the first catamaran in Canada to be certified for passenger service; family and group rates available; enjoy the wonders of nature as you sail past secluded beaches and uninhabited islands; educational program features demonstrations, exhibits and discussions as the marine ecosystem of the Bras d'Or is explored.

Our Lady of Guadalupe Shrine & Tepeyac Trail

Location: Johnstown, Rte 4, behind the church, which is across the road from the Johnstown Market. **Features:** the shrine commemorates the appearance of the Virgin Mary in Mexico back in the 1500's; the trail is a short groomed trail up the hill to a lookoff over Johnstown; a mini-gallery in the church depicts the story of Our Lady of Guadalupe and there is a painting that dates back to the 1700's which apparently was carried through the woods from Louisbourg to Johnstown to save it from being destroyed in the seige of the fortress.

Irish Cove

Located on Rte 4, about 30 km (20 mi) east of St. Peters and 55 km (33 mi) west of Sydney.

Irish Cove Provincial Picnic Park and Lookoff

On a hill, high above the Bras d'Or Lakes.

Location: Irish Cove, Rte 4. **Features:** picnic tables; toilet.

Big Pond

Located on Rte 4, about halfway between St. Peters and Sydney,40 km (24 mi) or so each way.

If you're a fan of singer Rita MacNeil, you've probably heard of Big Pond...it's her home turf and it's where you'll find her tearoom and shop.

Big Pond B & B

I predict you'll love the kitchen here. The ceiling beams are lavishly hung with wonderful lavender, rose and yellow coloured dried flowers, which you can purchase, or just enjoy.

Location: Big Pond Centre, Rte 4, 2 km (1.2 mi) east of Rita's Tearoom. **Mail Addr:** R. R. #1, Big Pond, N.S. B0A 1H0. **Tel:** 902-828-2476; Fax 902-828-3065. **Owners:** P. & K. Nelder. **Season:** May - Oct. **Rates:** med-low. **Cards:** VS, MC. **Features:** country setting with private beach on the Bras d'Or Lakes; walking trail; sailboat charters - crewed or bareboat (see below).

Cape Breton Lake Charters

Location, etc: Same as Big Pond B & B. **Rates:** various, depending on which sailing craft you choose and how you want to charter it - crewed and provisioned or bareboat. **Cards:** VS, MC. **Features:** bareboat and crewed charters on Bras d'Or Lake; learn-to-sail packages; beautiful sailboats, some of them hand constructed by the owner, Keith Nelder. (I know because I saw him working on his latest masterpiece.)

Rita's Tea Room and Gift Shop

Come have a cuppa with Rita's friends...you may even meet up with Rita herself. The original building was a one room school house and in the 1980's Rita lived there with her family. It's been renovated and enlarged and is now probably one of the most popular spots on the Island.

Location: Pig Pond, Route 4, about half-way between St. Peters and Sydney. **Tel:** 902-828-2667. **Hours:** 9 am - 7 pm, daily. **Season:** early Jun - mid-Oct. **Features:** Rita's own tea blend for sale in the Tea Room and by the box in the gift shop; lots of Rita's music and memorabilia.

MacIntyre's B & B

Location: Big Pond, Rte 4. **Mail Addr:** R. R. #1, Big Pond, N.S. B0A 1H0. **Tel:** 902-828-2184. **Owners:** A. and E. MacIntyre. **Season:** May - Oct; o/s by arrangement. **Rates:** med-low. **Features:** situated on the Big Pond outdoor Concert grounds; hiking trails; eagle and nature tours.

Big Pond Concert

Location: MacIntyre's Farm, Big Pond, Rte 4. **Features:** annual outdoor summer festival...heaps of fiddling, singing, dancing and socializing; benches available, but I would suggest you bring your own lawn chair if possible; fast food concessions stands, and toilets. See insert for this year's date and time.

Big Pond Public Beach

Location: across from the Church in Big Pond, Rte 4. **Features**: warm Bras d'Or water; canteen.

MacLeod's Grocery and Metro Station - Big Pond, Rte 4; 902-828-2286; summer hours - Mon to Fri 7 am to 10 pm, Sat & Sun from 8 am to 10 pm; o/s hours are Mon to Fri 7 am to 8 pm, Sat & Sun from 8 am to 8 pm; gas, groceries, fishing supplies, general merchandise; laundromat.

A. A. MacNeil General Merchant - gas and groceries; located at Big Pond, Rte 4; 902-828-3028; open from late Jun to Labour Day; 8 am to 7 pm daily.

Big Pond Eagle Tours

For nature lovers - a walking discovery tour down an old country road and through meadows.

Location: Tour begins at MacDonald's Consolidated School, next to St. Mary's Church, in Big Pond, on Rte 4. **Tel:** 902-828-3052. **Owner:** John Willie MacInnis. **Season:** summer and fall. **Hours:** by prior arrangement - just call ahead. **Rates:** $15 adults; $5 for under 12. **Features:** sighting of many birds, including bald eagle; introduction to plant life and trees; local history and stories.

Ben Eoin/East Bay

Pronounced by us non-Gaelic speakers 'Ben Yon'. Located on Rte 4 about 50 km (30 mi) east of St. Peters, and about 30 km (18 mi) west of Sydney.

Ben Eoin Crafts & Gifts

Located: Ben Eoin, Rte 4. **Tel:** 902-828-2890. **Owner:** B. Sophocleous. **Season:** late Jun to Thanksgiving. **Hours:** Jul to Labour Day 9 am to 8 pm; other months usually 10 am to 5 pm, but can vary a little. **Cards:** VS, MC, AE. **Features:** local handcrafts; large selection of Cape Breton music and books; souvenirs.

Ben Eoin Provincial Park

A small picnic park on an old farm property.

Location: Ben Eoin, Rte 4. **Features:** toilets, picnic tables, charcoal pits.

Me & The Mrs

Location: Ben Eoin, across from campground. **Tel**: 902-828-2808. **Season:** Jun - Sept (other months with reduced hours). **Hours:** 7 am to 11 pm daily. **Cards**: VS, MC. **Features**: small restaurant, convenience store, mini golf.

Ben Eoin Beach Campground and Trailer Park

Location: Ben Eoin, Route 4. **Mail Addr:** Box 1115, Sydney, N.S. B1P 6J7. **Tel:** 902-828-3100; o/s 902-562-4978. **Owners:** MacDonald family. **Season:** mid-Jun to Labour Day. **Rates:** avg and avg plus; beach day rates- 50 cents to $2. **Features:** serviced and unserviced sites;

canteen and fast food; washrooms, laundromat; launch area and dock; playground and recreation hall; canoe and pedal boat rental.

East Bay Bed & Breakfast

Location: East Bay, Rte 4. **Mail Addr:** Box 13, East Bay, N.S. B0A 1H0. **Tel:** 902-828-3140. **Owner:** A. Ryan. **Rates:** med-low. **Season:** year round. **Cards:** VS, MC. **Features:** quiet country setting; not suitable for small children.

East Bay Beach

This is a roadside beach with not a lot of shore area, but the water is clear and usually warm. Great for a quick dip on a hot day. **Location:** East Bay, Route 4 - turn onto the Northside East Bay Road, adjacent to the church, and drive a short distance - beach is along the causeway.

Julia Longacre

Sydney Forks

Located on Rte 4, between East Bay and Sydney. In addition to the facilities listed below, you'll also find several service staions, convenience stores and fast food outlets, more as you get closer to Sydney.

Meadows Motel

Location: 9 Meadows Rd, Sydney Forks. **Mail Addr:** 9 Meadows Rd, Sydney Forks, N.S. B1L 1A1. **Tel:** 902-562-7400. **Season:** year round. **Rates:** med-low. **Cards:** VS, MC. **Features:** outdoor pool; some units are housekeeping.

Garden Court Cabins

A peaceful spot on the Bras d'Or Lakes, a' hop, skip and a jump' from Sydney.

Location: Sydney Forks, Route 4, 9 km. (5.5 mi.) west of Sydney. **Mail Addr:** 2518 Kings Road, Sydney Forks, N.S. B1L 1A1. **Tel:** 902-564-6201; Fax same. **Owners:** L. A. MacDonald. **Season:** May to Oct. **Rates:** med-low. **Cards:** VS, MC. **Features:** some cabins are housekeeping; fishing in season; boat rentals; tennis; good place for windsurfing.

Christies B & B

This looks like it would be a great place for families.

Location: Sydney Forks, Rte 4, about 7 km (4 mi) west of Sydney. **Mail Addr:** 2486 Kings Rd, Sydney Forks, N.S. B1L 1A1. **Tel:** 902-564-9364. **Owner:** O. Christie. **Season:** Jun to mid-Nov. **Rates:** med-low. **Features:** guest lounge and games room; model ship display; good family accommodation.

Sydney

Located on the east coast of Cape Breton about 155 km (93 mi) from the Canso Causeway.

Sydney - A Little History Note

Sydney is thought to be one of the oldest settlements in North America. As far back as the sixteenth century Spanish fishermen used it as a refuge and when the French built the fortress at Louisbourg, Sydney Harbour provided access to food for the workers and bricks for the buildings.

In 1785 Loyalists fleeing the United States formally established Sydney and named it after the Colonial Secretary, Lord Sydney.

Between the late 1700's and early 1800's many Gaelic-speaking Scots settled in the colony and Sydney began to prosper.

The prosperity slowed down somewhat in 1820 when Nova Scotia annexed Cape Breton. But the growth of the coal mines and steel industry in the early 1900's brought prosperity back and people from all over the world came here to work. This accounts for Sydney's lively multicultural personality.

Sydney is the largest centre in Cape Breton, and in fact, is the only city on the Island.

Because of the large number of facilities in and around Sydney, I will only describe those on what I consider to be the four main streets in the City. These streets are **Kings Road, Charlotte Street, George Street** and **Prince St/ Welton St/Grand Lake Rd**.(see the map). Other relevant facilities will be listed with address and phone number for your convenience.

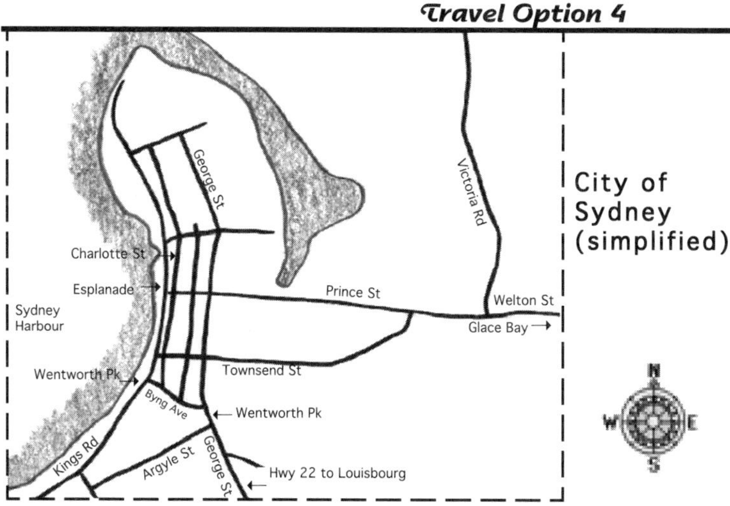

Kings Road/ Esplanade, Sydney

When you come into Sydney on Rte 4 from St. Peters, you'll eventually find yourself on Kings Road, one of Sydney's main thoroughfares. Drive under the overpass and keep straight. The first set of lights after the overpass is at Keltic Drive. In addition to the facilities listed below, you'll find fast food outlets, convenience stores, grocery stores (**Super Valu** 562-8258, open from 8 am to 10 pm Mon to Sat; **Lofood** 562-8274, same hours as Super Valu), and gas stations all along King's Rd.

Cape Breton Shopping Plaza

Walmart, Sobey's (groceries), Greenberg's (department store), a health food store, restaurant, postal outlet, pharmacy, liquor store and other stores.

Location: coming from Rte 4 - Kings Rd entrance - turn left a short distance after the underpass; Keltic Drive entrance - turn at the first set of lights after the underpass onto Keltic Drive. **Tel:** 564-5777. **Hours:** Walmart, Greenberg's and Sobey's open from 10 am to 10 pm; some of the smaller stores in the plaza close earlier, usually 5 or 6 pm.

Shoppers Drug Mart, Cape Breton Shopping Plaza; 902-539-8111; hours - 8 am to midnight, every day.

Nova Scotia Liquor Commission, Cape Breton Shopping Plaza,539-5588; open from 10 am to 10 pm Mon to Thurs; 10 am to 11 pm Fri & Sat.

Visitor Information Centre

Location: Keltic Drive, across from the Cape Breton Shopping Plaza, at the lights at Kings Rd. **Season:** mid-May to mid-Oct. **Hours:** 9 am to 9 pm, but could vary a little depending on demand.

Keltic Motel

A small motel about a km from the C.B. Shopping Plaza.(see above)

Location: 294 Keltic Drive, Sydney; turn at the first set of lights on Kings Rd coming in from Rte 4. **Mail Addr:** 294 Keltic Dr, Sydney, N.S. B1R 1V7. **Tel:** 902-562-3111. **Owner:** W. & S. Forrester. **Season:** year round. **Rates:** mid-range. **Cards:** VS.

Jasper's Restaurant

Location: Kings Road, Sydney. **Tel:** 902-564-6181. **Owner:** A. Wilson. **Season:** year round. **Hours:** 7am to 11pm daily (summer hours may be extended to midnight). **Cards:** most major cards. **Prices:** mid-range. **Features:** family-style restaurant.

Off the Dock

Fish & seafood market with fresh lobster, crab, muscles, halibut, etc.

Location: 1071 Kings Rd. **Tel:** 902-564-5541. **Owner:** K. Shaw. **Season:** year round. **Hours:** 9 am to 6 pm, Sat 9 am to 5 pm. **Features:** will pack for travel.

Keddy's Sydney Hotel and Dining Room

Location: 600 Kings Rd, Sydney. **Mail Addr:** 600 Kings Rd., Sydney, N.S. B1S 1B9. **Tel:** 902-539-1140; 1-800-561-7666; Fax 902-539-2258. **Owner:** C. MacQueen. **Season:** year round. **Rates:** med-high. **Cards:** all major cards. **Dng Rm Hrs:** 7 am to 10 am; 5 pm to 8 pm. **Dng Rm Prices:** mid-range.

Auberge Wandlyn Cape Bretoner and Dining Room

Location: 560 Kings Rd, Sydney. **Mail Addr:** 560 Kings Rd, Sydney, N.S. B1P 6C2. **Tel:** 902-539-8101; 1-800-561-0000 (central and eastern Canada); 1-800-561-0006 (continental USA); Fax 902-539-1743. **Owner:** V. Ramsey. **Season:** year round. **Rates:** med-high. **Cards:** all major cards. **Dng Rm Hrs:** Mon to Fri & Sun - 7 am to 2 pm and 5 pm to 8 pm; Sat - 7 am to 11 am and 5 pm to 8 pm. **Dng Rm Prices:** med-high.

Holiday Inn Sydney and Dining Room

Location: 480 Kings Rd. **Mail Addr:** 480 Kings Rd, Sydney, N.S. B1S 1A8. **Tel:** 902-5396750; 1-800-465-4329; Fax 902-2773. **Owner:** C. Greene. **Season:** year round. **Rates:** med-high to upper end. **Cards:** all major cards. **Dng Rm Hrs:** 7 am to 2 pm; 5 pm to 10 pm. **Dng Rm Prices:** med-high. **Features:** licensed; children's menu; pool; exercise room; outdoor lobster boil & barbecue.

Comfort Inn by Journey's End

Location: 368 Kings Road. **Mail Addr:** 368 Kings Rd, Sydney, N.S. B1S 1A8. **Tel:** 902-562-0200; 1-800-228-5150; Fax 902-564-6410. **Owner:** I. Carroll. **Season:** year round. **Rates:** mid-range to med-high. **Cards:** all major cards. **Features:** continental breakfast available.

Shoppers Drug Mart - located in the Medical Arts Bldg, 336 Kings Rd, Sydney; 902-564-0110; hours are generally Mon to Thurs 9 - 6; Fri 9 - 5, but in summer may be reduced to 9 - 5 every day.

Rockinghorse Inn and Dining Room

This is a wonderful old inn, newly renovated and furnished with antiques.

Location: 295 Kings Road, Sydney. **Mail Addr:** 295 Kings Rd, Sydney, N.S. B1S 1A7. **Tel:** 902-539-2696. **Owner:** M. Glabay. **Season:** year round. **Rates:** upper end. **Cards:** VS, MC. **Dng Rm Prices:** upper end - 4-course gourmet dinner - reservations preferred. **Features:** registred heritage property; breakfast in glassed sunroom; elegant and comfortable atmosphere.

City Lodge and Dining Room -

Location: 100 Kings Rd, Sydney. **Mail Addr:** 100 Kings Rd, Sydney, N.S. B1S 1A1. **Tel:** 902-567-3311; Fax 902-562-2640. **Owner:** B. Martin. **Season:** year round. **Rates:** med-low. **Cards:** most major cards. **Dng Rm Hrs:** 7 am to 2:30 pm; 5 pm to 9 pm. **Dng Rm Prices:** mid-range. **Features:** monthly rates available; room service available.

Wentworth Park

Location: Sydney, at the corner of Kings Rd and Byng Ave (stretches along Byng Ave to George St). **Features:** city park with fountain, ducks, tables and benches; bandshell with live entertainment on summer evenings.

➵ **EN ROUTE** - notice that Kings Rd becomes Esplanade at the intersection of Byng Ave (at Wentworth Park).

Cambridge Suites Hotel

Location: 380 Esplanade, Sydney. **Mail Addr:** 380 Esplanade, Sydney, N.S. B1P 1B1. **Tel:** 902-562-6500; 1-800-565-9466; Fax 902-564-6011. **Owner:** R. O'Beirne. **Season:** year round. **Rates:** med-high to upper end. **Cards:** all major cards. **Features:** complimentary continental breakfast; rooftop spa and pool.

Goodies Restaurant

Location: 380 Esplanade, Sydney, in Cambridge Suites Hotel. **Tel:** 562-6500. **Season:** year round. **Hours:** 11 am to 10 pm; Sun 5 pm to 10 pm. **Prices**: mid-range. **Cards:** most major cards. **Features:** daily lunch and dinner specials.

Royal Hotel

A small older-style hotel

Location: 345 Esplanade, Sydney. **Mail Addr:** 345 Esplanade, Sydney, N.S. B1P 1A9. **Tel:** 902-539-2148. **Owner:** I. Andrews. **Season:** year round. **Rates:** low.

The Boardwalk

Behind City Hall on Esplanade, you'll find a boardwalk where you can take a wonderful stroll along Sydney Harbour. There's an ice cream stand and often there's live entertainment. You might want to pick up a take-out lunch uptown and bring it down to the boardwalk. See book insert for some of the entertainment this summer.

Delta Sydney - Hotel and Dining Room

Location: 300 Esplanade, Sydney. **Mail Addr:** 300 Esplanade, Sydney, N.S. B1P 6J4. **Tel:** 902-562-7500; 1-800-268-1133 (Canada); 1-800-887-1133 (USA); Fax 562-3023. **Owner:** R. LeBlanc. **Season:** year round. **Rates:** med-high to upper end. **Cards:** most major cards. **Dng Rm Hrs:** 7 am to 9 pm. **Dng Rm Prices:** med-high to upper end. **Features:** pool with waterslide; sauna and exercise room; lounge.

Dream Nature Hiking Tours

If you'd like to 'take a hike' but don't know where to go, give Sylvia a call.

Guide: Sylvia Colbourne. **Tel:** 902-539-4828. **Season:** Apr to Oct. **Features:** guided hikes of all lengths in many of the great hiking spots on the Island; history notes and information.

Paul's Hotel

A small older-style hotel; some units are housekeeping.

Location: corner of Pitt St and Esplanade, Sydney. **Mail Addr:** Box 147, Sydney, N.S. B1P 6G9. **Tel:** 902-562-5747. **Owner:** E. Landry. **Season:** year round. **Rates:** med-low.

Royal Cape Breton Yacht Club

Location: 246 Esplanade, Sydney. **Tel:** 902-562-9086. **Facilities**: marina, mooring and launching facilities; engine and sail repair available; gas and diesel; washrooms, bar, etc. in clubhouse.

Governors Restaurant and Bunker's Peanut Bar

Location: 233 Esplanade, Sydney. **Tel:** 902-562-7646. **Season:** year round. **Hours:** summer 11 am to 11 pm (bar open until 2 am). **Prices**: mid-range to med-high. **Cards:** all major cards. **Features:** full menu, licensed.

St. Patrick's Church Museum

Built in 1828, operated by the Old Sydney Society.

Location: 87 Esplanade, Sydney. **Tel:** 902-562-8237. **Season:** mid-Jun to late Sept. **Hours:** 9:30 am to 5:30 pm. **Features:** artifacts from pioneer days in and around Sydney; pioneer cemetery; information; public washrooms; **walking tours** of Sydney's historic north end available by appointment.

This beautiful little church, the oldest Roman Catholic church in Cape Breton, was built in 1828 from hand-hewn local stones and wood. It is an example of the pioneer Gothic style of architecture. In it's heyday, St. Pat's served worshippers from as far away as Louisbourg who arrived by boat each Sunday.

At St. Pat's now you will find artifacts from these early pioneer days and out back a very old, intriguing cemetery.

Charlotte Street, Sydney

Location: Charlotte Street runs parallel to Esplanade. Since most of Charlotte is one-way, running from north (far end) to south, you'll have to drive north on Esplanade or George (see below) then turn onto a side street to get to Charlotte. (see map).

Since Charlotte is the City's main business street, you'll find banks, restaurants, clothings stores, convenience stores, etc. all along the way... as well as these facilities listed below, starting at the north end.

Jost House Museum

Originally built in the 1790's, it's reconstruction shows two distinctly different architectural styles - the Cape Cod 'salt box" style of the late 1700's and the Newfoundland style house of the early 1900's.

Location: 54 Charlotte Street (north end), Sydney. **Tel:** 902-539-0366. **Season:** Jun to Oct. **Hours:** Jul & Aug - Mon to Sat 9 am to 5 pm, Sun 1 pm to 4 pm; Jun & Sept open Tue to Fri 10 am to 4 pm. **Features:** marine display, artifacts and information.

Cossit House Museum

Believed to be the oldest house in Sydney, built in 1787 by Rev. Ranna Cossit, the first permanent Protestant minister in Cape Breton.

Location: 75 Charlotte Street (north end), Sydney. **Tel:** 902-539-7973. **Season:** Jun to mid-Oct. **Hours:** 10 am to 4 pm daily. **Features:** guides in period costume; rooms furnished according to an 1815 inventory of Rev Cossit's estate.

St. George's Church and pioneer cemetery

Location: Charlotte St (corner of Nepean), Sydney. **Features:** church built in 1785 as a garrison chapel and still used today.

Environmental Activities Centre

A community-based project run by the Atlantic Coastal Action Program.

Location: 180 Charlotte St, corner Charlotte and Dorchester, north end. **Tel:** 902-567-1628. **Hours:** Tue to Fri 10 am to 5 pm; Sat 12 noon to 4 pm. **Features:** displays and information on current environmental problems; general enviro-information; T-shirts and other items with and enviro-theme; a HUGE map of Cape Breton, in case you're lost!

Island Greek Donair

Location: 228 Charlotte St. **Tel**: 902-539-0003. **Features**: Greek dishes as well as donairs and pizza.

Cameo Card & Gift Shop

Location: 238 Charlotte St. **Tel:** 539-4718/6333. **Hours:** Mon to Thurs 9 am to 5 pm; Thurs 9 am to 9 pm. **Cards:** most major cards. **Features:** lots of greeting cards; gifts and souvenirs; art supplies,etc.

The Bean Bank

A cafe in the true sense, with dozens of specialty coffees, herbal teas galore and cafe-style food. Try their Espresso or Cappuccino made from freshly ground beans.

Location: 243 Charlotte St. **Tel:** 902-562-5400. **Owner:** S. Annesty/Udle. **Season:** year round. **Hours:** Mon to Wed 7:30 am to 5 pm; Thurs 7:30 to 9 pm; Fri 7:30 to 10 pm; Sat 8:30 to 5 pm; Sun 11 am to 5 pm; hours may be extended a bit during summer months. **Cards:** VS. **Features:** specialty coffee and tea; lunches; fresh homemade cheesecakes and pastries; cozy cafe setting.

Victoria Rose Gifts and Crafts

Location: 243 Charlotte St. **Tel:** 902-564-0208. **Features:** gifts, crafts.

Kula's Family Restaurant

Location: 16 Pitt St, just off Charlotte. **Tel**: 902-539-8844. **Owner**: J. Bedford. **Season**: year round. **Hours:** Mon to Fri - 7 am to 7 pm; Sat 7 am to 3 pm. **Prices**: low to mid-range. **Cards:** VS.

Maple Leaf Restuarant

Location: 272 Charlotte St. **Tel:** 902-564-6251. **Hours**: Mon to Wed 8 am to 8 pm; Thurs to Sat 8 am to 9 pm; hours may be extended a little in summer to 10 or 11 pm. **Cards**: VS. AE.

Annie Lore

"Unusual and artistic wares and wears"

Location: 270 Charlotte St. **Tel:** 902-562-6254. **Hours:** Mon to Wed 12 noon to 6 pm; Thurs 10 am to 9 pm; Fri 10 am to 6 pm; Sat 10 am to 5 pm (shop may stay open later some days). **Cards:** VS. **Features:** it's fun looking around in here - lots of neat things.

Alteens

Location: 276 Charlotte St. **Tel:** 902-564-5495. **Hours**: 9 am to 5 pm, except Thurs 9 am to 9 pm; closed Sunday. **Cards**: most major cards. **Features**: local crafts, china, souvenirs.

Le Brignolet

A large and fascinating collection of fine gifts and collectibles, and a year-round Christmas shop.

Location: 303 Charlotte St. **Tel:** 902- 539-7338. **Season:** year round. **Hours:** Mon to Wed plus Sat 9 am to 5 pm; Thurs & Fri 9 am to 9 pm. **Cards:** VS, MC, AE, Interac. **Features:** Maritime and Canadian handcrafts; Seagull pewter; quality souvenirs; imported gifts and collectibles; year round Christmas shop.

London Jewellers and Gifts

Another shop packed with lots of quality gifts.

Location: 307 Charlotte St. **Tel:** 902-539-5455. **Hours:** Mon to Sat from 9 am to 5 pm, except on Thurs open until 9 pm. **Cards:** VS, MC, AE, Interac. **Features:** lots of jewellery, gifts, china and souvenirs.

Crowells

This is one of those wonderful old department stores that are all but extinct these days. They still use the original pneumatic tube system for taking cash, the ones that shoot up the wall and land somewhere in the attic, then shoot back down with your change. Kids love it.

Location: 319 Charlotte St. **Tel:** 902-564-4431. **Hours:** open Mon to Fri from 9 am to 5 pm, except Thurs open until 9 pm. **Cards:** VS, MC, AE. **Features:** gift and china department on third floor (there's an elevator!)

Island Crafts

Location: 329 Charlotte St. **Tel:** 902-539-4424. **Features**: all locally handmade gifts and souvenirs including quilts, sweaters, etc.

Pharmasave (pharmacy) - 351 Charlotte St, 902-564-4141; open Mon to Fri 8 am to 9 pm; Sat 9am to 9 pm; Sun and holidays 11 am to 6 pm.

Peking Restaurant

Location: 355 Charlotte St. **Tel:** 902-539-7775. **Hours:** open at 11 am daily. **Features:** chinese cuisine; take out and delivery.

YMCA

In case you need a little loosening up after your long drive.

Location: 399 Charlotte St. **Tel:** 902-539-7880. **Hours:** Mon to Thurs 6 am to 10 pm; Fri 6 am to 9 pm; Sat 9 am to 6 pm; Sun 12 noon to 8 pm. **Features:** for $5 guests can spend the day at the "Y" in the weight room, pool, aerobics class; squash or raquet ball courts, etc. Sounds like a good deal!

Artist Teena Marie Saunders. See page 115.

Vogue Theatre

Location: Charlotte St, across from the YMCA. **Tel:** 902-564-8221. **Show times**: 7 pm and 9 pm generally; children's matinees on Sat, Sun and holidays.

Ike's Gourmet Delicatessen

A good place to pick up a sandwich to eat on the Boardwalk. You could even have them pack you a fancy picnic lunch.

Location: 413 Charlotte St. **Tel:** 902-564-8421 **Hours:** Mon to Wed 9 am to 6 pm; Thur & Fri 9 am to 7 pm; Sat 10 am to 5 pm. **Features:** imported goods, ethnic food, including kosher; gift baskets and party trays; picnic lunches; delivery; no eat-in facilities.

Joe's Warehouse & Food Emporium and Smooth Herman's Cabaret

Location: 424 Charlotte St. **Tel:** 902-539-6686 (restaurant); 539-0408 (cabaret). **Season:** year round. **Restr Hrs:** Mon to Thur 11:30 am to 11 pm; Fri & Sat 11:30 am to 12 pm; Sun and major holidays 5 pm to 11 pm; **Cabaret Hrs:** from 8 pm to 3:30 am daily, except on Friday there's Happy Hour from 4 pm to 8 pm. **Prices**: from mid-range to upper end. **Cards:** all major cards. **Features:** lots of room, pleasant atmosphere, good menu selection; salad bar; daily specials; live entertainment in cabaret.

Sit and Gids

Lebanese for Gramdma and Grandpa.

Location: 446 Charlotte St. **Tel:** 902- 564-9509. **Hours:** summer hours (starting Jun 1) Mon & Tue 11 am to 9 pm; Wed to Sat 11 am to 11 pm; Sun 4 pm to 10 pm; hours are a little less in o/s. **Prices:** mid-range. **Features:** tasty Lebanese fare.

Daniel's Pub

"The Cape Breton Pub"

Location: 456 Charlotte St. Tel. 902-562-8586. **Owner:** Blair Brown. **Season:** year round. **Hours:** 11 am to 2 am, every day. **Prices:** low to mid-range. **Cards:** all major cards. **Features**: pub food; lots of traditional Cape Breton music; Saturday afternoon Ceilidh's with Cape Breton music from 4 pm to 8 pm; Friday more Celtic and Maritime music from 5 pm to 8 pm; fresh lobsters; large outdoor patio.

The Treasure Cove and The Inlet

Quality gifts downstairs, children's toys and books upstairs.

Location: 74 Townsend St, at the corner of Charlotte. **Tel:** 902-564-8158. **Owners:** J. & H. Stewart. **Season:** year round. **Hours:** Mon, Tue, Wed, Sat 9 am to 5 pm; Thurs & Fri 9 am to 9 pm. **Cards:** VS, MC, Interac. **Features:** a large selection of fine gifts and souvenirs; kitchen wares; great selection of children's books and toys.

George Street, Sydney

Directions: From Hwy 125, the By-Pass, take Exit 8 to George St. Turn left off the ramp to go to downtown Sydney. A right turn will take you directly to Louisbourg.

On George St you'll find corner stores, gas stations, restaurants and other facilities, as well as the ones listed below:

Cape Breton Regional Hospital, located on George Street, Sydney, at first set of lights just off the ramp from Hwy 125. **OR**, if you're coming from downtown, drive up George St (south) to the top of what we call "Hardwood Hill" to the last set of lights, just before the overpass. **Tel: 902-567-8000.** Emergency entrance is at very front of building.

Lawton's Drug Store, 719 George St, Sydney, at the intersection of Byng Av and George St; 902-564-8200; hours Mon to Sat from 9 am to 9 pm; Sun 12 noon to 8 pm.

Wentworth Park

Location: Sydney, at the corner of George St and Byng Ave. **Features:** city park with fountain, ducks, tables and benches; bandshell with live entertainment on summer evenings.

Nova Scotia Liquor Commission, 500 George Street, Sydney; 902-564-6275; hours are Mon to Thurs 9 am to 6 pm; Fri and Sat 10 am to 10 pm.

Centre 200

Cape Breton's largest multi-purpose facility where you can enjoy hockey and other sports, concerts, ceilidhs, craft fairs, ice shows and many other events. Maximum seating capacity is about 5,500.

Location: 481 George St. **Tel:** information recording 902-539-1100; box office 539-2130;general 564-2200.

The Forum Pub & Eatery

Location: Centre 200 (above). **Tel:** 564-4442. **Hours:** open only on the day of Centre 200 events, from 11 am to 1 am.

Sheraton Casino

Location: Centre 200, George St. **Tel:** 902-563-7777. **Hours:** Mon to Wed 12 noon to 4 am; Thurs to Sun open 24 hours. **Features:** gaming tables, slot machines, restaurant, lounge, banking machine.

Outdoor Farmers' Market

Location: corner of George and Pitt Streets, on the Maritime Tel & Tel parking lot. **Season:** mid-Jul to end of Oct. **Hours:** Sat morning from about 7:30 'till the farmers run out...usually about mid-morning. **Features:** lots of seasonal fruit and vegetables, preserves and other goodies.

Jasper's Restaurant

Family-style eatery, open 24-hours a day.

Location: 268 George St. **Tel:** 902-539-7109. **Hours:** open 24 hours. **Prices:** mid-range. **Cards:** most major cards.

Cape Breton Centre for Heritage and Science

Location: The Lyceum, 225 George St. **Tel:** 539-1572. **Hours:** regular hours are Tue to Fri 10 am to 4 pm and Sat 1 pm to 4 pm; summer hours (Jun to Sept) - Mon to Sat 10 am to 4 pm. **Features:** travelling and in-house history-related exhibits (see book insert for this year's schedule); museum shop with some unique reproductions and gifts.

Cape Breton Centre for Craft and Design

A great place to spend some time mingling with Cape Breton craftspeople as they work. There's usually a group or two working on their weaving, rug hooking, quilting and other things.

Location: 225 George St, in the lovely old Lyceum building. **Tel:** 902-539-7491. **Hours:** Mon to Fri 9 am to 4 pm. **Features:** classes and workshops; exhibitions; craft and fine art library and resource centre.

Prince Street/Welton Street/Grand Lake Rd

This is really just one long street with three different names.

Location: Drive north on George Street (towards downtown) and at the traffic lights at Prince Street, turn right.

Alternatively: if you're coming into Sydney on Hwy 125, the By-Pass, drive to the end. A left turn will take you downtown, right turn will take you to the Mayflower Mall and Glace Bay.

Prince St becomes **Welton St** at Ashby Corner and somewhere around the K-Mart Plaza it turns into **Grand Lake Road** (see below). In addition to the facilities listed below, you'll also find service stations, corner stores, fast food outlets and many other shops along the way.

Acadian Lines

Bus service to Halifax and all points between Sydney and Halifax.

Location: Terminal Rd, just off Prince St by the tracks. **Tel:** 902-564-5533. **Bus times**: 7:30 am, 8:30 am, 11:00 am, 4:30 pm; terminal building is open every day from 7 am to midnight. **Cards:** VS.

Sydney Shopping Centre

Location: 322 Prince St. **Tel:** 902-539-6912. **Hours:** 10 am to 10 pm. **Features:** Sobey's (grocery store), pharmacy, Zellers (department store), clothing stores, bowling alley, Coles Book Store, bank, and others.

Empire 8

Movie theatres - 8 of 'em!

Location: Prince Street Plaza, across from Sydney Shop

ping Centre. **Tel:** for recording of movies playing 539-9049; for other inquiries 539-9050. **Show times**: there are generally two shows per night in each theatre - one around 7 pm and one around 9 pm - call for exact times, as they vary.

Kiwanis Pool

Location: 365 Prince, just up the hill from the Sydney Shopping Centre. **Tel:** 902- 564-4501. **Season:** closed July and Aug. **Hours:** Adult Swim (over 18) - Mon to Fri from noon to 1 pm; Tue & Thurs 8 to 9 pm; Public (Family) Swim: Mon, Wed & Fri 2 to 3 pm; Mon & Wed eve 8 to 9 pm; Tue eve 7 to 8 pm; Sun afternoon 2 to 5 pm.

Sydney Co-Op (groceries and general merchandise); Ashby Corner, 521 Prince St; 902-562-3904; **Hours:** Mon & Sat 8:30 am to 5 pm; Tue 8:30 am to 5:30 pm. Wed, Thurs, Fri 8:30 am to 9 pm.

Colleen's Cuisine

Location: 288 Welton St. **Tel:** 902-567-2177. **Season:** year round. **Hours:** Sun to Wed 7 am to 10 pm; Thurs, Fri & Sat 7 am to 12 pm. **Cards:** VS, MC, AE. **Prices:** mid-range. **Features:** family-style restaurant; breakfast, lunch and dinner specials each day; Italian, seafood, salads; etc; children's menu.

K-Mart Plaza

Location: 384 Welton St. **Features:** K-Mart (department store) open Mon to Fri 9 am to 10 pm; Sat 8 am to 10 pm. SuperValu (supermarket) open Mon to Sat 8 am to 10 pm; other stores in plaza as well.

Nova Scotia Liquor Commission, located in K-Mart Plaza, 384 Welton St; **Tel:** 567-2219. **Hours:** Mon to Sat 10 am to 10 pm.

Mayflower Mall

Location: 800 Grand Lake Rd. **Tel:** 902-539-0862. **Hours:** Mon to Sat 10 am to 9 p except Walmart which stays open until 10 pm. **Features:** Cape Breton's largest mall, has the usual assortment of stores - clothing and shoes, gifts, restaurant and fast food outlets; department stores (Walmart and The Bay); Coles Bookstore,etc.

Some restaurants on Grand Lake Rd

- √ **Simeon's II,** 427 Grand Lake Rd; 562-0251.
- √ **Chow Yan Foo**,460 Grand Lake Rd, 539-2825.
- √ **Swiss Chalet**,482 Grand Lake Rd,562-3232.
- √ **County Line Pub**, 581 Grand Lake Rd, 539-3003.

Bed & Breakfasts in Sydney

- √ **Anne's B & B**, 34 Amelia St, 539-3536
- √ **Anthony B & B**, 193 Bentnick St, 564-5937.
- √ **Century Manor B & B**, 212 Whitney Ave,567-1300.
- √ **Edna's B & B**, 17 Andrews Ave, 567-2239.
- √ **Gathering House B & B**, 148 Crescent St, 539-7172.
- √ **M. MacDonald's B & B**, 562-5070.
- √ **Country Post Office B & B**, 3 Strathcona St, 539-8033.
- √ **Park Place B & B,** 169 Park St, 562-3518.
- √ **Purcell Place B & B**, 196 Coxheath Rd, 562-4865.
- √ **White Maples B & B**, 72 Curry St, 564-4674.

Some other Sydney Restaurants

... in addition to these, you'll find lots and lots of fast food outlet - burgers, subs, donairs, pizza.

- √ **Cactus Cafe,** 100 Townsend, 564-0020
- √ **China Village**, C.B. Shopping Plaza,567-2838
- √ **E & L Italian Pasta Center**, 100 Townsend, 562-8241
- √ **Giorgio & Lim**, 536 George St, 539-8066
- √ **Italian Village**, 137 Victoria Rd, 539-1553
- √ **Kay's Kozy Korner**, 264 Townsend, 567-1414
- √ **Lam's Restaurant,** 439 Prince, 539-0313
- √ **New Moon,** 78 Townsend, 539-4422.
- √ **Pizza Den**, 1200 Kings Rd, 564-4483
- √ **Seabreeze Restaurant**, 300 Charlotte St, 539-2400

Alternate Route from Port Hawkesbury to St. Peters or from St. Peters to Port Hawkesbury

VIA

Dundee & Marble Mountain

If you're not in a hurry to get anywhere in particular, you should consider taking this Alternate Route from Port Hawkesbury to St. Peters or vice versa. It's a delightful drive along a lightly-travelled very scenic part of the Island. It takes you along the south-west shore of the Bras d'Or Lake - West Bay to be more specific.

There are some fine accommodations along this route, as well as, restaurants, an 18-hole golf course and a marina. At Marble Mountain there's a wonderful beach with marble sand, hiking trails and lots of peace and quiet.

Directions from St. Peters: in the centre of the village of St. Peters, turn onto Pepperell St next to the Irving station. Follow the route below in reverse.

Directions from Port Hawkesbury: drive straight past the Port Hawkesbury Centre (shopping mall). This will put you on Rte 4 to Cleveland. Follow the signs from Cleveland to West Bay. (about 35 km from Port Hawkesbury to West Bay).

➵ **EN ROUTE** -At the West Bay intersection, you can either go to **Marble Mountain** (a little side trip), or you can go to Dundee without taking the side trip.

Marble Mountain and Dundee

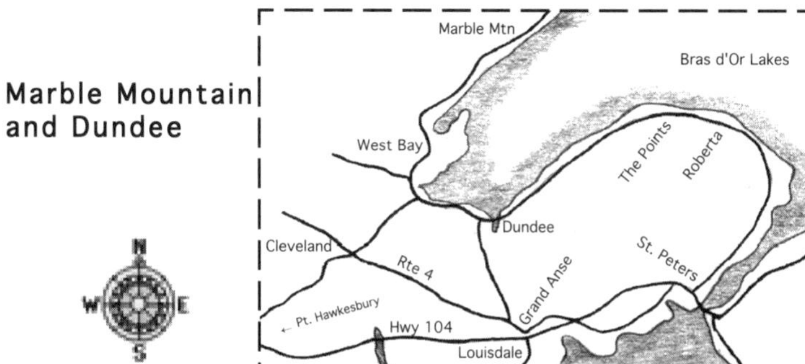

➵ To Marble Mountain

West Bay

Located at the western-most tip of the Bras d'Or Lakes, about 8 km (5 mi) west of Dundee. (see map and directions from Port Hawkesbury above)

LaFosse's Kwik Way - convenience store, gas, groceries.

Marble Mountain

Located about 15 km (9 mi) from West Bay. Although you'll find only a handful of people living here now, back in the early 1900's it was a thriving community. When the marble quarry was in full operation it employed 750 men. There were houses all along this road and over a thousand people living here.

Marble Mountain Community Museum

A short visit here is a great way to start your afternoon ...it sets your imagination adrift and takes you back to a time when Marble Mountain was a very different place!

Location: Marble Mountain, just past the two white churches. **Season:** Jul and Aug . **Hours:** Mon to Sat 10 am to 6 pm, Sun 1 to 6 pm. **Admission**: free. **Features**: Located in an old schoolhouse, this tiny museum houses a great collection of artifacts and photographs of a time, a hundred years ago, when Marble Mountain was bustling with activity; public washroom.

Marble Mountain Beach

This beach is exceptionally pleasant. The sand is actually crushed marble and the water is crystal clear.

Location: Marble Mountain. Driving in from West Bay, drive past the two white churches until you see two buildings close together on your right. One used to be MacLaughlin's General Store, a busy place indeed a hundred years ago. Take the road that runs in front of these buildings - it actually looks more like a driveway. Follow it down through the woods to the beach. Drive as far as you dare along the beach and park. **Features:** picnic tables, very basic toilet facilities- i.e. a classic outhouse; marble 'sand' beach; some grassy spots on the beach where, as far as I can find out, you are permitted to pitch a tent, but I wouldn't reallly recommend it.

Quarry Hike

A short, very steep climb to the top of the marble quarry, with a glorious view. Super place for a picnic, as long as you don't plan to take along the barbecue!

Location: Marble Mountain. Coming into the community from West Bay, drive a short distance past the road to the beach (see above) to a parking area along the road; pull over and park there. **Trail:** Across the road is another road with a gate. About two-thirds of the way up, before you reach the quarry, you'll come to a clearing to your right and a path that leads up the side of the quarry. Go slowly, it's very steep. The view from up there is wonderful! The hike is less than a kilometer long but once you're up there you can explore. Watch children carefully along the edge...it's a long way down!

➵ **EN ROUTE** - After you've poked around the Mountain and maybe had a swim, make your way back to West Bay and then on to Dundee.

➵ To Dundee

Dundee

Located about 20 km (12 mi) from Port Hawkesbury...8 km (5 mi) from the junction at West Bay.

Dundee Resort and Dining Room

A great spot on the shores of the Bras d'Or.

Location: Dundee, on the shores of West Bay, Bras d'Or Lakes, 20 km (12 mi) from Port Hawkesbury . **Mail Addr:** R. R. #2, West Bay, N.S. B0E 3K0. **Tel:** 902-345-2649; Fax 902-345-2697; 1-800-565-1774. Home Page: http://www.chatsubo.com/dundee. **Season:** May to Oct. **Rates**: med-high to upper end. **Cards:** most major cards. **Restr Prices:** mid-range to upper end. **Features:** 18-hole golf course with wonderful view; lighted tennis courts; pools; sun decks; marina; hiking trails; boat rentals; children's recreation; licenced.

Dundee Golf Course

A supurb view of the Bras d'Or Lakes.

Location: Dundee Resort (see above). **Tel:** 902-345-2639. **Features:** 18-hole, rating -70.0; slope -32; gas carts; pro shop with snack bar.

Dundee Marine

Offers ship supplies, moorings, maintenance, and full-service marina.

Location: Dundee Marina, across from Dundee Resort (see above). **Season:** year round. **Hours:** Jun to mid-Sept - 8:30 am to 9 pm; other months - 8:30 am to 5:30 pm. **Cards:** VS, MC. **Features:** fuel, sewage pump-out; shower and laundry services; launch; guest moorings; supplies.

St. George's Channel/The Points West Bay

Located between St. Peters and Dundee, on the West Bay segment of the Bras d'Or Lakes.

Bras d'Or Shores Resort

Location: St. George's Channel, about 1.5 (1 mi) east of Dundee. **Mail Addr:** R. R. #2, West Bay, N.S. B0E 3K0. **Tel:** 902-345-2896. **Owners:** T. & R. Burns. **Season:** May to Oct; o/s by arrangement. **Rates:** med-high to upper end. **Features:** 2- and 3-bedroom housekeeping units; heated pool; saltwater beach.

Artist Kenny Boone, Dominion. See page 276.

Dianna Lodge, Restaurant and Cottages

Location: The Points West Bay, between St. Peters and Dundee. **Mail Addr:** R. R. #2, West Bay, N.S. B0E 3K0. **Tel:** 902-345-2485; Fax 902-345-2858. **Owners:** S. & B. Winkler. **Season:** Apr to Nov. **Rates:** lodge mid-range (breakfast included); cottages upper end. **Cards:** VS, MC. **Dng Rm Hrs:** 8 am to 9 pm daily. **Features:** lodge and cottages; fireplace in cottages; fitness room; licenced restaurant.

Roberta

Located on the West Bay segment of the Bras d'Or Lakes, between Dundee and St. Peters.

Kayak Cape Breton and Cottages

Location: Roberta, about 20 km (12 mi) from St. Peters. **Mail Addr:** R. R. #2, West Bay, N.S. B0E 3K0. **Tel:** 902-535-3060; Fax same. **Owners:** E. & G. Witt. **Season:** May to mid-Nov. **Accommodation Rates:** mid range. **Cards:** VS. **Features:** secluded Lakeside setting; guided kayak tours and instruction; kayak, canoe and bike rentals; fishing; hiking; birdwatching.

The Pottery Garden

Don't pass this little gem of a studio without dropping in for a look around, or a chat.

Location: Roberta, 16 km (10 mi) from St. Peters. **Mail Addr:** R. R. #2, Roberta, West Bay, N.S. B0E 3K0. **Tel:** 902-535-2898. **Owner and Potter**: Anne Rogal. **Season:** year round. **Hours:** by chance or appointment - phone line has daily message with hours for the day; if you don't find Anne in the studio, go to the house or barn, she's usually around. **Cards:** VS, MC. **Features:** earthenware flowerpots, planters, vases, trinket boxes, candle holders - rustic, playful or elegant ... and definitely unique; Anne is happy to let you watch her work, she'll even let you try some clay if she's not too busy.

Cape George/Sampsonville

Located about between Dundee and St. Peters.

The Greenhouse Co-Op

Location: Cape George Harbour, on West Bay segment of the Bras d'Or Lakes, 13 km (8 mi) from St. Peters. **Tel:** 902-535-3129. **Owners:** a workers co-op with 5 members. **Season:** May, Jun, to mid-Jul. **Hours:** 9 am to 8 pm; Sun noon to 5 pm. **Features:** bedding plants: annuals, perennials, veggies; shrubs; garden supplies; advice; container gardens a specialty.

Bras d'Or Lighthouse Camp

Location: Cape George, 8 km (5 mi) from St. Peters, 25 km (16 mi) from Dundee. **Mail Addr:** Box 317, St. Peters, N.S. B0E 3B0. **Tel:** 902-227-7740. **Owners:** B. & M. Schinzig. **Season:** Jun to Oct. **Rates:** med-high; **Cards:** VS. **Features:** housekeeping cottages with fireplaces; beach; hiking trails; bike and canoe rentals.

Carter's Lakeside Cottages

Location: Sampsonville, about 5 km (3 mi) from St Peters. **Mail Addr:** R. R. #2, St.Peters, N.S. B0E 3B0. **Tel:** 902-535-2453. **Owner:** C. & A. Carter. **Season:** year round. **Rates:** mid-range. **Cards:** VS, MC. **Features:** located on Bras d'Or Lake; swimming.

➵ **EN ROUTE** - keep on this road until you get to St. Peters.

To continue on to Sydney from St. Peters, see page 182.

Alternate Route from Port Hawkesbury to St. Peters or from St. Peters to Port Hawkesbury

VIA
Isle Madame

This option takes you from Louisdale, across the Lennox Passage Bridge, around Isle Madame and back to the Lennox Passage Bridge.

Directions from Port Hawkesbury: take Hwy 104 east and take Exit 46. Turn right off the ramp and drive less than a kilometre to an intersection with a yellow overhead light. Keep straight through and you will find yourself, after two or three kilometres, crossing the Lennox Passage Bridge.

Directions from St. Peters: drive west out of the village until you come to the turnoff to the left to River Bourgeois. (see map on page 225) Then follow the route below in reverse.

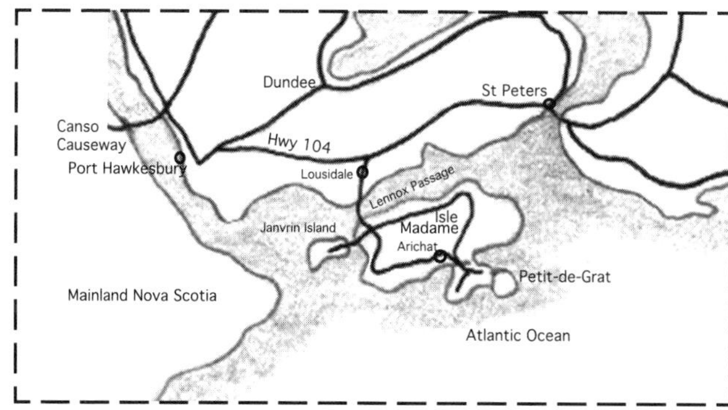

Pt Hawkesbury, St Peters & Isle Madame

Louisdale/Lennox Passage

Located on Rte 320, just north of the Lennox Passage Bridge to Isle Madame.

Cottage Bakery and Tearoom

Location: Lennox Passage, on the road to the Lennox Passage Bridge. **Tel:** 902-345-2229. **Season:** year round. **Hours:** Mon to Fri 7 am to 6 pm; Sat 10 am to 4 pm; closed Sun.

Britten's Ultramar - Lennox Passage, on road to the Lennox Passage Bridge; 902-223-2953; open from 7:30 am to 9 pm Mon to Sat, and on Sun from 10 am to 9 pm.

EN ROUTE - Once you cross the Lennox Passage Bridge (you're now, of course, on Isle Madame), you'll come to another junction. Turn right onto Rte 206.

Isle Madame

Isle Madame, one of Cape Breton's most picturesque and rugged seacoast communities, is situated off the south coast of Cape Breton, between Port Hawkesbury and St. Peters. It is decidedly Acadian and its French heritage goes way back to the 1600's when Basque and French fishermen set up temporary fishing huts there. You'll find the history intriguing, the beaches enchanting and the scenery inspiring.

West Arichat/Janvrin Island

West Arichat on Rte 206 begins about 3 km (1.8 mi) south of the junction of Routes 206 and 320. The Janvrin Island turnoff is in West Arichat.

Vollmer's Island Paradise

This is a wonderful, secluded, oceanside retreat.

Location: Janvrin Harbour, Janvrin Island. Turn off at West Arichat and follow signs to Janvrin Hbr. **Mail Addr:** Box 53, West Arichat, N.S. B0E 3J0. **Tel:** 902-226-1507; Fax 902-226-9853. **Owner:** A. Vollmer. **Season:** May to Oct. - other times by arrangement. **Rates:** mid-range. **Cards:** VS, MC. **Restaurant Hours:** 7 am to 10 pm daily, reservations required. **Restr Prices:** mid-range to med-high. **Features:** log cottages and a small, original fisherman's house; canoeing; bike rentals; walking trails; fishing; scuba diving - equipment & lessons; small restaurant (no smoking).

Bike Hike - Janvrin Island

This is not an official cycling route or anything, as far as I know, but I think it's a super place for a lovely leisurely bike ride along the ocean. In some places the road is so close to the ocean you can almost reach out and touch it as you go by. The road is very flat and there's very little traffic.

West Arichat Co-Op (grocery store) - Rte 206; 902-226-2220; open Mon to Sat 9 am to 9 pm; Sun 1 pm to 5 pm.

Chichton Island Hike

A walk around an island, off an island, off an island!

Location: West Arichat, Rte 206 about 7 km (4.3 mi) south of the junction of routes 206 and 320. **Directions to Trail**: Just past the Co-op store in West Arichat, turn onto Creighton Rd. and drive to the breakwater. Park there. There was a time when you could have driven your car across the breakwater, but no longer. As a matter of fact, I suggest you walk carefully as it is badly deteriorated...safe enough, but with large cracks and crevices.

Julia Longacre

Caution: do not attempt to walk across in a storm or high sea...you are at the ocean's mercy there and could easily get swept off! **Features:** the trail begins just up from the breakwater, takes you along the coast and through wooded areas, around the small island, about 4.5 km (2.8 mi) return; there are some roads leading across the island too which you can explore; lots and lots of wildflowers, berries, birds, and wonderful views of West Arichat and the ocean; keep your eye out for seals in the Harbour.

Isle Madame Service Stn - West Arichat, Rte 206; **Tel:** 902-226-3592; open year round Mon to Sat 7 am to 9 pm, Sun from 9 am to 9 pm; gas, deisel, propane.

Maison Emile-Mouchet B & B

Location: West Arichat, Rte 206. **Mail Addr:** General Del, West Arichat, N.S. B0E 3J0. **Tel:** 902-226-9740. **Owner:** M. LeBlanc. **Season:** May to Oct; o/s by arrangement. **Features:** ocean setting.

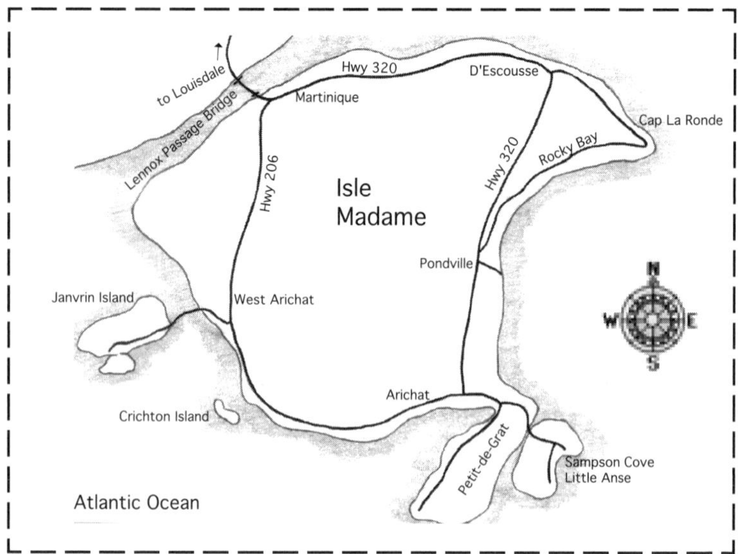

Arichat

Located on Isle Madame, on Rte 206, 11 km (6.6 mi) from the Lennox Passage Bridge. The name is Mi'kmaq for 'camping ground.

In Arichat you'll find service stations, grocery and convenience stores, churches, fast food outlets, as well as the facilities listed below.

Lower Road, Arichat

Located along the water; take any side street off the main street toward the water.

Le Noir Forge

This small museum will take you back to the days when Arichat was a bustling seaport and the forge a vital part of Isle Madame's thriving shipbuilding industry.

Location: Arichat, Lower Road. **Tel:** 902-226-2800. **Season:** May - Sept. **Features:** restored 18th century blacksmith shop; historical information about the area.

Turnstone Pottery (Studio)

Location: Lower Road, Arichat. **Tel:** 902-226-3004. **Owner and Potter**: Jack Outlette. **Season:** year round. **Hours:** by appointment only. **Cards:** MC. **Features:** distinct and beautiful pottery designs crafted on premises.

Gulliver's Landing Tea Room

Location: Lower Rd, Arichat. **Tel:** 902-226-9680. **Season:** year round. **Hours:** weekdays 10 am to 3 pm officially, but somewhat flexible; closed on weekends, but this may change in the summer. **Features:** cozy tearoom; home baked desserts; soups; salads; sandwiches; specialty teas and coffee.

High Road, Arichat

This is actually Rte 206, which runs through the village.

Isle Madame Customized Crafts

Location: High Rd, Arichat. **Tel:** 902-226-3132. **Owner:** B. Samson. **Season:** year round. **Hours:** 10 am - 5 pm daily. **Features:** crafts made with silk & dried flowers; ceramics.

Vina Motel

Location: High Rd, Arichat, Rte 206. **Mail Addr:** Box 91, Arichat, N.S. B0E 1A0. **Tel:** 902-226-2662/2774. **Owner**: Thai Luong. **Season:** year round. **Rates:** med-low. **Cards:** VS, MC.

L'Auberge Acadienne Inn and Restaurant

Location: Arichat, High Rd, Rte 206. **Mail Addr:**Box 59, Arichat, N.S. B0E 1A0. **Tel:** 902-226-2200/2150; Fax 902-226-1424. **Owner:** B. Boudreau. **Season:** May - Oct. **Rates:** med-high. **Cards:** VS, MC, AE. **Features:** 19-century style Acadian inn; licenced.

Dooley's Pharmacy - High Road, Arichat; 902-226-3133; open year round Mon to Fri 9 am to 9 pm, Sat 9 am to 5 pm and Sun 2 pm to 4 pm.

Nova Scotia Liquor Commission- High Road, Arichat; 902-226-2580; open in winter months Mon to Sat 9 am to 6 pm; Jul to Labour Day extended hours are Fri and Sat till 10 pm.

➼ **EN ROUTE**

Once you get through the village of Arichat, you'll come to a junction where Rte 206 meets again with Rte 320.

Keep straight on Rte 206 East, through this intersection to get to Petit-de-Grat. If you decide not to go to Petit-de-Grat, turn left at this junction onto Rte 320 north to Pondville/D'Escousse. (see map above)

Petit-de-Grat

(When it's said quickly it sounds like "petty de graw".)

Located on Isle Madame. Drive 3 km (1.8 mi) from the intersection of Rte 206 and Rte 320 in Arichat (see above) to a stop sign. Turn left.

'A spot where cod is dried'

The name **'Petit-de-Grat'** is a combination of French and Basque words that mean *a spot where cod is dried.* It is believed that the first resident of Petit-de-Grat was Gabriel Samson, a fisherman who came from Louisbourg in 1714. Other French and Acadian families followed his example and settled in the shelter of the coves, safe from their enemies.

Bonin Automotive - service station, Petit-de-Grat; 902-226-2343; open Mon to Sat from 8 am to 9 pm; Sun from 10 am to 9 pm; gas and deisel.

Centre Communautaire Acadien de Petit-de-Grat

Location: Petit-de-Grat, next to church **Tel:** 902-226-2800. **Season:** year round. **Hours:** generally in summer the centre is open from 8:30 am to 4 pm Mon to Fri and sometimes on the weekends. **Features:** historical and geneology records; information on Acadian culture and language; and general information about the Petit-de-Grat area.

Cachet de Cadeaux (Gift Shop)

Location: in the Centre Communautaire Acadien (see above). **Tel:** 902-226-2298. **Season:** Jun to Labour Day, other times by appointment. **Hours:** 9 am to 4:30 pm daily. **Cards:** VS, MC. **Features:** hand painted vases, canvases, plaques, etc by local Acadian artist Ronald a Gonzague.

Sampson Cove and Little Anse

While you're in Petit-de-Grat, you may want to take a short drive to **Sampson Cove** and **Little Anse**, two communities perched on the brink of the Atlantic.

Stop off for a picnic, or a walk along the beach - you'll enjoy every minute.

Directions: at the church in Petit-de-Grat, turn left and drive across the bridge; turn left at the Co-op store, then right up the hill.

Petit-de-Grat Co-op (grocery store) - at the church in Petit-de-Grat turn left and go across the bridge to the junction. **Tel:** 902-226-2023. **Hours:** open Mon & Tue from 9 am to 6 pm; Wed & Thurs from 9 am to 9 pm; Fri from 9 am to 6 pm; Sat from 9 am to 5 pm. **Note:** although this is a member co-op, I'm told tourists and visitors may shop there and will be treated just like members.

➵ EN ROUTE

Retrace your steps back from Sampson Cove and Little Anse, don't forget to turn right at Co-op Store to go back over the bridge, then turn right again. Once you drive through the village of Petit-de-Grat, past the service station, watch for the road that turns to your right. Drive about 3 km (1.8 mi) to an intersection. Turn right onto Rte 320 north. This will take you to Pondville and D'Escousse.

Pondville

Located on Rte 320, about 3 km (1.8 mi) northeast of junction of Rte 320 and Rte 206 at Arichat. (See map pg 218.)

Greg's Fuels - Service Station - located on Rte 320, just north of the junction of Rte 206 and 320; open Mon to Fri 7 am to 5 pm, Sat from 8 am to 4 pm, closed on Sun; 902-226-2172.

Acadian Campsite

Location: Pondville, Rte 320, 2.5 km (1.5 mi) northeast of Arichat. **Mail Addr:** Box 24, Arichat, N.S. B0E 1A0. **Tel:** 902-226-2447. **Owners:** C. & C. Davenport. **Season:** mid-May to mid-Oct. **Rates:** avg. **Features:** serviced and unserviced sites; washrooms and showers; lake swimming, boat rental, camping supplies.

Pondville Beach and Hike

Enjoy the sand dunes of this very pleasant ocean beach and park area. You also find here a large salt marsh with a fascinating assortment of birds.

Location: Take Rte 320 north from Arichat or Petit-de-Grat and drive about 3 km (1.8 mi). You'll see two roads close together off to the right. Take the first one - you should see the park sign (it's small). The beach is a short distance down this road. **Features:** picnic tables, toilets of the "out-house" variety, hiking trail along coast, lovely ocean beach. (water is a tad cool there, but very refreshing.); salt marsh;

D'Escousse

Located on Rte 320, about 10 km (6 mi) north of Arichat, and about the same distance east of the Lennox Passage Bridge. (see map pg 218)

Lennox Passage Yacht Club

Location: D'Escousse, Isle Madame, Rte 320. **Tel:** 902-226-1162. **Features:** marina facilities; launching and mooring facilities; engine and sail repair available; gas, diesel nearby.

D'Escousse B & B

Location: D'Escousse, Isle Madame, Rte 320. **Mail Addr:** R. R. #1, D'Escousse, N.S. B0E 1K0. **Tel:** 902-226-2936. **Owner:** S. & A. McDonald. **Season:** mid-May to mid-Oct. **Rates:** med-low. **Features:** ocean swimming.

Esso Station, D'Escousse, Isle Madame. **Tel:** 902-226-2998; open Mon to Sat 9 am to 9 pm; closed Sun.

Claire's Cafe and Restaurant

Location: D'Escousse, Isle Madame. **Tel:** 902-226-1432. **Season:** year round. **Hours:** Jun to early Oct - 8 am to midnight. **Cards:** VS, MC, AE.

Spring Tide Pottery

A working pottery studio and shop.

Location: D'Escousse, Isle Madame. **Tel:** 902-226-3456 **Season:** year round. **Hours:** Jun to Sept - 10 am to 5 pm, Tue to Sat; other months by chance or appointment. **Cards:** VS, MC. **Features:** functional earthenware; dinnerware and serving dishes; commission work; shipping available.

Martinique

Located on Rte 320 between D'Escousse and the Lennox Passage Bridge.

Lennox Passage Provincial Park

As you complete the loop of Isle Madame, you'll come upon this beautiful provincial park in Martinique, about 5 km (3 mi) past D'Escousse on Route 320. The park is situated on the site of the former Grandique Ferry crossing from Isle Madame to 'mainland' Cape Breton.

Location: Martinique, Isle Madame - Rte 320 about halfway between D'Escousse and Lennox Passage Bridge. **Features:** picnic tables; saltwater beach; hiking trail; lighthouse; great beachcombing; toilets.

➳ **EN ROUTE**

About 4 km (2.5 mi) from the Lennox Passage Provincial Park, you'll come back to the intersection where you started your journey around Isle Madame.

To leave the island, keep to your right here, drive back over the Lennox Passage Bridge to another junction [about 4 km (2.4 mi)]. At this junction, turn right to Louisdale, which will eventually take you to St. Peters.

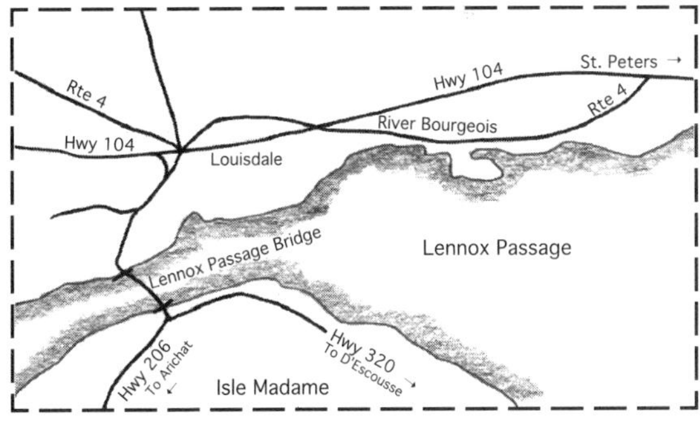

Louisdale/ River Bourgeois Area

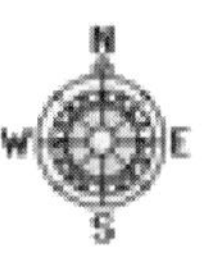

Louisdale/River Bourgeois

Coming from Isle Madame, Louisdale is about 4 km (2.4 mi) north of the Lennox Passage Bridge. Turn right at the yellow flashing light.

River Bourgeois is east of Louisdale (closer to St. Peters). Turn right at the intersection at Grand Anse, just past Louisdale.

Notice that the highway changes at this intersection from Rte 320 to Rte 4.

Note: You can get to Louisdale directly from Rte 104 from Port Hawkesbury or St. Peters by taking exit 46 or 47 off Rte 104. (see map above)

Margie's Village Cafe

Location: Main Street, Louisdale, Rte 320. **Tel:** 902-345-2472. **Owner:** M. Cornell. **Season:** year round. **Hours:** 7 am to 11 pm. **Prices:** low. **Cards:** MC. **Features:** full menu specializing in deep fried clams (they're great!); fully-licensed lounge.

La Cuisine Acadienne - Restaurant and Lounge

Location: Main Street, Louisdale, Route 320. **Tel:** 902-345-2817. **Owner:** L. Marchand. **Season:** year round. **Hours:** Sun to Thurs 6 am to 12 pm; Fri & Sat 6 am to 2 am. **Prices**: mid-range. **Cards:** all major cards. **Features:** homemade Acadian-style fare; view of harbour; not far from Dundee Golf Course and Resort.

Seal Cove B & B

This B & B is in a lovely location with the ocean and small islands almost in the back yard; deck overlooking harbour.

Location: 341 Main Street, Louisdale,Route 320. **Mail Addr:** Box 665, Louisdale, N.S. B0E 1V0. **Tel:** 902-345-2155. **Owner:** V. Sampson. **Season:** May to Oct. **Rates:** med-low. **Features:** picnic tables and deck; very clean and well kept.

J & C General Store and Take Out, River Bourgeois; 902-535-2050; open summer - Sun to Thurs 11 am to 11 pm; Fri & Sat 11 am - 12 pm; accepts VS, MC.

Grandma's House B & B

Antiques and gift shop as well as B & B.

Location: River Bourgeois, Rte 4 **Mail Addr:** R. R. #1, River Bourgeois, N.S. B0E 2X0. **Tel:** 902-535-2512. **Owners:** R. & T. Scott. **Season:** mid-May to mid-Oct. **Rates:** med-low. **Cards:** VS MC. **Features:** lovely restored Victorian house furnished with antiques; one room has private patio overlooking river; antique and gift shop on premises.

➛ **EN ROUTE** - About 3 km (1.8 mi) past River Bougeois you'll come to another intersection. Turn right towards St. Peters. (to continue on to Sydney, go to page 181.)

Artist Ollie MacKinnon, Sydney, 564-5166

The Legacy of the Sea

"It was medieval fishermen, drawn by the incredible abundance of northern cod on the teeming Grand Banks and Gulf of St. Lawrence, who first settled on Cape Breton, and for more than 500 years the fishery has been a dominant theme of island life. The origins of some of the tiny fishing villages, especially along the eastern shore, are lost in the mists of time, but men have been leaving them to work the fishing grounds since before the beginnings of recorded Cape Breton history, just as they continue to do today.

Fishing, and the toil, discomfort and danger of plying the trade on the stormy North Atlantic, winter and summer, have left an indelible mark on the character of both the island and its people."

...from *A Place Apart, The Cape Breton Story*, by James B. Lamb and Warren Gordon, Stone House Publishing, Inc. 1988.

Travel Option 5

Fleur-de-lis Trail

Canso Causeway to Louisbourg
Louisbourg to Canso Causeway
VIA L'Ardoise, Grand River, Gabarus

Some communities on *Travel Option 5*

- Port Hastings
- Port Hawkesbury
- St. Peters
- L'Ardoise
- Grand River
- Fourchu
- Louisbourg

Side Trips

- Isle Madame
- Dundee
- Marble Mountain
- Gabarus

Special Features

- √ St. Peter's Canal
- √ wonderful south coast beaches
- √ hiking trails
- √ light traffic on most roads
- √ museums
- √ Fortress of Louisbourg

Travel Option 5 takes you across the Island by way of the Fleur-de-lis Trail. You will travel through Port Hawkesbury and St. Peters, then along the south coast of the Island through L'Ardoise, Grand River, Fourchu and other coastal communities.

This is a lightly-travelled road with some wonderfully scenic spots. You'll have the option of taking a detour to **Gabarus** - a postcard perfect fishing village, or to take a Side Trip around the beautiful **Acadian** communities on **Isle Madame**. You can also choose to take an alternate route from Port Hawkesbury to St. Peters via **Dundee** and **Marble Mountain.**

At the present time, there are still some short stretches of the Fleur- de-lis Trail that are not paved, but the gravel portions of the road are in good condition.

I suggest that in order to really appreciate this wonder-fully unspoiled, uncluttered coast, (parts of the road are not in view of the ocean) you should take some time to drive down some of the side roads which lead you to beautiful ocean beaches.

➵ **EN ROUTE**

If you're travelling east, your travels begin in Port Hastings, just over the Canso Causeway. Once you cross the Causeway, you'll come to a rotary from which you can travel in several different directions.

If you're driving straight through on Travel Option 5, you won't have to actually go around the rotary. Just keep to your right, past the Visitor Information Centre, toward Port Hawkesbury on Route 104.

However, some of the facilities in this area are at various spots around the rotary so don't miss them.

I suggest as well that you stop off at the Visitor Information Centre...you'll find lots of brochures and information.

All the facilities are listed in order of appearance along the route. If any facility is 'off the beaten path', directions are given

Port Hastings

The village of **Port Hastings**, the "gateway to the Isle", is the first community you'll see after you cross the Causeway, and the last one you'll see before you cross to the mainland. It isn't a large community, but it does have motels, restaurants, gas stations and one of the Island's main Visitor Information Centres. All the roads leading east, south and north fan out from Port Hastings.

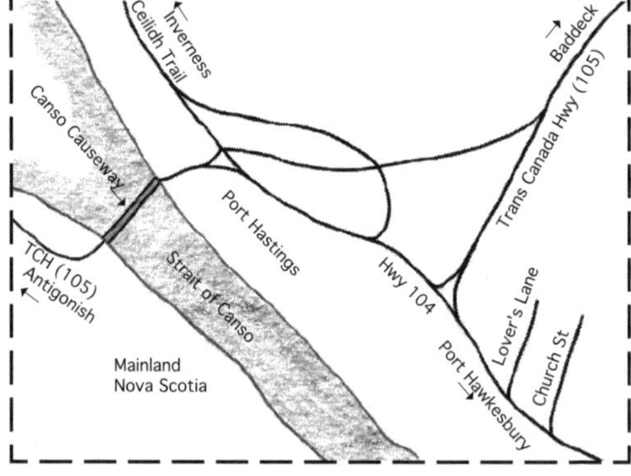

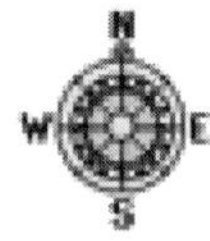

Nova Scotia Visitor Information Centre

This should probably be your first stop once you cross the Canso Causeway. It is located on the water side of the road, just over the Causeway.

Location: Port Hastings at the rotary. **Tel:** 902-625-1717. **Season**: mid-May to mid-Oct. **Hours**: generally from 9 am to 9 pm, but sometimes closes a little earlier, depending on demand.

Glen Auld Gifts

Located: Port Hastings, next to Visitor Information Centre. **Tel:** 902-625-1649. **Owner**: G. MacLean. **Season:** mid-May to Thanksgiving. **Hours:** summer months 8:30 am to 9 pm daily; other months 9 am - 5 pm daily. **Cards**: VS, MC. **Features**: large selection of gifts, crafts and souvenirs.

Keddy's Inn and Dining Room

Location: Port Hastings. Go part way around the rotary and turn right just before the Esso Station. **Mail Addr:** Box 50, Port Hastings, B0E 2T0. **Tel**: 625-0460; toll-free 1-800-

561-7666; Fax 625-1275. **Season:** year round. **Rates:** mid-range. **Cards**: most major cards. **Dng Rm Hrs:** 7 am to 11am; 5 pm to 10pm daily. **Prices**: mid-range. **Features**: licensed dining room and lounge; seniors discounts.

Port Hastings Esso - just over the Canso Causeway; 902-625-1100; open from 7 am to 11 pm daily; gas,deisel.

Smitty's Restaurant

Location: Port Hastings, at the rotary. **Owners:** M. & J. Chisholm. **Tel**: 902- 625-3346; Fax 902-625-2914. **Season**: year round. **Hours**: summer 6:30 am - 11pm; winter 7am - 10 pm daily. **Price**s: low to mid-range. **Cards:** VS, AE, debit cards. **Features:** large, bright family-style eatery; wide selection; specialty menu items for seniors, children and health conscious
.

Skye Travelodge and Dining Room

Location: Port Hastings, at the rotary. **Mail Addr**: Box 190, Port Hastings, N.S. B0E 2T0. **Tel:** 902-625-1300, Fax 902-625-1966, toll free 1-800-578-7878. **Season:** Year round. **Rates:** mid-range. **Cards:** most major cards. **Dng Rm Hrs:** 7 am to 10 pm daily. **Dng Rm Prices**: low to mid-range. **Features:** award-winning licensed dining room; overlooking Strait of Canso.

Artist Thorn Morrow, Sydney. **See page 258.**

MacPuffin Inn, Dining Room and Gift Shop

Location: Lover's Lane, Port Hastings - first street to your left after the Skye Travelodge. **Mail Addr**: Box 558, Port Hawkesbury N.S. B0E 2V0. **Tel:** 902-625-2283; toll free 1-800-867-2212; Fax 625-1525. **Owner**: Kenzie Jones. **Season**: Jun - Oct **Rates:** from mid-range to upper end. **Cards:** most major cards. **Features:** complimentary continental breakfast, family rates: gift shop; putting green; swimming pool.

Port Hastings Museum and Archives

Location: 367 Church St, Port Hastings - second street to your left after you pass the Skye Travelodge. **Mail Addr:** Box 115, Port Hastings, N.S. B0E 2T0. **Tel:** 902-625-1295. **Season**: Jun - Oct. **Hours:** Jul & Aug - Mon to Fri 9 am to 8 pm; Sat & Sun 12 noon to 4 pm; other months - Mon to Fri 9 am to 5 pm. **Features**: genealogy records, artifacts, newspapers relating to the Strait of Canso area.

MacPuffin Motel, Dining Room & Gift Shop

Location: Port Hastings, about 3 km (1.8 mi) from the rotary on Rte 104. **Mail Addr:** Box 558, Port Hawkesbury, N.S. B0E 2V0. **Tel:** 902-625-0621; Fax 902-625-1525; 1-800-867-2212. **Owner:** K. Jones. **Season:** May - Dec. **Rates:** rooms mid-range; suites upper end. **Cards:** most major cards. **Dng Rm Hrs:** 7 am - 10 am; 6pm - 9 pm. **Prices**: mid-range. **Features:** Licensed; air purified rooms available; laundromat; gift shop; indoor pool.

Port Hawkesbury Motel and Dining Room

Location: Port Hastings - 3 km (1.8 mi) from the rotary on Rte 104. **Mail Addr:** Box 549, Port Hawkesbury, N.S. B0E 2V0. **Tel:** 902-625-2480. **Owner:** M. Adams. **Season:** year round. **Rates:** mid-range. **Cards:** VS, MC, AE. **Dng Rm Hrs:** 6 am to 9 pm. **Dng Rm Prices:** mid-range.

➵ **EN ROUTE** - About 6 km (3.5 mi) from the Canso Causeway on Rte 104 (straight past the Visitor Information Centre) you'll come to the turnoff to Granville Street. This will take you to the 'downtown' part of Port Hawkesbury.

Downtown Port Hawkesbury (Granville St)

Turn down Granville Street off Rte 104 (see above) and drive along the water to the business district of the Town.

Harbourview B & B

Location: 209 Granville St, Port Hawkesbury. **Mail Addr:** 209 Granville St, Port Hawkesbury, N.S. B0E 2V0. **Tel:** 902-625-3224. **Owner:** M. Pase. **Season:** mid-May to mid-Oct. **Rates:** med-low. **Cards:** VS. **Features:** restored heritage property; located on Strait of Canso; smoke-free property; full breakfast.

The Creamery

On the Waterfront.

Location: Granville St, Port Hawkesbury. Farmers market, craft market, ceilidhs, concerts, and much more...see below.

The Waterfront
Granville St, Port Hawkesbury.

The citizens of Port Hawkesbury have been busy these last couple of years, and things are really starting to take shape there on the waterfront. On Granville St you'll find **The Creamery** (see below), a centre for lots and lots of activities. For instance...from Jun to Oct a farmers' market and craft fair every Sat from 9 am to 3 pm; Tuesday evening Ceilidhs (fiddling, stepdancing, etc) at 7 pm,July to Sept; and outdoor concerts every Sun night from Jul to Sept; boat and scuba diving tours and scuba diving; deck for picnics and relaxing; ice cream parlour and lunch counter; Pub for special events (weekly schedule posted); dinner theatre. See book insert for dates of events.

At the Waterfront, too, you'll find a Pirate Ship playground, horse and buggy rides during the Farmer's Market; and a train ride that will take you from Port Hawkesbury to the Railway Museum in Orangedale.

And a little farther down the street, there'll be a boat builder for you to watch, an art gallery and gift shop (below) and a cafe.

For more information on the Waterfront activities call **902-625-3224** during business hours.

Customs House Gallery & Gifts

See local marine artist J. Franklin Wright's originals and prints, as well as other local art work and crafts.

Location: on the Waterfront, Granville St, Port Hawkesbury. **Tel:** 902-625-2747. **Owner:** B. MacKinnon. **Season:** year round (opening 1996 on July 1). **Hours:** 9 am to 8 pm daily. **Cards:** VS, MC, Interac. **Features:** original art, sculpture, wrought iron; pottery; handcrafted gifts and souvenirs; information on where you can find other artists and craftspeople on the Island.

Reeves Street, Port Hawkesbury

Located along Rte 104, about 7 km (4 mi) from the Canso Causeway, Reeves St. is actually part of Rte 104.

Along here you'll find several service stations and quite a few fast food restaurants like Subway, Dairy Queen ,Tim Hortons, KFC and others. You'll also find three small shopping plazas... the Causeway Shopping Centre and the Island Gateway Plaza, both on your left, and a little further up on your right is the Chediac Plaza.

In these plazas you'll find an assortment of grocery stores, convenience stores,department stores, banks etc.

The following are some of the facilities you'll find in the Reeves St. area:

MacKeigan's Pharmacy, Causeway Shopping Centre, Reeves St, Port Hawkesbury; **Tel:** 902-625-1113; **Hours:** Mon to Fri open 9 am to 9 pm; Sat 9 am to 6 pm.

Nova Scotia Liquor Commission, Causeway Shopping Centre, Reeves St, Port Hawkesbury; **Tel:** 902-625-2010; regular hours are Mon to Wed 10 am to 6 pm; Thurs to Sat 10 am to 10 pm; in summer hours are extended a bit so you might want to call ahead.

Some Restaurants on Reeves St

- Papa's Pub & Eatery, Island Gateway Plaza; 902-625-3270
- Rose Garden Restr, Island Gateway Plaza; 902-625-5600.
- Louis' Family Restr, Reeves St; 902-625-0111
- Billy Joe's Place, Reeves St.

Auberge Wandlyn Inn and Dining Room

Location: 689 Reeves Street, Port Hawkesbury, N.S. B0E 2V0. **Mail Addr:** Box 759, Port Hawkesbury, N.S. B0E 2V0. **Tel:** 902-625-0320; Fax 902-625-3876; 1-800-561-0000 (cntrl & easternCanada); 1-800-561-0006 (USA). **Season:** year round. **Rates:** med-high to upper end. **Cards:** major cards. **Dng Rm Hrs:** 7 am - 9:30 pm. **Prices**: mid-range. **Features:** licensed; outdoor and indoor pool.

➵ **EN ROUTE**

At the east end of Reeves St, Port Hawkesbury, there is a junction.

Turn left off Reeves St if you're heading east toward St. Peters.

If you're coming **from** St. Peters, turn left **onto** Reeves St.

Port Hawkesbury Centre

Location: Rte 104 (directions above); **Tel:** 902-625-0382. **Hours:** Mon to Wed 10 am to 6 pm; Thurs & Fri 10 am to 9 pm; Sat 10 am to 5 pm. **Features:** clothing stores, jeweller, Walmart, supermarket, bookstore etc.

Shoppers Drug Mart, located in Port Hawkesbury Centre (above); **Tel:** 902-625-1801. **Hours**: Mon to Fri 9 am to 9 pm; Sat 9 am to 6 pm; Sun and holidays 1 pm to 5 pm.

More Travel Options

If you're heading east, you have **three** choices now as to how you'll travel to St. Peters from Port Hawkesbury:

Opt (a)- you can drive **directly** to St. Peters on Hwy 104 (details are below);
Opt (b) - you can take an alternative route via **Isle Madame** (details are at the end of Travel Option 4, page 215)
Opt (c) - you can take a detour through **Dundee**. (details are at the end of Travel Option 4, page 208)

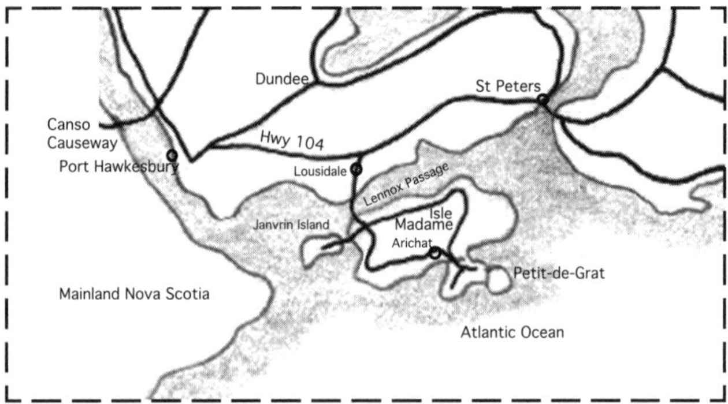

Port Hawkesbury, St Peters & Isle Madame

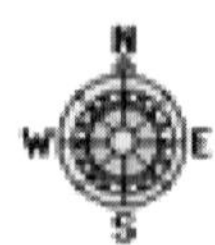

Port Hawkesbury to St. Peters
The DIRECT ROUTE ↔ Hwy 104

Directions: Just past the Port Hawkesbury Centre, is a turnoff ramp to St. Peters. Turn here onto Hwy 104, which is a limited access highway with no facilities on it except the hospital below. Follow Hwy 104 until you get to St. Peters.

Coming west from St. Peters, just drive on Hwy 104 to the end and follow the signs.

The Strait Richmond Hospital at Evanston; **902-625-3100**, about 12 km (7 mi) or so from Port Hawkesbury.

St. Peter's

Located about 43 km (25.5 mi) east of Port Hawkesbury and 85 km (51 mi) west of Sydney.

St. Peters is a busy little village in which the main business street is actually part of the highway. You'll find convenience and grocery stores, post office and service stations (open until at least 10 pm in summer months) as well as the facilities listed below.

Glad Tidings (Christmas shop)

Location: St. Peters, as you come into the village from the west. **Tel:** 902-535-2248. **Season:** May to Dec 24. **Hours**: Mon, Tue, Wed & Sat - 9 am to 5 pm; Thurs & Fri - 9 am to 9 pm; Sun - 9 am to 7 pm. **Cards:** VS, MC, Interac. **Features:** a great place to find gifts for those Christmasy friends back home.

Wallace MacAskill Museum and Gift Shop

...St. Peters is the birthplace of renowned marine photographer Wallace R. MacAskill.

Location: St. Peters. **Season:** Jul- Sept. **Hours:** 10 am - 6 pm. **Features:** restored original residence of W. MacAskill; display of his hand-tinted photographs; artifacts relating to his sailing hobby and his life

Presents of Mine Crafts and Gifts

A lovely selection of gift and souvenir items.

Location: Main St, St. Peters. **Tel:** 902-535-3199; Fax same. **Owner:** Fran Doyle. **Season:** year round. **Cards:** VS, MC, Interac.

Lynn's Flowers & Gifts

Location: Main St, St. Peter's. **Owner:** C. MacPhail. **Tel:** 902-535-2377, fax 902-535-2084. **Season:** year round. **Hours**: 9 am - 5 pm, Mon - Sat. **Cards:** VS, AE.

Parker's Restaurant and Coffee Shop

Location: Main St, St Peter's. **Tel:** 902-535-2405. **Season:** year round. **Hours:** weekdays - May to Oct 7 am to 10 pm; weekends - 7 am to 11 pm; coffee shop open from 6 am to midndight. (restaurant hours may be slightly longer in summer) **Cards:** VS, MC, AE. **Features:** family-style restaurant.

Lawton's Drugs - Main St, St. Peters; 902-535-2203; open Mon to Wed 9 am to 8 pm; Thurs & Fri 9 am to 9 pm; Sat 9 am to 5 pm; Sun 1 pm to 3 pm; extended summer hours are Sun from 12 noon to 5 pm.

River Tillard Hiking Trail

An old railway bed converted to a super nature trail along the shores of St. Peters Bay.

Location: St. Peters - in the centre of the village, turn down Pepperell St toward the water (right if you're heading toward Sydney); trail begins a couple of hundred yards down Pepperell St. **Features:** wonderful oceanside hike with views of lighthouse, Isle Madame; trail is 2 km (1.2 mi) to an old railway trestle at River Tillard; beaches and picnic tables; watch for blue herons, eagles and osprey.

> ➻ **EN ROUTE** - If you're heading west and want to take the Alternate Route through Dundee and Marble Mountain (page 208), turn off here at the Irving station.

MacDonald's Hotel and Dining Room

An older style hotel with continental breakfast.

Location: 9383 Pepperell St, St. Peter's. Turn at the Irving Station in the centre of the village. **Mail Addr**: Box 70, St. Peters, N.S. B0E 3B0. **Tel:** 902-535-2997; 535-2996. **Season:** Apr - Dec. **Rates:** low. **Cards:** most major cards. **Dng Rm Hrs:** 8 - 10 am; 11 am - 3 pm; 4:30 - 10 pm.

Nova Scotia Liquor Commission, St. Peters, 902-535-2117; open Mon to Thurs & Sat 10 am to 6 pm; Fri 10 am to 9 pm; extended summer hours - open Sat until 9 pm. -hours 535-2117?

MacDonnell Pharmacy - Main St, St. Peters, close to Canal; 902-535-3196; **emergency number** when store is closed **902-535-2173**; open Mon & Tue from 9am to 6 pm; Wed, Thurs & Fri from 9 am to 8 pm; Sat from 9 am to 5 pm; closed Sun.

Country Lane Crafts

Location: Main St, St. Peter's, near Canal. **Tel:** 902-535-3126, fax 902-535-3089. **Owners:** A. & M. Touesnard. **Season:** year round **Hours:** Mon - Wed & Sat 10 am to 5 pm; Thurs & Fri 10 am to 8 pm; Sun 1 to 4 pm. **Cards:** VS, MC, AE. **Features:** usually someone is working on a craft in the store so you can watch...maybe even learn how it's done.

Bras d'Or Lakes Inn and Restaurant

Large family-style restuarant.

Location: St. Peter's, by the Canal. **Mail Addr:** St. Peters, N.S. B0E 3B0. **Tel:** 902-535-2200; Fax 902-535-2784; 1-800-818-5885. **Season:** year round. **Rates:** mid-range. **Cards:** VS, MC, AE. **Dng Rm Hrs:** 7 am to 9 pm **Restr Prices:** mid-range. **Features:** lovely view of the lake; licensed.

St. Peters Marina

Location: St. Peters, at the Canal. **Mail Addr:** St. Peters, N.S. B0E 3B0. **Tel:** 902-535-2729. **Features:** floating finger docks for 15 - 20 boats; gas, diesel, water and power; washrooms with showers; laundry facilities; club room; picnic area.

Artist Ollie MacKinnon, Sydney, 564-5166.

St. Peter's Canal

The only functioning tidal lock system in Nova Scotia.

St. Peter's Canal

The area around the Canal at St. Peters has a long and fascinating history.

Before the builders of the canal blasted and dug away the solid granite isthmus that once separated the Altantic Ocean and the Bras d'Or Lakes, ocean-going ships had to be hauled overland from the Ocean to the Lake.

As early as 1520, Portugese fishermen used the isthmus as a seasonal fishing station. And before that the Mi'kmaqs used the isthmus to portage their canoes.

Its history is linked, too, with the activities at Fortress Louisbourg in the 1700's, providing the first line of defense to the fort via the "French Road", which ran eastward through the woods.

Location: St. Peters, east end of Village. **Tel:** 902-535-2118. **Season:** Canal is accessible year round. **Features:** interpretive exhibit outside; picnic facilities; mooring for boats; washrooms; wheelchair accessible.

Nicolas Denys Museum

Location: St. Peters, next to Canal, take road up along the canal on St. Peter's side. **Tel:** 535-2379. **Season:** Jun - Sept. **Hours:** 9 am - 5 pm daily. **Admission**: adults 50 cents, children 25 cents. **Features:** building is reminiscent of the original 1650 trading post built here by Nicolas Denys of France; washrooms, picnic area.

Battery Provincial Park

Location: St. Peters, on the Canal; take the road up along the Canal, on the Sydney side. **Tel:** 902-535-3094. **Season:** mid-Jun to early Sept. **Rates:** avg. **Features:** picnic area; unserviced sites; toilets, disposal station; cold water taps; fire grills; wood; beach; frontage on Canal.

Campbell's Dairy Freeze - Route 4 near the St. Peter's Canal - fast food, ice cream.

Nicolas Denys was one of Cape Breton's first true entrepreneurs. Apparently in 1677 he pursuaded the French government to give him the right to exact a duty from all persons who took coal or gypsum from Cape Breton...a tidy income, I'm sure, in itself; but in addition he was also granted permission to require all traders of fur to buy a license from him.

Joyce's Motel and Cottages

Location: St. Peters, 1.6 km. (1 mi.) east of village on Rte 4. **Mail Addr:** Box 193, St. Peter's N.S. B0E 3B0. **Tel:** 902-535-2404; o/s 902-535-2231. **Owners:** M.& R. Robertson. **Season:** mid-May to Oct. **Rates:** mid-range. **Cards:** VS, MC. **Features:** overlooking Bras d'Or Lakes; pool; launching dock; laundromat, playground; fishing; boat rental.

➵ **EN ROUTE** - About a km east of the St. Peter's Canal, just past the RCMP station, you'll come to a turnoff to Route 247 to L'Ardoise and Pt. Michaud. Turn here.

St. Peter's R.V. Campground

Location: St. Peters - just as you turn onto Rte 247. **Mail Addr:** Box 226, St. Peters, N.S. B0E 3B0. **Tel:** 535-3333; Fax 535-2202. **Owners:** R. & L. Wambolt. **Season:** Jun to Sept. **Rates:** avg. **Cards:** VS, Good Sam. **Features:** serviced and unserviced sites overlooking Bras d'Or Lake; washrooms; laundromat; camp cabins, fire pits; playground; heated pool.

Grand Greve

Located on Rte 247, about a km or so from the turnoff from Rte 4.

Grand Greve Beach

Location: Grand Greve, drive about 2 km (1.6 mi) on Rte 247 to a gravel road on your right. Drive down this road another 2 km (1.6 mi) to the beach. **Features:** This is a gorgeous sprawling beach with inlets and coves and a salt marsh; lots of birds, wildflowers and plants.

L'Ardoise

This French name has been anglicized over the years and you'll probably hear it pronounced "lordways".

Located on Rte 247. As you drive through the community of L'Ardoise you may want to take a short detour onto Chapel Cove Rd, which takes you on a very picturesque drive along the ocean where you'll find many of the homes of the community, as well as the school and church.

Fleur-de-lis Cafe

Location: L'Ardoise. **Tel:**902-587-2755. **Season:** May to Nov. **Hours:** 11 am to 11 pm daily.

➛ **EN ROUTE** - about 10 km (6 mi) from L'Ardoise you'll come to a crossroads. Keep straight to Pt. Michaud.

Crossroads Grocery Store - about 4 km (2.5 mi) from L'Ardoise; summer hours Mon to Sat 8 am to 10 pm; in winter store closes at 9 pm.

L'Ardoise, Grand River

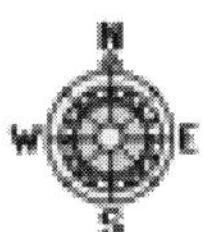

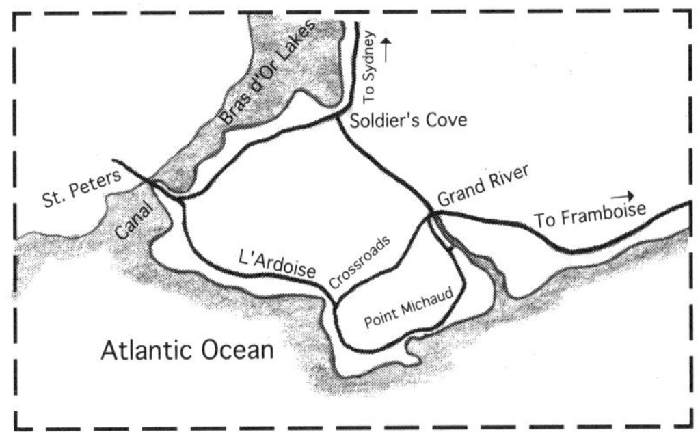

Pt. Michaud

Located on Rte 247 - about 7 km (4 mi) from crossroads. You actually leave the Fleur-de-lis Trail for a bit along here.

Point Michaud Provincial Park and Beach

A glorious sand beach that stretches for miles.

Location: About 7 or 8 km (4 mi) from the crossroads, watch for small "Park Entrance" sign. **Features:** a 3 km (1.8 mi) long sandy beach that's perfect for walking and beach-combing; water can be a little cool as it is the open Atlantic, but it has a long rolling surf that's fun for children. If there's a high sea, watch for undertows - beach is not supervised.; picnic area up the hill overlooking the ocean; picnic tables, toilets,changing rooms.

Grey Seal Weaving Studio

Location: Pt. Michaud Beach. Park in parking lot, or on top of hill in picnic area and walk down the hill to a small grey cabin. **Tel:** 902-587-2777. **Owner & Weaver**: Del Zoppo. **Season:** summer and fall. **Hours:** by chance or appointment. **Cards:** no. **Features:** working studio specializing in drawloom damask; silk scarves and shawls.

➵ EN ROUTE

Heading east: Not far from of Point Michaud Beach you'll come to the end of the pavement and then an intersection. Keep to your left to Grand River. Although this is a gravel road, it is wide and in good condition. About 4 km (2.5 mi) or so past the intersection you'll come to another unpaved road. This is the road to Indian Point Lodge (see below). Keep straight to get to Grand River.

Indian Point Lodge

A truly delightful hideaway for lovers of nature, solitude and outdoor activities.

Location: take the Indian Point Rd (see En Route above) and drive 2 km. **Mail Addr:** Grand River, N.S. B0E 1M0. **Tel:** 902-587-2410; Fax same. **Owners:** P. & B. Christians. **Season:** May - Oct. **Rates:** med-high to upper end. **Features:** housekeeping log cabins snuggled in among the trees; canoe with every cabin; hiking and other nature activities; river and ocean setting; fishing; swimming.

Julia Longacre

Grand River

Located about 12 km (7 mi) east of L'Ardoise.

> An **alternative** way to get to Grand River from Rte 4 (St. Peters) is to drive east from St. Peter's to Soldier's Cove, about10 km (6 mi) then turn off at Grand River sign and drive 8 km (5 mi).

Riverside Confectionery, Grand River; 902- 587-2725; summer hours 7 am to 9 pm, except Sun 10 am to 9 pm.

Salmon View Housekeeping Log Cabins

Location: Grand River, across from Riverside Confectionery. **Mail Addr:** Grand River N.S. B0E 1M0. **Tel:** 902-587-2725; after 9 pm 587-2264. **Owner:** Ian MacLeod. **Rates:**med-low. **Season:** Apr - Dec. **Cards:** VS, MC, AE. **Features:** housekeeping log cabins, fishing, swimming, boat rentals, canoeing.

Bonnach and Molasses

Motel rooms and restaurant.

Location: Across the road from the Salmon View cottages, there's a one-lane bridge. Bonnach and Molasses is across the bridge .**Mail Addr:** 1826 Grand River, N.S. B0E 1M0. **Tel:** 902-587-2554. **Season:** May to Dec; Jan to Apr - weekends only. **Rates:** med-low. **Restr Hours:** summer 7 am - 10 pm; fall 7 am - 7 pm; winter weekends 11 am - 7 pm. **Restr Prices:** mid-range. **Cards:** VS, MC, Interac. **Features:** overlooks beautiful Grand River; canoeing nearby; fresh seafood in season.

L'Archeveque

This tiny fishing community is about 9 km (5.5 mi) east of Grand River. There's a road heading toward the water, you'll see the sign. It's only about a km down that road.

It's a great place for taking photographs, having a picnic or walking along the beach.

> There are several small communities spread quite widely along this road and you won't find any stores or gas until you get to Framboise, about 32 km (20 mi) away.
>
> To really appreciate this travel route, I advise you to take the time to drive down some of the side roads...stop off for a swim or a stroll along one of the gorgeous beaches, or take a short detour into Gabarus and explore a little.
>
> Because this south coast is not heavily travelled, or for that matter, populated, it has maintained it's unspoiled ruggedness and beauty and is a wonderful place to spend time.

Framboise

French for "raspberry", of which, no doubt, there are plenty.

Located on the Fleur-de-lis Trail, about 32 km (20 mi) east of Grand River.

Pioneer Cemetery

If you have a penchant for poking around old graveyards, this is an interesting little one overlooking the ocean. Sometimes you can learn a lot of history from the old headstones.

Location: at Framboise, just before the store, turn down the Crooked Lake Road and watch for the sign.

Village Store, Gas Bar and Tea Room

Your last chance to stock up on food and supplies for quite a few kilometres.

Location: Framboise, on the Fleur-de-lis Trail, about 32 km (20 mi) east of Grand River. **Tel:** 902-884-2356. **Hours:** 7 am to 8 pm daily. **Cards:** VS, MC, AE. **Features:** gas, take-out food; tea room; army surplus, crafts, minor car repairs and information.

➵ EN ROUTE

A few km east of Framboise you'll come to a junction. Turn here toward Fourchu. This will take you around Fourchu Harbour and through the fishing community of **Fourchu**, another one of the Island's truly quaint and charming coastal communities.

This was once a busy harbour, in the days of sail, with upwards of a thousand residents along its shores.

Fourchu

From french word 'fourchette' meaning 'fork'...referring, I presume, to the road. Located on the Fleur-de-lis Trail between Framboise and Gabarus.

Forchu Head Trail

A coastal hike and a shipwreck to explore.

Location: Back at the intersection where you turned off from Framboise, take the gravel road at the intersection and drive along the south side of the Harbour to the end; park there and walk to the beach on your right. **Features:** a walk along the shore to a shipwrecked trawler that broke up on the rocks in 1967, taking 10 lives. It's not exactly a Spanish galleon, but it **is** interesting and it's a lovely beach for exploring.

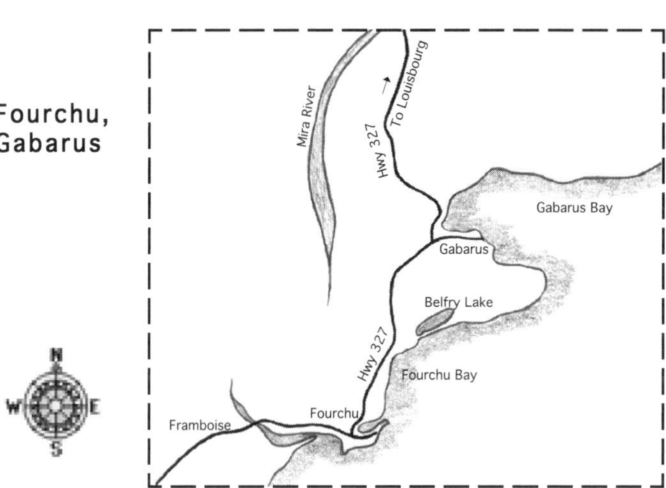

Fourchu, Gabarus

Belfry Beach

A glorious south shore beach situated on a narrow strip of land that separates Fourchu Bay from Belfry Lake. There's a channel that's great for kids to swim in (at high tide) and the beach and coast is a walker's paradise.

Location: Fleur de lis Trail, between Fourchu and Gabarus about 7 km (4 mi) northeast of Fourchu. Turn down a gravel road where you see the sign and just before you reach the beach, take the road to your left. This will take you to the channel and a good place to stop off.

➳ **EN ROUTE**
On your travels **eastward**, you'll come to a junction about 17 km (10 mi) northeast of Fourchu. A left turn here will take you north toward Marion Bridge and Louisbourg. However, if you want to visit the village of Gabarus, keep straight and drive for about 4 km (2.5 mi) into the village.

If you're travelling **westward** toward Grand River, turn right at the junction at Fourchu. If you want to visit Gabarus, turn left.

Gabarus

A short detour off the Fleur-de-lis takes you to the fishing village of Gabarus. It's a paradise for photographers and a super place, too, for those who just like to explore a beach, or take a hike.

When you reach the sea wall, you can park there and walk along the beach, or explore the village. If you'd like to take a more challenging hike along the coast, make your way to Gull Cove (below).

Julia Longacre

Gull Cove Hike

A lovely hike through woodlands and along the barren sea coast.

Location: When you come to the sea wall at Gabarus, turn right and drive (or walk) about a km to a cemetery. You'll see the trail heading into the woods. **Features:** If you go all the way - about 12 km (7 mi) return - you'll come to the remains of a very old fishing village - parts of the foundations of buildings. However, you can just go part way and turn back if you're not up for the entire trail.

➻ **EN ROUTE** - When you're finished poking around Gabarus, drive back to the intersection of Route 327 [about 4 km (2.5 mi) or so and turn right toward Marion Bridge, or keep straight to Grand River.

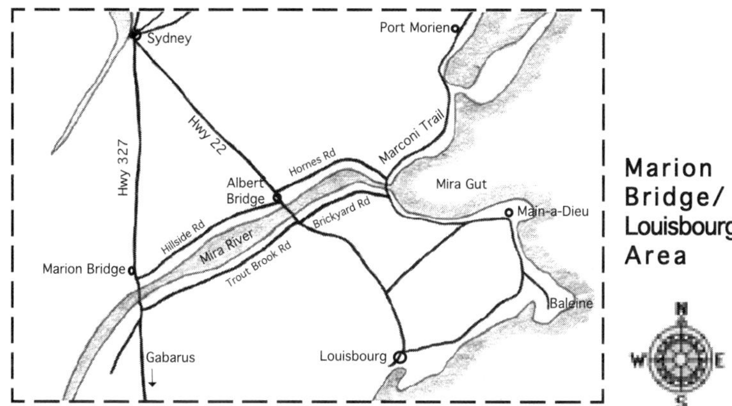

Marion Bridge/ Louisbourg Area

Marion Bridge

From Fourchu drive north on Rte 327 for about 20 km (12 mi) to a junction. Turn right and drive a km to Marion Bridge. The bridge takes you across the renowned Mira River.

Li'l Bit of Heaven B & B

Location: 371 Trout Brook Rd, Marion Bridge. Turn onto the Trout Brook Rd, just south of the bridge, and drive 2.5 km (1.5 mi). **Mail Addr:** 371 Trout Brook Rd, Marion Bridge, N.S. B0A 1P0. **Tel:** 902-727-2936. **Owners:** B. & C. Butts. **Season:** May - Oct; o/s by arrangement. **Rates:** med-low. **Features:** river swimming; boating; fishing.

Church's Cloverfarm Supermarket and Gas Bar

Location: Marion Bridge, Rte 327, just on the north side of the bridge. **Tel:** 902-727-2685; Fax same. **Owners:** J. & C. Church. **Season:** year round. **Hours:** daily until 9 pm. **Cards:** most major cards. **Features:** full line of groceries, bakery; gas bar.

MacKeigan's Bay Beach Park

Location: Sandfield Road, Marion Bridge - turn next to Church's Cloverfarm store. **Mail Addr:** Sandfield Rd, Marion Bridge, B0A 1P0. **Tel:** 902-727-2369. **Season:** Jun to Sept. **Rates:** avg. **Features:** serviced and unserviced sites; swimming; some groceries.

Two Rivers Wildlife Park

Location: Sandfield Road, Marion Bridge - turn next to Church's Cloverfarm store and drive about 10 km (6 mi). **Season:** mid-May to mid-Oct. **Hours:** 9 am to 7 pm daily. **Features:** black bears, cougars, moose, red deer, Sable Island ponies, bald eagles and others; picnic area on the Mira River with tables; toilets.

Victoria Bridge Housekeeping Cottages

Location: Victoria Bridge turn next to Church's Cloverfarm store and drive to Victoria Bridge. **Mail Addr:** Box 176, Glace Bay, N.S. B1A SV2. **Tel:** 902-727-2920. **Owner:** D. Gillis. **Season:** Jun to Oct. **Rates:** mid-range. **Cards:** VS, MC. **Features:** river swimming.

Tiggers

Location: Marion Bridge, Rte 327, on the north side of the bridge; 902-727-2653. **Features**: gifts, souvenirs, handcrafts.

➵ EN ROUTE

At Marion Bridge, on the north side of the bridge, you'll come to Hillside Road. This will take you along the Mira River for 14 km (8.5 mi) to Albert Bridge. From there you'll to on to Louisbourg.

Riverside B & B

Location: 1818 Hillside Road - turn onto Hilllside Rd at Marion Bridge and drive 4.5 km (3 mi) toward Albert Bridge. **Mail Addr:** Box 140, Marion Bridge, N.S., B0A 1P0. **Tel:**

902-727-2615. **Owner:** L. Ferguson. **Season:** May - Oct. **Rates:** med-low. **Cards:** VS, MC. **Features:** close to Fortress and other attractions; swimming and boating.

Mira Water Park and Campground

Location: Hillside Rd. Turn onto Hillside Rd at Marion Bridge, and drive about 7 km (4.2 mi) toward Albert Bridge. **Mail Addr:** Box 63, Marion Bridge, N.S. B0A 1P0. **Tel:** 902-564-1824/1674. **Season:** late May to Labour Day. **Rates:** avg. **Features:** serviced and unserviced sites on Mira River; washrooms; laundromat; disposal station; shelter; camping supplies.

Apple Tree Croft Antiques and Uniques

Location: Hillside Road, Turn onto Hillside Rd at Marion Bridge and drive 9 km (5.5 mi) toward Albert Bridge. **Tel:** 902-562-3433. **Season:** mid-Jun to Sept; other times by appointment. **Hours:** 11 am to 5 pm, Wed to Sun. **Cards:** VS. **Features:** quality glass, country and formal furniture, jewellry and uniques.

➼ **EN ROUTE** - After driving 14 km (8.5 mi) on Hillside Road from Marion Bridge, you'll come to Hwy 22, the Louisbourg Hwy, at Albert Bridge.

Albert Bridge

Located on Hwy 22, the Louisbourg Hwy, about 20 km (12 mi) north of Louisbourg.

Mira Ferry Convenience Store

Take Out and Gas Bar

Location: Albert Bridge, just on the Sydney side of the bridge. **Tel:** 562-4142. **Season:** year round. **Hours:** Jul and Aug - 6 am to 11 pm daily; other months 6 am to 10 pm. **Cards:** most major cards. **Features:** gas, diesel; take out, bakery,dockside service on Mira River.

Mullins Mini Mart

Gas station, restaurant, convenience store and postal outlet, all in one.

Location: Albert Bridge, just on the Louisbourg side of the bridge. **Tel:** 902-562-1070. **Season:** year round. **Hours:**

summer 6:30 am to 10:30 pm.; winter 7 am to 9 pm, daily. **Cards:** most major cards. **Features:** gas, diesel, propane, bakery.

Mira River Provincial Picnic Park and Campground

Location: Brickyard Rd off Hwy 22. At Albert Bridge, on the south side of the bridge, turn onto Brickyard Rd (left if you're heading toward Lousibourg. Drive about 2 km (1.2 mi) east to Park. **Tel:** 902-563-3373 **Season:** mid-May to Oct. **Rates:** avg. **Facilities**: unserviced camp sites; washrooms; disposal station; fire grills; picnic tables; river swimming; boat launch.

Bill Dalton Lobsters

Fresh out of the water, or the pot!

Location: Mason Pt Rd. At Albert Bridge turn off Hwy 22 onto Brickyard Rd and drive about 2.4 km to Mason Pt Rd. (about a half km east of the Provincial Park). **Tel:** 902-562-2173. **Season:** mid-May to end of July. **Features:** very fresh lobsters - live or cooked; Bill is usually home from fishing by noon or so.

Sunlit Valley Farms B & B

Location: 821 Brickyard Road. Turn onto Brickyard Rd from Hwy 22 and drive 1.6 km past the Provincial Park (see above). **Mail Addr:** R. R. #2, Marion Bridge, N.S. B0A 1P0. **Tel:** 902- 562-7663/562-2222 **Owner:** Hazel Ferguson. **Season:** May to Oct; o/s by arrangement. **Rates:** med-low. **Cards:** VS, MC. **Features:** close to beaches and Fortress.

✶ **Note**: To continue on to Louisbourg from here, see details starting on page 260.

Julia Longacre

Travel Option 6

Sydney to Louisbourg
Louisbourg to Sydney
VIA
Direct Route
Colliery Route
Marconi Trail

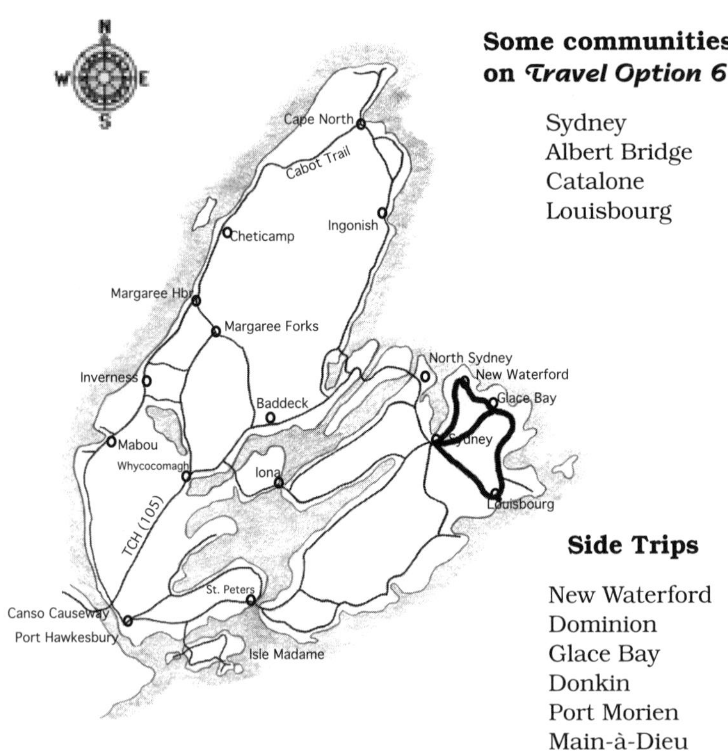

Some communities on Travel Option 6

Sydney
Albert Bridge
Catalone
Louisbourg

Side Trips

New Waterford
Dominion
Glace Bay
Donkin
Port Morien
Main-à-Dieu

Special Features

- √ museums
- √ restaurants and accommodations
- √ shopping
- √ coastal drives
- √ entertainment and activities
- √ Fortress of Louisbourg

This Travel Option takes you the short distance from Sydney to Louisbourg and vice versa. And just to make things interesting, it gives you three choices as to how you want to get there.

The **direct route** is shorter, but less scenic. The other two choices take you through the smaller towns of Industrial Cape Breton like **New Waterford** and **Glace Bay** and along the east coast of the Island through places like **Dominion**, **Donkin**, **Port Morien** and **Main-à-Dieu**.

If you follow this route **from** Sydney **to** Louisbourg, all three options begin in Sydney. If you follow this route **from** Louisbourg **to** Sydney, all three options begin in Louisbourg.

➺ **EN ROUTE**

Coming into Sydney from the west (Canso Causeway/Baddeck) you will either come in on the Hwy 125 (the By-Pass) (Travel Option 1) or on Rte 4 from St. Peters (Travel Option 4)

If you come in on Hwy 125 (The By-Pass) you will take one of four Exits into the city...Exit 6(e) Kings Road. Exit 7 Alexandra St. Exit 8 George St. Or the Welton St/Grand Lake Rd exit which is the end of the By-Pass.

If you come in from St. Peters via Rte 4, keep straight and you'll eventually find yourself on Kings Road, one of Sydney's main thoroughfares. Drive under the overpass and keep straight.

Sydney

Located on the east coast of Cape Breton, 140 km (84 mi) east of the Canso Causeway.

Sydney - A Little History Note

Sydney is thought to be one of the oldest settlements in North America. As far back as the sixteenth century Spanish fisher-men used it as a refuge and when the French built the fortress at Louisbourg, Sydney Harbour provided access to food for the workers and bricks for the buildings.

In 1785 Loyalists fleeing the United States formally established Sydney and named it after the Colonial Secretary, Lord Sydney.

Between the late 1700's and early 1800's many Gaelic-speaking Scots settled in the colony and Sydney began to prosper.

The prosperity slowed down somewhat in 1820 when Nova Scotia annexed Cape Breton. But the growth of the coal mines and steel industry in the early 1900's brought prosperity back and people from all over the world came here to work. This accounts for Sydney's lively multicultural personality.

✻ **Note:** For details of Sydney, see Travel Option 4, page 192.

AND SO ON TO LOUISBOURG....

More Travel Options

The most **direct** way to get to Louisbourg from Sydney is to take **Hwy 22**, the Louisbourg Highway (directions below).

But...if you have the inclination to take a more round about route to see more of the Island, you can take an Alternative Route from Sydney to Glace Bay via the **Colliery Route** through the mining towns of New Waterford and Dominion - a surprisingly beautiful and interesting drive along the ocean.

Or you can take the **Marconi Trail** from Sydney to Louisbourg through places like Port Morien and Main-a-Dieu.

You will find the **Colliery Route** and the **Marconi Trail** alternatives at the end of this Travel Option starting on page 270.

The **direct route** is below.

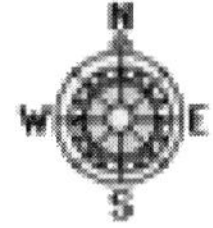

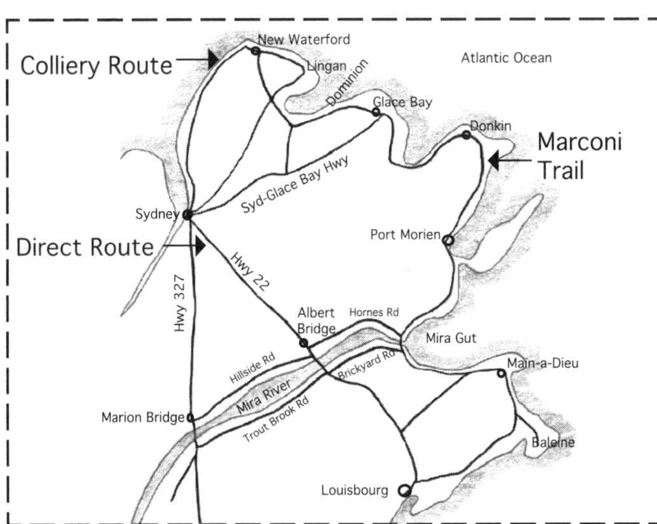

Three Travel Options from Sydney to Louisbourg

Sydney to Louisbourg

VIA

Direct Route (Hwy 22)

Highway 22, the Louisbourg Highway, is really just an extension of Sydney's George Street. (See map page 193.) This is the most direct way to get from Sydney to Louisbourg and back. If you're coming into Sydney from Hwy 125, the By-Pass, take the George Street/ Louisbourg Exit #8, and turn right off the ramp toward Louisbourg.

If you are coming from downtown Sydney, drive up George Street (away from the downtown area). Keep in mind that you are now travelling in a south east direction toward the ocean.

It's about 33 km (20 mi) to Louisbourg from Sydney.

Thorn Morrow Gallery

A quaint ittle shop filled with oils, watercolours and prints, mostly of Cape Breton, by artist Thorn Morrow.

Location: 1860 George Street - beginning of Hwy 22, about a km past the overpass. **Tel:** 902-564-8238. **Hours:** all day, 7 days a week, by chance or appointment. **Season:** Apr to Oct. Sample painting on page 175.

Apple Tree Croft Antiques and Uniques

Location: Hillside Road. From Hwy 22 turn right onto Hills Rd and drive to the end; turn right again onto Hillside Rd and drive a short distance to the sign. **Tel:** 902-562-3433. **Season:** mid-Jun to Sept; other times by appointment. **Hours:** 11 am to 5 pm, Wed to Sun. **Cards:** VS. **Features:** quality glass, country and formal furniture, jewellry and uniques.

Jennifer's Country B & B

Location: #33 Wilford Place, off Hornes Rd. Turn onto Hornes Rd off Hwy 22 and drive 2.9 km (1.8 mi) to Wilford Place. **Mail Addr:** R. R. #2 Hornes Rd, Mira, N.S. B0A 1P0. **Tel:** 902-564-0589./737-5184. **Owner:** J. Thomas. **Season:** May to mid-Oct. **Rates:** low. **Features:** close to swimming, clam digging, hiking and Fortress; horse stables on property; boat tours available.

Albert Bridge

Located on Hwy 22, the Louisbourg Hwy, about 15 km (9 mi) south of Sydney and the same from Louisbourg. The bridge takes you across the renowned Mira River.

Riverside B & B

A short detour off Hwy 22.

Location: 181 Hillside Rd. From Hwy 22 at Albert Bridge, turn onto Hillside Rd (before the bridge if you're heading south) and drive 9.5 (6 mi.) toward Marion Bridge. **Mail Addr:** Box 140, Marion Bridge, N.S., B0A 1P0. **Tel:** 902-727-2615. **Owner:** L. Ferguson. **Season:** May - Oct. Credit **Cards:** VS, MC. **Features:** close to Fortress and other attractions; swimming and boating.

Mira Ferry Convenience Store, Take Out and Gas Bar

Location: Albert Bridge, Louisbourg Hwy 22, just on the Sydney side of the bridge. **Tel:** 562-4142. **Season:** year round. **Hours:** Jul and Aug - 6 am to 11 pm daily; 6 am to 10 pm other months. **Cards:** most major cards. **Features:** gas, diesel; take out, bakery,dockside service on Mira River.

Mullins Mini Mart

Gas station, restaurant, convenience store and postal outlet, all in one.

Location: Albert Bridge, on Louisbourg Hwy 22, just on the Louisbourg side of the bridge. **Tel:** 902-562-1070. **Season:** year round. **Hours:** summer 6:30 am to 10:30 pm; winter 7 am to 9 pm daily. **Cards:** most major cards. **Features:** gas, diesel, propane, bakery.

Mira River Provincial Picnic Park and Campground

Location: Brickyard Rd, off Hwy 22 at Albert Bridge. On the south side of the bridge turn onto Brickyard Rd (left if you're heading toward Louisbourg). Drive 3 km (1.8 mi) to Park. **Tel:** 902-563-3373 **Season:** mid-May to Oct. **Rates:** avg. **Facilities**: unserviced camp sites; washrooms; disposal station; fire grills; picnic tables; river swimming; boat launch.

Sunlit Valley Farms B & B

Location: 821 Brickyard Rd, off Hwy 22 at Albert Bridge. On the south side of the bridge turn onto Brickyard Rd and drive 1.6 km (1 mi) past the Provincial Park (see above). **Mail Addr:** R. R. #2, Marion Bridge, N.S. B0A 1P0. **Tel:** 902- 562-7663/562-2222 **Owner:** H. Ferguson. **Season:** May to Oct; o/s by arrangement. **Rates:** med-low. **Cards:** VS, MC. **Features:** close to beaches and Fortress.

Li'l Bit of Heaven B & B

Location: 371 Trout Brook Rd. On south side of bridge, turn right (if you're heading toward Louisbourg) onto Trout Brook Rd and drive about 10 km (6 mi). **Mail Addr:** 371 Trout Brook Rd, Marion Bridge, N.S. B0A 1P0. **Tel:** 902-727-2936. **Owners:** B. & C. Butts. **Season:** May - Oct; o/s by arrangement. **Rates:** med-low. **Features:** river swimming; boating; fishing.

Artist Beryl Davis, Glace Bay, 849-3938.

Catalone

Located on Hwy 22, the Louisbourg Hwy, about 20 km (12 mi) south of Sydney.

MacLeod's B & B

Location: Catalone, on Hwy 22, between Albert Bridge and Louisbourg. **Mail Addr:** R. R. #1, Louisbourg, N.S. B0A

1M0. **Tel:** 902-733-2456. **Owner:** R. MacLeod. **Season:** May to Sept, o/s by appointment **Rates:** med-low. **Features:** close to Fortress Louisbourg.

Camilla Peck's Tourist Home B & B

Location: Catalone, 23 km (14 mi) from Sydney, on Louisbourg Hwy #22. **Mail Addr:** 5353 Louisbourg Hwy, Louisbourg, N.S. B0A 1M0. **Tel:** 902-733-2649. **Owner:** C. Peck. **Season:** Jun - Oct. **Rates:** med-low. **Features:** a turn-of-the-century farm with animals, situated off the highway; close to Fortress Louisbourg.

Stonewall Trailer Park and Campground

An open and wooded campground on Catalone Lake.

Location: Catalone, on Louisbourg Hwy #22. **Mail Addr:** 5785 Louisbourg Hwy, N.S. B0A 1M0; 902-733-2058, o/s 902-733-2612. **Owner:** S. Ogilvie. **Season:** mid-May to mid-Oct. **Rates:** avg & avg plus. **Features:** quiet tourist campground; serviced sites; trout and salmon fishing; swimming pool, canteen.

Catalone General Store & Irving Station - on Hwy 22 at Catalone; 902-733-2597; **summer hours:** 7 am to 10 pm daily; accepts all credit cards; groceries, camping and fishing supplies, gas, diesel, etc.

Island Seafari

Sea kayaking tours.

Location: Catalone. Take the Main-à-Dieu turnoff from Hwy 22, about 24 km (14 mi) from Sydney; and drive about 3 km (2 mi) to Paddy's Lane. Watch for sign. **Internet Addr**: http//www.cideo.com/websites/seafari **Tel:** 902-733-2309. **Owners:** F. Kennedy and R. Girard. **Season:** mid-May to Oct. **Hours:** calls taken 24 hours a day. **Cards:** VS, MC. **Features:** half-day and day trips, as well as overnight and custom-designed tours.

Louisbourg

Located 33 km (20 mi) south of Sydney on Hwy 22, the Louisbourg Hwy.

In the town you'll find convenience stores, fast food outlets, gas stations, bank, gift shops, a bakery or two, as well as the facilities listed below.

Sydney and Louisbourg Railway Museum.

Location: Main St, Louisbourg, just as you enter the town on Hwy 22. **Mail Addr:** Box 225, Louisbourg, N.S. B0A 1M0. **Tel:** 902-733-2720. **Season:** mid-May to Oct. **Hours:** Jul & Aug 9 am to 7 pm; o/s 9 am to 5 pm **Admission**: free, donations accepted. **Features:** station dates back to 1895; rolling stock, original freight shed, lots of artifacts and information.

This museum is a must for railroad buffs and anyone interested in a unique glimpse into our very colourful past.

The S & L Railway Museum brings you back to a time when trains ran constantly between Sydney and Louisbourg carrying millions of tons of freight and hundreds of thousands of passengers.

Tourist Informaton Centre

This is located in the S & L Railway Museum. **Season:** mid-May to mid-Oct. **Hours:** same as museum above.

Lighthouse Trail

This is a wonderful walk along Louisbourg Harbour in view of the Fortress across the water. The trail begins at Lighthouse Point, the site of the oldest lighthouse in Canada, built by the French in 1733.

As you can imagine, the history of this coast is fascinating, with the French and British vying for the great Fortress. At one point, in the mid 1700's, the British slipped into a cove (now called Wolfe's Cove, just up the shore from the lighthouse) and dragged their cannons over the rocks and bogs to Lighthouse Point. From there they attacked the French on Battery Island, in Louisbourg Harbour.

Directions: take Havenside Rd, just past the S & L Railway Museum, and drive along the Harbour to the lighthouse site. There's a parking lot and a sign marking the trail.

Caution: you may want to bring along a sweater or jacket as it can be a tad cool along this coast...especially if the fog rolls in, which it has been known to do occasionally!

LeMoyne's Wharf

If you want seafood right off the boats (like lobster, crab and shrimp, depending on season), stop off here.

Location: Havenside Rd, Louisbourg. Coming into town, turn left just past the S & L Railway Museum. Watch for the wharf and LeMoyne's sign. **Tel:** 902-733-3258. **Season:** May to Oct.

The Stacey House

Location: 7438 Main St, Louisbourg, near corner of Pepperell. **Mail Addr:** 7438 Main St, Louisbourg, N.S. B0A 1M0. **Tel:** 902-733-2317; o/s 564-1011. **Owner:** G. Beaver. **Season:** Jun to Oct. **Rates:** med-low. **Cards:** VS, MC. **Features:** house is a former Victorian Methodist Parsonage; full breakfast.

Greta Cross B & B

Location: 48 Pepperell St, Louisbourg. Take the second right (coming from Sydney) off Main St after the Railway Museum. **Mail Addr:** Box 153, Louisbourg, N.S. B0A 1M0 **Tel:** 902-733-2833. **Owner:** G. Cross. **Season:** May to Oct. **Rates:** low. **Features:** kitchen and laundry facilities; scenic view of harbour and Fortress; outdoor picnic area; children welcome.

Levy's B & B

Location: 7 Marvin St, Louisbourg. Take the second left (coming from Sydney) off Main St after the Railway Museum. **Mail Addr:** Box 175, Louisbourg, N.S. B0A 1M0. **Tel:** 902-733-2793. **Owner:** A. Levy. **Season:** May to Oct. **Rates:** med-low. **Features:** located on the waterfront, close to shopping and restaurants.

The Coastal Inn

Location: Main St, Louisbourg. **Mail Addr:** Box 197, Louisbourg, N.S. B0A 1M0. **Tel:** 902-733-2844. **Owner:** M. MacDonald. **Season:** May - Oct, partial service other months. **Rates:** mid-range. **Cards:** major cards. **Dng Rm Hrs:** 7:30 to 1030 am; 11:40am to 1:40 pm; 5:30 to 9 pm. **Dng Rm Prices:** mid-range. **Features:** gift shop; licenced; central.

Louisbourg Motorhome Park & Campground

Location: waterfront, near boardwalk, Louisbourg. **Mail Addr:** Box 10, Louisbourg, N.S. B0A 1M0. **Tel:** 902-733-3631. **Season:** Jun - Sept. **Rates:** avg. **Features:** situated on waterfront; serviced and unserviced sites; washrooms; showers; disposal station.

Grandmother's Place B & B

Location: 6 Brittanic St, Louisbourg. Turn off Main St in the centre of town. **Mail Addr:** Box 185, Sydney, N.S. B1P 6H1. **Tel:** 902-733-2375; o/s 562-1130. **Owner:** J. Pope. **Season:** mid-May to mid-Sept. **Rates:** low. **Cards:** VS, MC. **Features:** centrally located.

The Grubstake Restaurant

Location: 1274 Main St, Louisbourg, next to town hall. **Owners:** K. & M. Fulmer. **Tel:** 902-733-2308. **Season:** late Jun to late Sept. **Hours:** noon til 9 pm daily. **Prices:** mid-range to upper end. **Cards:** VS, MC, AE. **Features:** recommended in several travel publications over the years; large menu selection.

Fortress View Restaurant

Location: Main St, Louisbourg. **Tel:** 902-733-3131; Fax 902-733-3140. **Owner:** J. Lawrence. **Season:** May to mid-Oct. **Hours:** Jul & Aug 7 am to 10 pm; other months 11 am to 6 pm. **Prices**: mid-range. **Cards:** all major cards. **Features:** seafood, fish and chips, children's menu; gift shop.

Station House Restaurant and Amusements

Location: Harbour Front Cr, Louisbourg; turn down toward the harbour at town hall. **Tel:** 902-733-3033. **Season:** May to Oct. **Hours:** 8 am to 9 pm daily. **Cards:** VS, MC, AE. **Features:** short orders; mini golf and go-carts.

Lupine Tours B & B

Location: Main St, Louisbourg. **Mail Addr:** Main St, Louisbourg, N.S. B0A 1M0. **Tel:** 902-733-2122. **Owner:** S. Stevens. **Season:** year round. **Rates:** med-low. **Cards:** VS, MC. **Features:** kitchen facilities; central.

Mid Town Housekeeping Cottages

Location: Main St, Louisbourg. **Mail Addr:** Box 304, Louisbourg, N.S. B0A 1M0. **Tel:** 902-733-2330. **Owner:** J. W. Price. **Season:** year round. **Rates:** mid-range. **Cards:** VS, MC, Interac. **Features:** centrally located.

Atlantic Stadiquarium Marine Museum

Location: Main St, Louisbourg. **Tel:** 902-733-2721. **Season:** Jun to Oct. **Hours:** 10 am to 9 pm. **Features:** displays of recovered sunken treasures; marine artifacts and saltwater aquarium.

Louisbourg Harbour Inn

Location: 9 Warren St, Louisbourg - off Main St in the centre of town, down toward the Harbour. **Mail Addr:** 9 Warren St, Louisbourg, N.S. B0A 1M0. **Tel:** 902-733-3222; Fax same. **Owner:** P. Bagnell. **Season:** May to Oct. **Rates:** upper end. **Cards:** most major cards. **Dng Rm Hrs:** 7:30 - 9 am; 5 - 9 pm. **Prices**: med-high. **Features:** renovated century-old home overlooking Harbour; some rooms have patios with Harbour view and jacuzzi.

Kathy's B & B

Location: Warren St, Louisbourg - off Main St. **Mail Addr:** Box 133, Louisbourg, N.S. B0A 1M0. **Tel:** 902-733-2264. **Owner:** K. Rudderham. **Season:** May - Oct; o/s by arrangement. **Rates:** med-low. **Features:** central location.

Evensong B & B

Location: 30 Upper Warren St, Louisbourg - off Main St in centre of town. **Mail Addr:** Box 272, Louisbourg, N.S. B0A 1M0. **Tel:** 902-733-3691; Fax same. **Owner:** M. Marshall. **Season:** May to Oct. **Rates:** med-low. **Features:** Victorian home, close to shopping and Fortress.

The Manse B & B

Location: 10 Strathcona St, just off Main St, down toward the water. **Mail Addr:** Box 56, Louisbourg, N.S. B0A 1M0. **Tel:** 902-733-3155. **Owners:** D. Brooks. **Season:** Apr to Nov. **Rates:** med-low. **Features:** close to Fortress and shopping; overlooking harbour.

Julia Longacre

Nova Scotia Liquor Commission - Main St, Louisbourg; open Mon to Thurs & Sat - 9 am to 6pm; Fri. 9 am to 10 pm (may be open slightly longer hours in summer months.) 902-733-2335.

Ashly Manor B & B

Location: 7590 Main St, Louisbourg. **Mail Addr:** Box 127, Louisbourg, N.S. B0A 1M0. **Tel:** 902-733-3268. **Owner:** S. Simpson. **Season:** year round. **Rates:** med-low. **Features:** adults only; central.

Along Main Street you'll find several gift and souvenir **shops**:

- √ F M Crafts
- √ Arlies' Crafts
- √ Bagnell's Gift Boutique
- √ House of Dolls

Peck's Housekeeping Cottages

Location: Wolfe St, Louisbourg - at the end of Main St by the fountain. **Mail Addr:** Box 10, Louisbourg, N.S. B0A 1M0. **Tel:** 902-733-2210. **Owners:** G.& E. Peck. **Season:** year round. **Rates:** mid-range. **Cards:** most major cards. **Features:** groceries; laundromat; five minutes from Fortress.

Cranberry Cove Inn and Dining Room

This is one of the Island's most appealing accommodations - an elegant renovated Victorian house.

Location: Wolfe St, Louisbourg - at end of Main St, keep left at the fountain. **Mail Addr:** Box 27, Louisbourg, N.S. B0A 1M0. **Tel:** 902-733-2171; fax 902-733-2449. **Owner:** C. Swander. **Season:** year round. **Rates:** upper end. **Cards:** VS, MC, AE. **Dng Rm Hrs:** evening meal served from 5 - 8 (reservations suggested). **Prices**: med-high (breakfast included). **Features:** beautiful cozy rooms all with private bath, Jacuzzi tubs & gas fireplaces; full breakfast included; very close to Fortress and shopping; licenced.

Point of View Suites and RV Park

Location: Commercial St Ext, Louisbourg. Drive to end of Main St, turn left at fountain (Wolfe St) - turn left across from entrance to Fortress Visitor Reception Ctr. **Mail Addr:** 5 Commercial St Ext, Louisbourg, N.S. B0A 1M0. **Tel:** 902-733-2080/3254. **Owners:** T. & L. Kennedy. **Season:** mid-May - Oct. **Rates:** suites med-high; RV sites avg plus.. **Cards:** VS, MC. **Features:** situated on Harbour; luxury suites; light housekeeping; saltwater beach, lobster & crab boils in season; serviced and unserviced sites; 3-way hook-ups; showers, laundry facilities.

Kennington Cove Beach

How would you like to break away for awhile to a glorious beach where you can lie back, soak up the warmth of the sun, watch the gulls dip into the waves and listen to the rhythm of the rolling surf? Sounds inviting, doesn't it?

A little detour to Kennington Cove, along the coast from Louisbourg, is just what you're looking for.

Location: Kennington Cove, about 20 km (12 mi) from Louisbourg. Drive down Main St in Louisbourg until you come to the fountain. Turn right and drive about a km to the Park Administration sign. Turn left and drive to the intersection. You'll get a wonderful distant view of the Fortress. Turn right and drive to the beach. **Facilities:** two sandy ocean beaches (just drive a little further for second beach); small fresh water pools to dip in; picnic area. **Caution**: there can be undertows when the sea is high, so be careful.

History Note...

Back in 1758, when the French were getting pretty comfortable at the Fortress, shiploads of British military men (27,000 to be exact!) landed at Kennington Cove and set up camp.

They travelled overland to the Fortress, attacked the French who were not expecting an attack from land, and eventually took the Fortress away from the French.

Fortress of Louisbourg National Historic Site

Location: Wolfe St, Louisbourg. Drive to the end of Main St and turn left at the fountain onto Wolfe St; watch for sign. **Mail Addr:** P.O. Box 160, Louisbourg, N.S. B0A 1M0. **Tel:** 902-733-2280. **Season:** Jun to Oct. **Hours:** May, Jun, Sept, Oct - 9:30 am - 5 pm; Jul & Aug - 9 am - 7 pm. **Admission:** from $5 to $10; family $25; fees less in off-season. **Features:** reconstructed 18th century fortified town; 3 eighteenth-century-style restaurants; bakery; gift shop; children's interpretive centre; guided tours; picnic areas; walking trails.

The Great Fortress

This exerpt from an old visitor information brochure seems to capture the magic of the Louisbourg experience.

"The reconstructed Fortress of Louisbourg is a unique place that recreates a moment in time - the summer of 1744. Once again it is the military capital of a colony and the centre of a valuable commerce, about to plunge into a global war.

A visit to the Fortress is a series of small experiences that set a mood: a file of marching soldiers...a drink at a sailor's tavern...a shingled roofline...the swirl of a woolen cape...a fisherman at work...a child engrossed in play...looming fog...the scent of tallow candles...the sound of a windslammed shutter.

About a fifth of 18th century Louisbourg now stands as it did in 1744. Ramparts, streets and households recreate not only the look but the texture and the mood of another century. Heavy cannon on stone ramparts, a busy waterfront tavern, a roasting spit turning in a crowded kitchen, tell how people of a different age lived and worked. The Fortress of Louisbourg stands and lives again."

Fortress of Louisbourg Period Restaurants

Where original 18th century recipes are the order of the day. All restaurants are located within the Fortress. Most major credit cards are accepted. Hours are slightly less than those of the Fortress itself.

√ **Hotel de la Marine** - a lively tavern located on the waterfront where you'll very often find live traditional entertainment.

√ **Destouches House** - for a light, 18th century-style lunch.

√ **L'Épee Royale,** for a more sophisticated dinner.

Julia Longacre

Alternate Route from Sydney to Glace Bay

VIA Colliery Rte

This alternate route takes you from **Whitney Pier** in Sydney along the shore through **New Victoria** and **New Waterford** and on to **Glace Bay**. When you get to Glace Bay you can pick up the Marconi Trail to Louisbourg.

I have to admit that until very recently I had no idea just how fascinating the history is along this part of the Island and just how wonderful the scenery.

Directions: As you can see, this route is written for those who are driving **from** Sydney **to** Glace Bay. However, you can, of course, also take the Colliery Route **from** Glace Bay **to** Sydney, by taking Main St out of Glace Bay (see map of Glace Bay page 277) and following this route in reverse.

Below are details of this route from Sydney to Glace Bay.

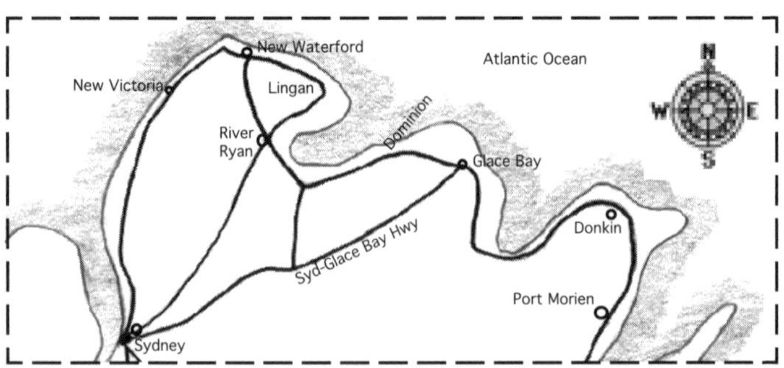

Sydney, New Waterford, Glace Bay - The Colliery Route

Sydney

The Colliery Route begins in Sydney on Victoria Rd, which you will find if you take Prince St from downtown to the lights at Ashby Corner. Turn left onto Victoria Road, which will take you to Whitney Pier ("The Pier" as we call it locally). For a map and more information on Sydney see page 193.

Whitney Pier, Sydney

This is an interesting part of Sydney as the population here is made up of many different nationalities. Most of the Pier residents' fathers or grandfathers came from places like Poland, Hungary, Barbados, Italy, Lebanon and Greece, to find work at the steel plant, which you will see as you cross the "overpass" from Sydney proper.

Along Victoria Rd, running through the Pier, you'll find service stations, bank, convenience stores, pharmacy and some small restaurants.

You'll also see rows of the "company houses" that were built and owned by the steel company and rented to its employees.

The Whitney Pier Historical Society

Location: 88 Mt. Pleasant St, Whitney Pier. Coming from Sydney, turn left off Victoria Rd soon after you cross the overpass. **Tel:** 902-564-9819. **Season:** late May to Sept. **Hours**: May and June - Mon to Fri 1 pm to 4 pm; Jul & Aug - Mon to Sat 9 am to 5 pm (closed from 12 to 1 pm). **Features**: artifacts and records of this interesting multicultural community; art exhibits and other activities.

New Victoria

Located on the coastal Hwy 28 between Sydney and New Waterford; about 14 km (8 mi) from Whitney Pier (Sydney) and about 3 km (1.8 mi) from New Waterford.

Julia Longacre

Fort Petrie

Location: New Victoria, on Hwy 28, between Sydney and New Waterford.

Features: This is an interesting spot for World War II buffs.

It is the remains of a fortification built during the war as part of a coastal defense network all along Sydney Harbour. These fortifications protected the many supply ships coming in and out of the Harbour during the war and kept a sharp eye out for enemy submarines that may have slipped into the area.

There is no development on the site yet, but hopefully there will be in the future.

There's a beautiful view from here across to North Sydney, and if the time is right you can see the ferry to Newfoundland either beginning or ending it's journey across the Strait.

New Waterford

Located about 18 km (11 mi) east of Sydney on Hwy 28, the Colliery Route.

Colliery Lands Park

Location: Ellsworth Avenue, New Waterford. **Features**: monuments to coal miners who lost their lives in local collieries; other memorabilia of coal mining in the area; New Waterford Historical Society offices.

➵ **EN ROUTE** -The shore road from New Victoria will take you into New Waterford on Ellsworth Avenue. Turn right onto Heelan St, then after a short distance turn left onto Plummer Ave. This is the main street of the town.

Davis Square

Location: Plummer Ave, New Waterford. **Features:** A small park dedicated to the memory of Bill Davis, a miner who was shot and killed by a coal company official on June 11, 1925. Since then June 11, "Davis Day", has been a holiday in all the mining towns in the area. A war memorial, a monument commemorating the miners' strike of 1925 and a monument to the memory of miners killed in the 1917 mine explosion, are also in the square.

A Few Facts About Coal Mining

- The Town of **Glace Bay** once had 12 coal mines in operation; today it has none.
- you can tour an underground coal mine at the Miner's Museum in Glace Bay.
- A horse-drawn railroad took coal from the town of Dominion as early as the 1820's.
- Between 1907 and 1911 four collieries opened in **New Waterford** and a total of 11 mines were in production over the years. Now there is only one...Phalen Colliery at Lingan.
- 65 miners were killed in an underground explosion in No.12 Colliery in 1917.

Young's Irving - 3477 Plummer Ave, New Waterford; 902-862-7767; open 7 am to 10 pm Mon to Sat; 8 am to 10 pm Sun.

Simeons Restaurant

Location: Plummer Ave, New Waterford; **Tel:** 862-8090. **Season:** Year round. **Hours:** 11 am to 12 pm; Sunday 11:30 am to 12 pm. **Cards:** most major cards. **Features:** family-style dining.

Nova Scotia Liquor Commission - 3434 Plummer Ave, New Waterford; 902-. 862-8012; open Mon to Wed - 10 am to 6 pm; Thurs, Fri & Sat - 10 am to 10 pm.

Midtown Pharmasave - 3435 Plummer Ave, New Waterford; 902-862-7186; open Mon to Sat 9 am to 9 pm; Sun and holidays 12 noon to 8 pm.

MacSween's Flowers and Gifts

Location: Plummer Ave, New Waterford. **Tel:** 902-862-6468. **Hours:** 9 am to 5 pm, Mon to Sat. **Cards:** VS, MC.

Lawton's Drugs - 3415 Plummer Ave, New Waterford; 902-862-7105/6409; open 9 am to 9 pm Mon to Sat; 12 noon to 8 pm Sun & holidays.

China Kitchen Restaurant

Location: 3321 Plummer Ave, New Waterford. **Tel:** 902-862-7000. **Hours:** Mon to Thurs 11am to 11 pm; Fri 11 am to 2 am; Sat 2 pm to 11 pm; Sun 3 pm to 10 pm. **Cards:** VS.

Ross Service Ctr - 3302 Plummer Ave; 902-862-8262; open 7 am to 12 midnight Mon to Fri; 8 am to 12 Sat; 9 am to 12 Sun.

New Waterford Consolidated Hospital - 716 King St; turn right at the east end of Plummer Ave; **902-862-6411**.

> ➼ **EN ROUTE** - To keep going on the Colliery Route to Glace Bay, turn left onto King Street at the end of Plummer Ave. You'll see a well-preserved sampling of the company houses that were once owned by the coal company and rented to the miners and their families. From King St. turn right onto Hinchey Ave. This will take you to Lingan.

Lingan

From New Waterford, take Hinchey Ave along the shore. It's interesting to note that in the early 1700's French colonists from Louisbourg settled here and extracted coal from the many seams along the ocean. Probably most of it was used to meet what must have been a huge demand for fuel at the mighty Fortress.

Phalen Colliery

Location: Lingan, just east of New Waterford. Owned by the Cape Breton Development Corporation. The working face of this coal mine is about 5 km (3 mi) out under the Atlantic Ocean.

River Ryan

Located on Colliery Route, Hwy 28 , about 3 km (1.8 mi) from New Waterford. Coming from Lingan, drive to the Nova Scotia Power facility and turn onto Lingan Road. Drive to the intersection, yellow light, and turn left.

River Ryan Campground

Open and wooded campground on Lingan Bay.

Location: River Ryan, on Hwy 28, between New Waterford and Glace Bay. **Mail Addr:** R. R. #1, River Ryan, N.S. B1H 4K2. **Tel:** 902-862-8367. **Owner:** P. Grezel. **Season:** May to Sept. **Rates:** avg. **Features:** washrooms;showers; laundromat;fire pots; store; swimming; mini putt; fishing.

New Waterford Fish and Game Picnic Spot , located at the bridge at River Ryan. Picnic tables on the water.

Bayside Drive In

Location: River Ryan, Hwy 28. **Tel:** 902-862-6842. **Season:** Apr to Nov. **Hours:** 12 noon to midnight daily. **Tel:** 862-6842. **Features:** fast food.

Lionel's Golf Centre

Location: Gardiner Mines. Turn right at the intersection just east of River Ryan. **Tel:** 902-842-0474.

➳ **EN ROUTE** - The drive from New Waterford to Dominion and Glace Bay is very scenic, along Lingan Bay, through Gardiner Mines. At the intersection just past River Ryan, keep straight through on the Colliery Rte toward Dominion.

Dominion

Located on the Colliery Route, about 1 km west of Glace Bay. The Dominion Coal Company opened its first colliery here in 1893.

Dominion Heritage Building (Schoolhouse)

This late 1800's schoolhouse on the original site contains artifacts and photos, desks and documents from that era.

Location: Dominion, on highway coming in from New Waterford, adjacent to Dominion Beach (see below). **Season:** Jul & Aug. **Hours:** 9 am - 5 pm daily. **Admission:** free - donations welcom. **Features:** information centre; platform for bird watching over Lingan Bay.

Dominion Beach Provincial Park

Location: Dominion - coming in from New Waterford on Hwy 28, Colliery Route, just past the Dominion Heritage Building (see above). **Features:** long, sandy beach; boardwalk; shore birds; washrooms and showers; canteen; change houses.

> ➵ **EN ROUTE**: - In Dominion, turn onto Commercial Street (which turns into King St) and keep on to Glace Bay.

Dominion Pharmasave - Commercial St, Dominion; 902-849-0200; open 9 am to 9 pm Mon to Fri; 9 am to 5 pm Sat; closed Sun.

Kenny Boone - Art Studio and Gallery

Kenny's work as a commercial artist helped him develop a keen sense of colour and harmony, which is really evident in his beautiful watercolours.

Location: 230 Neville St, Dominion - turn off King St to Neville (King St is a continuation of Commercial St); studio is in back of house. **Tel:** 902-849-5820. **Hours:** by chance or appointment. **Features:** original watercolors, most of them Cape Breton land- and seascapes, as well as limited edition prints. See page 212 for a sample of his work.

Glace Bay

Located on the east coast of Cape Breton, about 18 km (11 mi) from Sydney.

As you drive into Glace Bay from Dominion, you'll find yourself on Main Street.

Making Waves...

"...have honour send through Times, inventor's first wireless transatlantic message of greetings."

That was the message Guglielmo Marconi sent from Glace Bay, Cape Breton, to the Times of London in 1902, proving to the world his theory that it was indeed possible to send a message across the ocean using electro-magnetic waves instead of wires.

He really started something that day!

At the Marconi National Historic Site, at Table Head, Glace Bay, you'll find out all about the "Wizard of the Wireless" and his contribution to our lives.

Marconi National Historic Site

Location: Timmerman St, Glace Bay. Coming into Glace Bay from Dominion, keep on Main St to King Edward, take King Edward to Sterling, and following Sterling to Timmerman (see map below) **Tel:** 902-295-2069. **Season:** Jun to mid-Sept. **Hours:** daily 10 am to 6 pm. **Admission:** free. **Features:** wheelchair accessible interpretive exhibit and wash-rooms; picnic area.

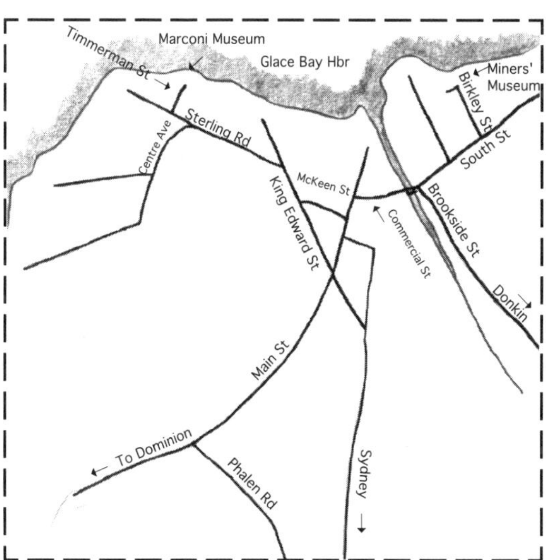

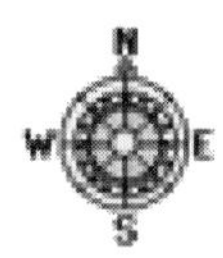

Glace Bay (Simplified)

➵ **EN ROUTE**

This is the end of this travel alternative as such, but you can continue your coastal drive right to Louisbourg by picking up the Marconi Trail at the Marconi Museum in Glace Bay (see next page for details.)

Along the **Marconi Trail** you'll see the Marconi National Historic Site, the Glace Bay Miners' Museum, the Town of Glace Bay and all the beautiful coastal communities along the way like Donkin, Port Morien, Main-a-Dieu and others.

Alternate Route from Sydney to Louisbourg

VIA Marconi Trail

This route takes you from Sydney to Louisbourg (and vice versa) through the coastal commuinities of Donkin, Port Morien and Main-à-Dieu. It's a wonderful drive along the Atlantic with lots beaches, hikes and history.

Marconi Trail

EN ROUTE

➺ To get from Sydney to Glace Bay, take Prince/ Welton Street (aka Grand Lake Rd or the Glace Bay Hwy) drive east (away from the downtown district).

⇠ To get from Glace Bay to Sydney, take the Glace Bay Hwy out of Glace Bay through Reserve to Sydney. (See map of Glace Bay page 277.)

You'll find several gas stations between Sydney and Glace Bay, as well as the facilities listed below (east of the Mayflower Mall on Grand Lake Rd).

For details of other Sydney facilities, see Travel Option 1, page 192.

Sydney

Grand Lake Rd (Glace Bay Hwy), east of the Mayflower Mall. For details on the rest of Sydney, see page 192.

Lingan Golf and Country Club

Location: Glace Bay Hwy, about 8 km (4.8 mi) from Sydney. **Tel**: 562-1112/5700. **Season:** May to Oct. **Hours**: 6 am in Jul and Aug; 7 am or 8 am other months; closes at dark. **Green Fees**: $37 per day. **Features**: 18-hole; pro shop.

University College of Cape Breton

Location: Glace Bay Highway, about 9 km (5.5 mi) from Sydney. **Tel:** 902-539-5300.

University College of Cape Breton

UCCB is Canada's first university college. That means it's an innovative blend of degree and diploma programs providing a unique opportunity for students.

UCCB is heavily involved in community development and applied research, and has a very active cooperative education program. Its commitment to the culture of the Island is evident in its Mi'kmaq Studies program, Art Gallery, Playhouse and Beaton Institute of Cape Breton Studies.

Beaton Institute of Cape Breton Studies

This research centre and archives had its beginnings back in the late 1950's when Sister Margaret Beaton began collecting material pertaining to the Gaelic language and culture. Today it incorporates all aspects of the Island's life and history. It contains a manuscript collection (Gaelic and otherswise), published works, photo and painting collection; audio and video tapes; parish records; school registers; censuses and more. It also offers genealogical services if you have a notion to look up your ancestors. **Location:** University College of Cape Breton, Glace Bay Hwy. **Hours:** Mon to Fri 8:30 am - 4 pm. **Tel:** 902-539-5300, ext 327.

Jaques Cartier Motel

Location: Sydney-Glace Bay Hwy. **Mail Addr:** Box 555, Sydney, N.S. B1P 6H4. **Tel:** 902-539-4375. **Owner:** R. Poirier. **Season:** year round. **Rates:** mid-range. **Cards:** VS, MC.

Sydney Airport

Location: Glace Bay Highway, about 14 km (8.4 mi) from Sydney and 4 km (2.4 mi) from Glace Bay. **Facilities:** two runways; terminal features car rentals, restaurant, lounge, gift shop, washrooms, ground transportation, etc.

Some Important Telephone Numbers

Airport: 902-564-7720; 564-7730
Airlines:
Air Atlantic 902-539-2500
Air Nova 902-539-7501
Provincial Airlines 902-567-0001
Air St-Pierre 902-562-3140.
Car rentals:
Avis 902-564-8265
Hertz 539-5623
Budget 562-1223
Tilden 564-6417.
Canada Customs 564-7012
Immigration 564-7045
Weather info 564-7299.

Reserve Mines/Reserve

Located about 15 km (9 mi) from Sydney on the Sydney-Glace Bay Hwy. You'll find several service stations, grocery stores (SuperValu and Co-Op), some fast food outlets and convenience stores along this highway, as well as the facilities listed below.

Becky's B & B

Also has apartment available for longer stay

Location: 208 Main St, Reserve Mines - 3 km (1.8 mi) past the Sydney Airport turn onto Main St, across from the fire hall. **Mail Addr:** 208 Main St, Reserve Mines, N.S. B0A 1V0. **Tel:** 902-849-2974. **Owner:** L. & R. Oliver. **Season:** year round. **Rates:** low. **Features:** light lunch served in evening; kitchen available for guests use.

Tompkins Historical Museum

Location: Tompkins Centre, Reserve Mines, Sydney-Glace Bay Hwy. **Tel:** 902-849-4583. **Features:** Museum is dedicated to the founder of the Credit Union Movement, Father Jimmy Tomkins.

Blossoms & Lace B & B

Location: 127 Haulage Rd Turn left onto Haulage Rd about a km from the turnoff to Donkin/Port Morien. **Mail Addr:** 127 Haulage Rd, Reserve Mines, N.S. B0A 1V0. **Tel:** 902-849-3550. **Owner:** L. Aucoin. **Season:** year round. **Rates:** low. **Features:** full breakfast.

Kenny Boone - Art Studio and Gallery

Kenny's work as a commercial artist helped him develop a keen sense of colour and harmony, which is really evident in his beautiful watercolours. See page 212 for a sample of his work.

Location: 230 Neville St, Dominion. Turn off the Glace Bay Highway in Reserve at Tim Horton's; drive to the intersection of Neville St, then turn right and drive about 2 km 1.2 mi) or so. Studio is in back of house. **Tel:** 902-849-5820. **Hours:** by chance or appointment. **Features:** original watercolors, most of them Cape Breton land- and seascapes, as well as limited edition prints.

Glace Bay

Located about 18km (11 mi) east of Sydney on Glace Bay Hwy, Rte 4.

Since Glace Bay is a large town, it wouldn't be practical to try and set out all of the streets in town. The following is the most direct route through Glace Bay that will get you to the Marconi Museum, through the business district of town, to the Miner's Museum, then out of town to continue on to Donkin, Port Morien and eventually Louisbourg.

The simplified map of Glace Bay on page 277 should help you find what ever else you may be looking for in the Town.

King Edward Street, Glace Bay.

Coming into Glace Bay from Sydney on the Glace Bay Hwy, turn left onto King Edward Street, just past the Co Op store.

Will Brig House B & B

Location: 322 King Edward St. **Mail Addr:** 322 King Edward St, Glace Bay, N.S. B1A 3W3. **Tel:** 902-8496585. **Owner:** E. Curry. **Season:** year round. **Rates:** med-low. **Features:** one housekeeping suite available as well.

Sterling Rd, Downtown Glace Bay

Turn left off King Edward St after you cross the tracks.

Sterling Mall

Location: Sterling Rd, Glace Bay. **Tel**: 902-539-6912. **Hours:** 9 am to 9 pm Mon to Fri; 9 am to 5 pm Sat. **Features**: department store, supermarket, clothing stores and other smaller stores.

Mike's Lunch

Location: Sterling Rd, Glace Bay, across from the Sterling Mall. **Tel:** 902-849-1010. **Season:** year round. **Hours:** Mon to Fri & Sun - 7 am to 12 pm; Sat 7 am to 2 am. **Cards**: VS, MC, AE. **Features**: family dining.

Marconi National Historic Site

Location: Timmerman St, Table Head, Glace Bay. Keep on Sterling Rd. As you get closer to the ocean you'll come to a sharp turn to the left - don't turn, keep straight and you'll see Timmerman St on your right (see map page277). **Tel:** 902-295-2069. **Season:** Jun to mid-Sept. **Hours:** daily 10 am to 6 pm. **Admission:** free. **Features:** wheelchair accessible interpretive exhibit and washrooms; picnic area.

Making Waves...

"...have honour send through Times, inventor's first wireless transatlantic message of greetings."

That was the message Guglielmo Marconi sent from Glace Bay, Cape Breton, to the Times of London in 1902, proving to the world his theory that it was indeed possible to sent a message across the ocean using electromagnetic waves instead of wires.

He really started something that day!

At the Marconi National Historic Site, at Table Head, Glace Bay, you'll find out all about the "Wizard of the Wireless" and his contribution to our lives.

➵ **EN ROUTE**

The **Marconi Trail** begins or ends, depending on which way you're travelling, at the Marconi National Historic Site.

If you're heading to Louisbourg, follow these directions to get through Glace Bay and on to Donkin and Port Morien, or watch for the Marconi Trail signs.

Directions: From the Marconi site, turn left off Timmerman Street onto Sterling Rd. Drive straight on Sterling Rd, past the Sterling Mall and take a left at McKeen St at the tracks. At the Irving station turn left then make a quick right. This is Commercial St.

If you're heading toward Sydney, follow Sterling Rd until you cross the tracks and take a right at King Edward St. Follow King Edward to Reserve St (Glace Bay Hwy) and turn right. This will take you to Sydney.

Commercial Street, Glace Bay

This is the main business district of Glace Bay where you'll find an assortment of clothing, convenience and other stores, a small restuarant or two, as well as the facilities listed below.

Savoy Theatre

A beautiful old theatre, restored to its former glory...concerts, live theatre, revues and other live entertainment.

Location: 19 Union St - just off Commercial St. **Tel:** 902-849-5192.

Pharmacies on Commercial St:

Medical Hall Pharmasave, 15 Commercial St; 902-849-6552; open 9 am to 9 pm Mon to Fri; 9 am to 8 pm Sat; 12 noon to 8 pm Sun.

Shopper's Drug Mart, 39 Commercial St; 902-849-2920; open 9 am to 9 pm Mon to Fri; 9 am to 6 pm Sat; 12 noon to 6 pm Sun.

Lawton's, 48 Commercial St; 902-849-7573 open 9 am to 9 pm Mon to Sat; 12 noon to 8 pm Sun.

Renwick Brook Park - A quiet shady park along a brook...great place to have a picnic lunch.

Glace Bay Miners' Museum & Ocean Deeps Colliery

Exhibits focusing on coal miners' lives and livelihood. Take a guided tour into an underground coal mine. A special treat - Tuesday evening concerts by the Men of the Deeps - a well-known and much-travelled choir of working and retired coal miners.

Location: Quarry Point, 42 Birkley St - drive down Commercial St, which turns into South Street somewhere around the bridge, until you come to Birkley St on your left. **Tel:** 902-849-4522. **Season:** year round. **Hours:** early Jun to early Sept 10 am to 6 pm daily; Tue evening concerts; other months open Mon to Fri 9 am to 4 pm. **Rates:** small fee charged for admission to museum and for mine tour. **Features:** underground mine; artifacts and exhibits relating to coal mining; public washrooms; information.

The Miners' Village & Miners' Village Restaurant

Features a "company store', miner's home circa 1850-1900 and a restaurant.

Location: adjacent to Miners' Museum, operated in conjunction with museum.

Glace Bay Hospital, one of two locations - this one is located on South St, which is an extension of Commercial Street; **Tel:** 902-849-5511.

Justamere B & B

Location: 2489 Tower Rd. **Mail Addr:** R. R. #1, Glace Bay, N.S. B1A 5T9. **Tel:** 902-849-0218. **Owner:** A. & B. MacDonald. **Season:** May to Oct. **Rates:** low to med-low. **Features:** full breakfast.

➵ **EN ROUTE** - to get back onto the Marconi Trail toward Donkin/Port Morien from downtown Glace Bay, drive down Commercial St to the bridge (or if you're coming from the Miners' Museum come up South St to bridge), and turn onto Brookside St. Drive on Brookside St. After about 2 km (1.2 mi) you'll come to a sharp turn - keep to your left). You'll soon come to an intersection, about 5 km (3 mi) from downtown Glace Bay - keep straight to Donkin.

Big Glace Bay Beach

Location: on road between Glace Bay and Donkin (see opposite page for directions). **Features**: large public beach; convenience store nearby.

Donkin

Located on the Marconi Trail just east of Glace Bay - (see directions opposite). A village literally perched on the edge of the ocean, Donkin is a perfect spot for photographers and lovers of the sea.

South Street General Store - South Street, Donkin; 902-737-5055; open 8 am to 10 pm Mon to Sat; 11 am to 10 pm Sun.

Julia Longacre

Cape Perce Hiking Trail

A walking trail, about 3 or 4 km (2 or 2.5 mi). return, that leads along the headland of Cape Perce overlooking the Atlantic. In lobster season (May, June and part of July) you can see the fishermen hauling their traps in their boats far below you.

Location: Donkin on the Marconi Trail. Drive through Donkin and at Schooner Cove take a left turn onto the dirt road. Drive less than a km to the end. Trail is uphill to your left. **Features:** a beautiful barren headland along the ocean; lots of plants, berries and seabirds; of special interest is the kittiwake colony at the very tip, an unusual sight as they usually nest on remote islands. **Caution**: Don't walk too close to the edge as the overhangs are very unstable and dangerous...especially watch children. And don't disturb the birds when they're nesting.

Cape Perce Nature Tours

If you would prefer a guided tour with a naturalist and birder, give this number a call. **Tel:** 902-737-2684. **Owner:** Cathy Murrant. **Season:** year round **Prices:** Adults $15, children and youths to 16 yrs.$5. **Features:** very knowledgeable tour guides; lots of seabirds, seals and sometimes whales; view of Flint Island lighthouse; an unusual mainland colony of nesting black-legged kittiwakes.

Port Morien

Located on Marconi Trail, about 7 km (4 mi) south of Donkin. This community has a fascinating history as it is the site of the very first coal mine, **and** the site of the very first boy scout troup, in North America.

Old French Mine Site

Location: Port Morien - drive from Donkin to Port Morien on the Marconi Trail until you come to the end of the road and a stop sign. To your left is a ball field. If you walk down along the fence you'll find a path near the bleachers that takes you down to the water.

This is the site of the very first coal mine in North America. In the early 1700's, the French were building their fortress at Louisbourg, just south along the coast. To fuel the great fortress, they began extracting coal from exposed seams all along the cliffs, and in 1720 the first coal mine in North America was opened here on the shore of Baie de Mordienne (as it was then called).

Later on, in the 1800's when business was really booming, there were three rows of company houses on that site and hundreds of men and their families living and working on that now-deserted slice of Cape Breton seashore.

Hopper's Grocery - Port Morien; 902-737-2388; open 7:30 am to 8:30 pm; Sun 9:30 am to 8:30 p.m; convenience store.

Mira Gut

Located on the Marconi Trail, between Port Morien and Main-à-Dieu; keep south from Port Morien.

Mira Gut Beach

This beach is situated where the Mira River empties into the Atlantic Ocean. There's a boardwalk and lots of sand.

Location: Mira Gut, Marconi Trail, next to the Mira Gut Bridge. **Features**: sandy beach; boardwalk; parking. **Caution**: stay on the Port Morien (north) side of the breakwater as there can be currents and undertows where the river flows into the ocean.

Out on the Mira Boat Tours and Charters

Location: Mira Gut, at the wharf near the bridge. **Tel**: 902-564-8790. **Owner**: Don Messenger. **Season:** mid-July to Oct. **Hours**: anytime - call ahead. **Rates**: variable, best to call and ask. **Features:** tours of Mira River, Scatarie Island, cliffs at Port Morien, Flint Island, etc.

Mira River Provincial Picnic Park and Campground

If you prefer a river swim, try Mira Park.

Location: On Mira River, just a short detour off the Marconi Trail. On the south side of the bridge at Mira Gut take Brickyard Rd; drive for 4.8 km.(3 mi) to Park. **Tel:** 902-563-3373 **Season:** mid-May to Oct. **Rates:** avg. **Features**: unserviced camp sites; washrooms; disposal station; fire grills; picnic tables; river swimming; boat launch.

Catalone Gut

Located on the Marconi Trail about 18 km (11 mi) south of Port Morien and 6 km (3.6 mi) north of Main-à-Dieu.

There are some wonderful places to stop off along here where the narrow sandbar on which you're driving separates Catalone Lake from Mira Bay. It's a super place to canoe, snap some photos, or take a stroll along the beach. You can swim too, if you don't mind the "chilly" Atlantic water.

Main-à-Dieu

Located about 30 km (18 mi) south of Port Morien on the Marconi Trail. Keep left at stop sign at Bateston, then at the next intersection, turn left to get into the main part of the village. (If you want to keep going to Louisbourg, and not go into the village of Main-à-Dieu, turn right at this intersection.)

This is a postcard perfect fishing village with bright colored boats in the harbour, bustling wharf and wonderful rocky landscape.

Peter A Mullins

Grocery store and gas bar.

Location: Village of Main-à-Dieu, across from the wharf. **Tel:** 902-733-2676. **Season:** May - Oct. **Hours:** 8 am to 9 pm; Sun 1 pm to 4 pm.

Fresh Fish

...you can usually get fish and seafood right out of the water in season either at the Main-a-Dieu wharf or at Peter A. Mullins store (above). Lobster season is May 15 to July 15 and crab season is July until quotas are reached.

Fishermen's Museum

A fascinating collection of fishing paraphanalia and memorabilia from years past when the fishing industry was thriving in villages like Main-à-Dieu.

Location: Village of Main-à-Dieu. Drive through village and up the hill. **Tel:** 902-733-3042. **Hours:** 9 am to 9 pm, daily. **Season:** Jul & Aug. **Features:** very interesting display of artifacts, newspaper clippings, photos, etc; picnic area outside overlooking Main-à-Dieu Passage. There's a replica of a boat's wheelhouse on the hill outside that you can stand in and imagine you're a fishing boat captain. Kids think it's great!

Moque Head Hiking Trail

This is a coastal walk that takes you along the shore of Main-à-Dieu Passage, uphill to a headland and back down along the beach again for miles, if you're so inclined.

Location: drive through the Village of Main-à-Dieu and

up to the top of the hill. Park there and look for the beginning of the trail. **Distance:** you could probably hike for several kilometres but the trail does deteriorate into not much more than an animal track. You can make the walk as short or as long as you like. **Caution**: Stick to the boardwalk and path and walk carefully as some parts of the trail are very close to the edge due to erosion. **Features:** wonderfully scenic walk along a rugged coastline; view of Scatarie Island.

> ➛ **EN ROUTE** - to continue on the Marconi Trail from the village, drive back through the village and keep straight at the intersection.

Main-à-Dieu Boardwalk

Location: Main-à-Dieu, on the Marconi Trail. This boardwalk was built by unemployed fishermen a few years ago; it's about 2 km (1.5 mi) in length overall. You can also cross the road and walk in woods over a wooden bridge and along another boardwalk.

Artist Teena Marie Saunders. See page 115.

Sandy's Take Out and Gift Shop

A good place for a quick bite, right across from the Boardwalk. **Location:** Main-à-Dieu, on the Marconi Trail, directly across from the boardwalk. **Season:** year round. **Hours:** May to Sept 9 am - 12 pm; Oct to Apr 11 am to 10 pm. **Prices:** low. **Features:** picnic tables overlooking the Bay.

Baleine

Located just off the the Marconi Trail,just south of Main-à-Dieu. Watch for the dirt road and the Baleine sign.

Baleine Coastal Hiking Trail

This stretch of coastline is oozing with history and intrigue. It's the most easterly point on the "mainland" of Cape Breton and almost 400 years ago it was the Island's first permanent settlement. In the 1930's a British flier named Beryl Markham crash-landed her plane here during a solo flight across the Atlantic. And more recently, Baleine was the site of a police seizure of a very large shipment of illegal drugs.

All that aside, though, it is a marvellous walk along the beach and headland, where you can enjoy the abundant plant life and the salt sea air, and let the rest of the world hurry on. **Caution**: watch edges of cliffs, overhang is loose and dangerous; stay on path as hard-to-see bog holes can be hard on the ankles. **Parking**: park you car at the beach and walk along the beach to pick up the trail, which heads north, toward Main-à-Dieu.

➵ EN ROUTE

About 14 km (8.5 mi) from Main-à-Dieu, on this in-case-you-hadn't-noticed-by-now very 'curvy' road, there's an intersection and the end of the Marconi Trail. (There's a one-lane bridge along here with a bit of a dangerous approach, so be careful.)

At the intersection you will turn onto Hwy 22, the Louisbourg Hwy and continue on to Louisbourg. For details of Louisbourg see page 261.

← If you're coming **from** Louisbourg **toward** Glace Bay on this Marconi Trail, take Hwy 22 out of Louisbourg and turn off just a short distance from the town onto the Little Lorraine turnoff and follow the Marconi Trail above in reverse.

The Last Word

When your travels around Cape Breton have come to an end (at least for now), I hope you will take with you fond memories of a happy holiday. I hope you discovered things about our Island that enchanted, delighted and astounded you. And I hope you will come back again.

Because *A Traveller's Guide to Cape Breton*, by its nature, must contain up-to-date and useful information for travellers, it will be updated each year. If you have any comments or suggestions for changing or improving the book, I would appreciate hearing from you. Please contact Pat O'Neil, c/o Solus Publishing, 14 Beacon St, Sydney, Nova Scotia, Canada, B1P 4S9; 902-562-8195 (Fax same).

"**Cape Breton**, so long untouched by the onward march of commercial progress, is now alive with productive activities, and its own people, as well as hundreds who have come to its favored shores, are beginning to reap the fruits of its prosperity. Furthermore, Cape Breton, already famous for the beauty of its scenery of sea and mountain, lake and hill, deserves that the brightness of its skies, the envigorating properties of its pure air, the splendor of its crystal waters, and the loveliness of its landscapes, should be still more widely known and appreciated."
...from *Cape Breton Canada* by C. W. Vernon, Nation Pub. Co., Toronto, 1903.

Index

Boat Tours and Charters

Golf Courses

Hospitals

Information Centres

Malls and Shopping Plazas

Maps

Marinas

Museums, Historic Sites

Outdoor Adventures

Tours

Trails

Transportation

Note:

Accommodations and **Restaurants** can be located by looking through the listings in the body of the book. Just look in the Index above under 'Cities, Towns, Villages' and turn to the page indicated.

Churches in Cape Breton number in the hundreds and it is not possible to list them all. You will find them listed in the Yellow Pages of the Cape Breton Island Telephone Book.